European Union Constitutionalism in Crisis

Several years after the first Greek bailout, the integration project of the European Union faces an interlocking set of political, economic, legal and social challenges that go to the very core of its existence. Austerity is the order of the day, and citizens in both debtor and creditor states increasingly turn to the political movements of the far left and right, anti-politics and street protests to vent their frustration.

This book demonstrates the limits of constitutionalism in the EU. It explores the 'twin crises' – the failure of the Constitutional Treaty in 2005 and the more recent Eurozone crisis – to illuminate both the possibilities and pitfalls of the integration project. It argues that European integration overburdened law in an attempt to overcome deep-seated political deficiencies. It further contends that the EU shifted from an unsuccessful attempt at democratisation via politicisation (the Constitutional Treaty), to an unintended politicisation without democratisation (the Eurozone crisis) only a few years later. The book makes the case that this course is unsustainable and threatens the goal of European unity.

This text will be of key interest to students and scholars in the fields of EU studies, EU law, democracy studies, constitutional studies and international relations.

Nicole Scicluna is a researcher at Collegio Carlo Alberto, Italy.

Routledge/UACES Contemporary European Studies

Edited by Federica Bicchi, London School of Economics and Political Science, Tanja Börzel, Free University of Berlin, and Mark Pollack, Temple University, on behalf of the University Association for Contemporary European Studies

The primary objective of the new Contemporary European Studies series is to provide a research outlet for scholars of European Studies from all disciplines. The series publishes important scholarly works and aims to forge for itself an international reputation.

European Union Constitutionalism in Crisis

Nicole Scicluna

LONDON AND NEW YORK

First published 2015
by Routledge
2 Park Square, Milton Park, Abingdon, Oxon OX14 4RN

and by Routledge
711 Third Avenue, New York, NY 10017

Routledge is an imprint of the Taylor & Francis Group, an informa business

British Library Cataloguing in Publication Data
A catalogue record for this book is available from the British Library

Library of Congress Cataloging in Publication Data
Scicluna, Nicole, author.
  European Union constitutionalism in crisis / Nicole Scicluna.
    pages cm. – (Routledge/UACES contemporary European studies; 26)
  Includes bibliographical references and index.
  1. Constitutional law–European Union countries. 2. European Union countries–Politics and government. I. Title.
  KJE4445.S374 2015
  342.24–dc23
                2014022900

ISBN: 978-1-138-80160-8 (hbk)
ISBN: 978-1-315-75454-3 (ebk)

Typeset in Times New Roman
by Taylor & Francis Books

Contents

Acknowledgements

This book is the culmination of several years of hard work. It would not have been possible without the assistance and encouragement of many people, as well as the institutional support of La Trobe University, Melbourne and Collegio Carlo Alberto, Turin. For their endorsement of the project, I would like to thank Andrew Taylor at Routledge and the editors of the UACES Contemporary European Studies series. I am also very grateful to Charlotte Endersby, Kris Wischenkamper and Ruth Bradley for their help in preparing the manuscript. I would like to thank Gabriel Bielek, who took the photograph on the cover, and Hanneke Beaumont for allowing the image of her sculpture to be used.

The book is based on my doctoral thesis and I am thankful to several of my colleagues at La Trobe, without whose help it would not have gotten to this point. My biggest debt of gratitude is to Stefan Auer for his excellent supervision, astute feedback, and enthusiasm for the project. I would also like to thank Nick Bisley, Raul Sanchez-Urribarri, Robert Horvath, Michael O'Keefe and Gwenda Tavan. I am grateful to John Hirst for his sage advice, often dispensed over lunch, on structure, argument and the all-important issue of headings. Finally, I'm thankful to Jane Rowe, Louise Saw and Lee Shore for their helpful and friendly administrative support.

I was fortunate to have the opportunity to conduct some of my doctoral research in Germany. I would like to thank Thomas Risse and Tanja Boerzel at the Free University of Berlin, and Antje Wiener at the University of Hamburg's Centre for Globalisation and Governance for facilitating my stay at their respective institutions and for including me in the activities of their programmes.

The manuscript was completed during my postdoctoral fellowship at Collegio Carlo Alberto and it was improved immensely by the feedback I received from several colleagues there. I would like to thank Margarita Estevez-Abe, Stefano Sacchi, Tiziana Caponio, Giulia Dotti Sani, Angela Garcia Calvo, Josef Hien, Juana Lamote de Grignon Perez and Pier Domenico Tortola for their support and advice.

I am also grateful to Christian Joerges, Wojciech Sadurski and Richard Bellamy, who examined my thesis. The final product benefitted considerably from their valuable insights.

Parts of earlier versions of some chapters were published in the *Journal of Common Market Studies*, the *European Law Journal* and the *International Journal of Constitutional Law*. I am grateful to the editors of those journals as well as to the anonymous reviewers for their feedback. I have also benefitted from participation in numerous conferences over the past four years. I am grateful to the participants in those conferences and, particularly, to Andreas Dür and John Leslie for their valuable comments, which helped to strengthen and refine my arguments. I would especially like to thank Matthew Zagor for inviting me to participate in the ANU Centre for European Studies' round-table on constitutional patriotism and identity in August 2010. This was the first conference I presented at and it laid the foundations for some of the key ideas in the thesis.

Writing this book was a long and sometimes challenging process. I am grateful to my friends, including Steffen Joeris, Sejal Amin, Thao Pham and Minerva Livanidis for their encouragement along the way. Thanks also to Mashitah Hamidi, Trevor Wilson and Leila Alkassab, with whom I shared an office as well as the journey of undertaking a PhD. Finally, I would like to thank my family for their constant love and support.

List of abbreviations

CAP	Common Agricultural Policy
CT	Constitutional Treaty
EC	European Community
ECB	European Central Bank
ECJ	European Court of Justice
ECSC	European Coal and Steel Community
EEC	European Economic Community
EFSF	European Financial Stability Facility
EFSM	European Financial Stabilisation Mechanism
EMU	Economic and Monetary Union
EP	European Parliament
EPP	Group of the European People's Party
ESM	European Stability Mechanism
EU	European Union
FRG	Federal Republic of Germany
GCC	German Constitutional Court
GDR	German Democratic Republic
IGC	Inter-Governmental Conference
IMF	International Monetary Fund
ITL	Integration through Law
LT	Lisbon Treaty
OLP	Ordinary Legislative Procedure
OMT	Outright Monetary Transactions
QMV	Qualified Majority Voting
S&D	Group of the Progressive Alliance of Socialists and Democrats
SEA	Single European Act
SGP	Stability and Growth Pact
TEC	Treaty on European Community
TESM	Treaty Establishing the European Stability Mechanism
TEU	Treaty on European Union
TFEU	Treaty on the Functioning of the European Union
TSCG	Treaty on Stability, Coordination and Governance in the Economic and Monetary Union (Fiscal Compact)
UN	United Nations
WTO	World Trade Organization

Introduction

Reframing EU constitutionalism

Europe is in crisis and so is European Union (EU) scholarship. Several years after the first Greek bailout put paid to the conceit that the Global Financial Crisis was merely a disease of American capitalism, the integration project faces an interlocking set of political, economic, legal and social challenges that go to the very core of its existence. Austerity is the order of the day across the continent, and citizens in both debtor and creditor states increasingly turn to political movements of the far left and right, anti-politics and street protests to vent their frustration. Yet, while these events receive scholarly attention, what is less widely recognised is that they have also triggered a crisis of integration *theory*. That our scholarly conceptualisations of the EU – as a community of law, as a *demoicracy*, as a post-national *sui generis* polity – are also in need of a radical rethink. This book aims to contribute to that rethink – a necessary process if the EU is to find a viable path out of its travails.

The book is framed by the *twin crises* of twenty-first-century EU con-stitutionalism: the failure of the Constitutional Treaty (CT) in 2005, and the euro crisis, which followed several years later. In analysing these crises, I draw on the rich theoretical framework of Integration through Law (ITL) in order to embed and explicate EU constitutionalism. However, in contrast to tradi-tional legal integration theories, law is used to investigate the *limits* of integration, and the potential for partial *disintegration*. In particular, I will demonstrate how the integration process overburdened law in an attempt to overcome political deficiencies, with serious consequences for the EU's 'democratic deficit'. Part of the legacy of the first crisis was a retreat from the Constitution's lofty ideal of democratisation via politicisation. Now, as a result of the second crisis, the integration project has become well and truly politicised and European policies highly salient for national voters. However, this process has occurred largely against the will of EU leaders, who have sought technocratic solutions to what are inherently political problems. Thus, over the past decade, the EU has moved from an unsuccessful attempt at democratisation via politicisation, to an unintended politicisation without democratisation. This development poses a serious threat to the maintenance of European unity in the medium-to-long-term.

ITL rose to prominence in the 1980s, bringing to light the enduring centrality of law to a Community whose political fortunes had waxed and waned. This was a significant contribution to the scholarly literature, which helped to popularise interdisciplinary approaches to EU studies and bridge the gap between political scientists and legal scholars. Early ITL studies focused on the role of the European Court of Justice (ECJ) and the impact of doctrines such as direct effect and supremacy, as well as the Court's path-breaking human rights jurisprudence, during the European Community's formative years (Haltern 2004). The Court's towering achievement of moving the Community from the realm of traditional international law into its own, *sui generis*, category of federal-like constitutionalism – termed the 'transformation thesis' by Joseph Weiler (1999) – is now a conventional wisdom of EU studies. Ever since the 1980s, the study of European law in context has been a mainstay of the scholarly literature. The focus, however, has shifted from specific institutions and doctrines to a more holistic assessment of legal systems, with extensive subsections of the literature emerging around new theories of governance and constitutionalism in the EU (see, for example, Everson 1998; Walker 2009; Wiener 2011).

ITL scholarship, therefore, was critical in theorising the construction of the EU as a constitutionalised non-state actor *par excellence*, but it is not without its flaws and oversights. In particular, some ITL scholarship has been criticised for its tendency – occasionally verging on triumphalism – to regard law almost exclusively as an instrument of progress towards a more federal Europe (Shaw 1996; Everson 1998: 389). This emphasis on law's integrative force runs parallel to the tendency, in the broader field of EU studies, to treat the process of integration as quasi-teleological, and its putative federal end point as self-evidently a good thing (see, for example, Della Sala 2012; Zimmerman and Dür 2012: 2–6). During the euro crisis, this tendency has manifested itself in the elite consensus – maintained by political figures and academics alike – that no matter the question, 'more Europe' is the answer.

However, as conditions in the eurozone failed to substantially improve, cracks began to appear in this consensus, with a number of academics becoming much more openly negative about the euro's prospects and critical of the undemocratic and austerity-focused manner in which its rescue was proceeding (see, for example, Joerges 2012a, 2012b; Majone 2011, 2012; Marsh 2013; Scharpf 2011). In a notable contribution to the debate, Francois Heisbourg (2013), an avowed pro-European and an expert on European security policy, called for an orderly dissolution of the currency union in order to save the larger integration project. Whilst still in a minority, such views are no longer the province of an anti-EU fringe and ought to be given due consideration. I will revisit them in the chapters that follow.

One of the tasks of this book, then, will be to explicate a general integration fatigue that was signalled – not for the first time, but perhaps most strikingly – by the failure of the CT, and that has since escalated into a full-blown existential crisis. Again, in an inversion of the conventional understanding of integration through law, it is law's *disintegrative* potential that I am primarily interested in. Put another way, the focus is on law as a *constraint* on, rather than enabler of, ever-closer union. Thus, I follow Jo Shaw in treating the disintegrationist elements of the EU legal order 'not as *exceptions* to an integrationist norm, but as autonomous facets of the whole' (Shaw 1996: 241, emphasis in original). This is not to claim that law has no part to play in the construction and reconstruction of the European project, but rather to suggest that there are limits to the extent to which it can advance an integrationist agenda without major political reform.[1] In this respect, the currency union (and its crisis) serves as a prime illustration of EU actors' overconfidence in the ability of formal law to overcome political deficiencies (Everson and Joerges 2012: 645–49; Joerges 2012b).

Legalisation and de-legalisation: the impact of the twin crises

Early scholars of European law in context rightly observed that the nature of the EC/EU was defined, to a significant extent, by its legal order (Stein 1981; Weiler 1994).[2] The project was forged in international treaty law, took root in the member states via national law, and extended its breadth and depth through the development of a supranational legal order with a certain (though disputed) degree of autonomy (Schilling 1996). The EU has been conceptualised as everything from an 'experimental union' (Laffan, O'Donnell and Smith 2000), to a 'Europe of bits and pieces' (Curtin 1993), a 'regional state' (Schmidt 2006, 2009) and a 'neo-medieval empire' (Zielonka 2006), amongst many other labels. How best then to understand its peculiar constitutional character?

Since the traditional categories of international organisation and federal state are insufficient to capture the constitutional structure of the European polity, an alternative suggestion is that the EU be conceptualised as a Kelsenian *Rechtsgemeinschaft* (community of law). For Hans Kelsen (1989: 286–88), a political community was identical to its legal order and their shared legal bond, the only factor capable of uniting the individual community members. Accordingly, and in contrast to notions of a pre-political *demos*, Kelsen regarded 'the people' as a fictional construct that 'exists only from a juridical and normative perspective' (Ragazzoni 2011: 19). Kelsen focused on *states* as legal communities, but his ideas may be extrapolated to the EU as an entity that is both framed by law and is in search of a non-ethno-culturally based identity. The applicability of the *Rechtsgemeinschaft* concept to the EU relies partly on the potential of the Union's non-national category of citizenship to construct a purely legal, and thereby neutral, bond amongst Europeans. In other words, to create a situation whereby – in the absence of any pre-political criteria of belonging – whosoever is subject to the European legal order is a citizen of the European polity (Busch and Ehs 2008: 5–7, 10–11).[3]

Kelsen's concept of a *Rechtsgemeinschaft* was linked to his theory of legal monism. Since, for Kelsen, the state was identical to its legal order, there was nothing outside of the law; every norm was valid only insofar as it was derived from another, higher norm. This process of norm derivation could be traced back to a basic norm (*Grundnorm*), which was the state's constitution and, therefore, equal to the state itself. Taken to its logical conclusion, legal monism implies that there is only one, international legal system, of which all national and regional legal orders are sub-systems. It follows that all legal norms across all sub-systems, if they were to be considered valid, would have to be reconcilable with each other and would have to coexist in a hierarchical system leading ultimately to one, international *Grundnorm* (Kelsen 1989: 221–24; MacCormick 1998: 527–32; Vinx 2011). The normative appeal of Kelsen's theories is clear. Political conflicts are eliminated through their transformation into legal conflicts, which turn out not to be conflicts at all once the correct hierarchy of norms is determined and the appropriate (higher) norm applied. Monism, thus understood, may be applied in an international or transnational arena to resolve seemingly irreconcilable claims and counterclaims by competing sovereign authorities in a rational and consistent manner. It is in this respect that monist theories are potentially attractive as a means of understanding EU constitutionalism (Vinx 2011).

Certainly, the ECJ has advanced a monist view of the relationship between the EU's (autonomous) legal order and those of the member states, particularly through its uncompromising stand on the supremacy and self-validating nature of EU law (de Witte 2009: 26–32). However, the idea that national legal orders are subordinate to the EU's supranational legal order is logically incoherent, not only because many of the ECJ's jurisprudential claims (including those regarding the extent and origins of supremacy) are contested by national actors, but also because the EU's legal authority derives originally from treaties created by the member states and legitimated by the international law principle *pacta sunt servanda* (MacCormick 1995, 1998). Therefore, in line with Neil MacCormick (1995: 259), I reject monist interpretations of EC/EU law and instead advance an argument in favour of a 'more subtle understanding of the meaning of sovereignty and its locus'. That is, one that treats Europe's legal order as heterarchical rather than hierarchical, and national and supranational legal spheres as interdependent but co-equal (MacCormick 1999; Cooper 2010).[4]

Kelsen's approach to intra- and cross-societal conflict management may be contrasted with that of Carl Schmitt, who criticised legal monism as a purely normative fantasy. Kelsen's theory of sovereignty, according to Schmitt, was no theory at all; as the latter wrote in *Political Theology*, 'Kelsen solved the problem of the concept of sovereignty by negating it' (Schmitt 2005: 21). Schmitt regarded Kelsen's equation of a state's legal system with the state itself as an idealistic disjunction between the juristic and sociological aspects of the state that had no basis in reality (Schmitt 2005: 18–22). It was completely at odds with Schmitt's own conception of sovereignty, which was centred on the *exception*, rather than the norm. Schmitt's sovereign was necessarily situated outside the legal order because he had the power to take the ultimate decision – that is the decision as to whether or not the normal state of affairs existed and, accordingly, whether or not the legal order was valid (Schmitt 2005: 13–15).

Though both are problematic in their own ways, the theories of Kelsen and Schmitt may still offer insights into how (and how effectively) the EU system manages conflict. Their theories may also shed light on the difficult question of the *nature* of intra-EU conflicts: To what extent are they political and, hence, beyond the limits of the law to adjudicate and resolve? This line of inquiry points us towards ever more difficult questions that, in normal times, did not really need to be answered. If conflicts between different actors or interests within the EU are political, who has the authority to decide on them? Is this authority legitimate? If so, whence does this legitimacy derive? In addressing these issues in the chapters that follow, I will suggest that Schmitt's theories are the more compelling in times of crisis (or, 'states of exception') because of his insistence on directly confronting the problem of sovereignty, *contra* the tendency in EU studies to treat it as an outdated concept that was subsumed by the Union's *sui generis Rechtsstaat*.

What impact is the current state of exception having on EU constitutionalism, then? The twin crises have caused a fundamental, and potentially permanent, shift in the predominant mode of EU governance. From the origins of the European Coal and Steel Community (ECSC) in the 1950s until around the time of the Maastricht Treaty in the early 1990s, European integration was characterised by a highly legalised mode of governance (i.e. the European Community as a community of law). Throughout this period, open political contestation was often suppressed in favour of integration via the proliferation of rules and regulations, with judicial and administrative bodies leading the way. By Maastricht, the limitations of this approach were becoming apparent, as popular 'permissive consensus' gave way to 'constraining dissensus' (Hooghe and Marks 2009). The Constitutional Treaty was the most important initiative in the subsequent push to promote a more inclusive, participatory and democratic mode of governance that would lend the EU the legitimacy to match its ambitious political agendas.

The CT's failure was a watershed moment. Its significance, for my purposes, lay in its exposure of the limits of law as an integrationist tool and the difficulty of transforming European integration from an elite to a mass project. However, its full import can only be appreciated in light of the euro crisis – that is, that insufficient public support exists to build the sort of political union that would make monetary union viable. It is in this respect that the two crises are 'twinned'. The problem of the EU's democratisation that was left open by the CT's defeat is now more pressing than ever. The euro crisis has led to a 'de-legalisation' of Economic and Monetary Union (EMU) that is pushing the EU towards new forms of technocratic and administrative rule (Everson and Joerges 2012). This is not to say that the instruments of the new economic governance are not legally codified, but that they lack the formal legitimacy of the constitutional order they bypass and that this lacuna is not made up for by other forms of democratic accountability. EU constitutionalism looks like becoming a casualty of the crisis, but it is also implicated in its own demise. The reasons behind this lie in the limitations of court-led integration through law.

During decades in which the European project looked to have stagnated politically, the ECJ was successfully deepening legal integration. That was the breakthrough insight offered by Weiler's famous distinction between the legal and political facets of supranational governance. Weiler (1981, 1991) observed and described a 'foundational equilibrium' in the EC between 'normative supranationalism' (the constitutionalisation of Community law as the supreme and directly effective law of the land) and 'decisional intergovernmentalism' (member state control over law-making in the Council of Ministers via the national veto). He posited that the retention of governmental control in the Council was largely responsible for member states' support for, or at least acquiescence in, the ECJ's constitutionalising work.

However, national authorities were more than passive receptors of EC/EU law, they also contributed actively to the constitutionalisation process. As Weiler (1994: 516) put it, it was one thing for the ECJ to use its jurisprudence to position itself as the ultimate authority over the Community legal system, but quite another for the Court's manoeuvring to be accepted by its inter-locutors, be they the other Community institutions, national governments, or national courts. Thus, the ECJ's constitutional achievements were the result of its ability to 'persuade, co-opt, and cajole most, if not all, of [the] other principal actors to accept the fundamentals of its doctrine', as well as its position as 'final arbiter' of Community law (Weiler 1994: 517). Indeed, national courts were empowered, to a certain extent, by their integration into the enforcement mechanisms of EC law, especially lower courts and those in states with traditionally strong legislatures and weak powers of judicial review (Alter 2001).[5]

The ECJ itself was traditionally portrayed in ITL literature as a 'hero' of integration and the great 'constitutionaliser' of the treaties (Haltern 2004). ITL scholarship was quick to comprehend and celebrate the ECJ's singular achievement in harnessing the power of law and using it to pursue the Treaty of Rome's headline goal of 'ever closer union', thereby taming Europe's pre-viously warring nation states.[6] However, particularly in ITL's early phase, much of the work in the field failed to appreciate the negative repercussions of taking such a narrow view of good governance; a view that privileged outcome-driven administration over democratic political will formation. I take a different approach here, in recognition of the fact that a full assessment of the effectiveness of EU constitutionalism requires a move away from the 'over-eager, and sometimes arrogant, substitution of juridification for politi-cisation which marked much of European governance in the 1980s' (Everson 1998: 389).[7]

The ECJ's role in fashioning the contemporary EU is, then, less clear-cut and more controversial than it first appears. There is considerable scope for conflict between the impartiality required of any court, and the ECJ's treaty-based mission, as an institution of the European Union, to advance the cause of integration. Perhaps more than any other Union institution, the Court has undertaken its mission with vigour and great success. As a result, judicially created principles such as direct effect and supremacy form the core of the Union's legal architecture. Advances in legal integration have circumvented the lack of political will that may otherwise have left the European project as nothing more than an intergovernmental organisation of states, as envisioned, for example, by Charles De Gaulle in the 1960s. Yet, 'integration by stealth' (Majone 2009: 12) comes at a cost to a polity's legitimacy and, for the EU, these costs are mounting.

It is clear that the pro-integrative constellation so usefully theorised by ITL is changing. Since the high point of the Maastricht Treaty in 1992, the path towards further legal integration has been strewn with obstacles. This was evidenced by the laboured process of treaty reform that saw painstakingly negotiated compromises at Amsterdam (1997) and Nice (2001), followed by a failed Constitution, followed by the symbolically de-constitutionalised Lisbon Treaty (LT) (2009). Even after Lisbon there has been no respite, two international agreements intended to strengthen the eurozone were signed in 2012 (the European Stability Mechanism (ESM) Treaty and the Fiscal Compact) and the EU treaties may be reopened in the near future. The twin crises of twenty-first-century EU constitutionalism have exposed the Union's deeply political core, rendering attempts to cloak it under the supposedly benign neutrality of law and other technocratic instruments futile. In fact, EU leaders' and policymakers' efforts to keep democratic politics out of the eurozone crisis – for example, through the elevation of the European Central Bank (ECB), the creation of 'special purpose vehicles' to administer bailout funds, and the introduction of supranational budgetary oversight and automatic triggers for sanctions – are damaging the fabric of the integration project.[8]

Over the same period of time, the ECJ's influence as an instigator and driver of European integration has waned. This trend is partly crisis-induced. The need for quick, effective action privileges executive authority, while more ponderous and cumbersome institutions, such as courts and parliaments, are marginalised. However, the European Court is also, to some extent, a victim of its own success. The rate of legal integration the ECJ established between the 1960s and 1980s became increasingly difficult to sustain, especially since supranational political integration did not keep pace. A high degree of legal federalisation combined with a post-Maastricht increase in EU competences magnified the Union's democracy and legitimacy deficits and made further legal integration more difficult to achieve. Furthermore, at the national level, some member state courts have become less amenable to the ECJ's rigid supranationalist doctrines, reasserting their ultimate authority as national constitutional guardians, and suggesting that European integration may go so far, but no farther (see, for example, Grimm 2009; Phelan 2010; Steinbach 2010). This issue will be considered with respect to Germany and its constitutional court in Chapter 3. Suffice it to note here that the pressure on Europe's constitutional order has multiple sources including judicial unease over encroachments on national constitutional sovereignty, public disillusionment with a European Union that seems remote and indifferent, and a loss of market faith in stalling economies.

Structure of the book

The scope of this book is broad. However, breadth is precisely what the study of European integration needs at this critical juncture in the EU's history. The gap between elites and publics over the nature and direction of the EU, which has been widening since the ratification of the Maastricht Treaty, now threatens to engulf the integration project. Concomitant with this development, in the academic world, has been the 'pragmatic turn' in European integration studies. That is, the turn away from overarching theories that explore the 'nature of the beast', towards a micro focus on the dynamics of policymaking and the intricacies of individual policies and policy areas. Thus, another gap has opened up – one between EU studies and ordinary people – whereby the former 'tends to reproduce the "priestly mysteries" through which the EU governs itself' to the bewilderment and bemusement of the latter (Bickerton 2012: 4). Unsurprisingly, this second gap hardly contributes to the bridging of the first, especially at a time when publics and the political realm are grappling with big questions of purpose and legitimacy: What is the EU? What should it aspire to? How do its institutions represent Europeans? Who makes political decisions in Europe and through what processes (Bickerton 2012: 2–12)?

This book returns to that earlier tradition of regarding the Union as a polity-in-the-making, rather than as a *sui generis* collection of institutions and processes. To be sure, the parts are important, but their in-depth study should not come at the expense of attempts to comprehend the whole. My own attempt to do so uses the prism of constitutionalism, which Weiler (1997: 97–99) described as the 'operating system' of the European Union. This is a useful metaphor for two main reasons; firstly, it conveys the importance of constitutionalism to the functioning of every facet of EU activity. Secondly, it highlights how easy it is to take constitutionalism for granted as part of the background of integration when it is, in fact, its essence. Therefore, one is well placed to gain a more comprehensive picture of the European polity through the study of its constitutional order. What is presented in the following chapters is an analysis of the *reconfiguration of EU constitutionalism through crisis*. In some ways, this is a necessary reconfiguration, especially insofar as it involves a re-evaluation of the relationship between law and politics (Everson and Joerges 2012: 644–45). However, the constitutional configuration that emerges from this period of crisis will not necessarily be more stable and sustainable than the over-reliance on law that characterised previous decades of European integration. As the integrationist power of law wanes, it is increasingly being supplanted by new forms of administrative governance, instead of – and to the detriment of – participatory democracy in Europe (Habermas 2012: 50–53).

Chapter 1 maps out and defines the different strands of EU constitutionalism. It then briefly sketches the contours of the EU's 'uncodified constitution', by which I mean the founding treaties as constitutionalised by the ECJ. This story is, by now, fairly well known, but its essential features are worth recapitulating because they chronicle the formative period of the Union's political and legal culture. In this way, a process that at first seemed to be an overwhelming success (from a federalist viewpoint) is revealed as being far more complex and ambiguous insofar as it also embedded a preference for non-majoritarian, technocratic modes of governance, a hubristic sense of integration as mission and end point in itself, and other habits that inform the Union's present predicament (Weiler 2011).

In Chapter 2, I contrast the EU's uncodified constitutionalism with the ill-fated project to give Europe a formal constitution. This effort grew out of dissatisfaction with the messy compromises of the Nice Treaty and culminated in the CT being signed on 29 October 2004, in the very same room as the original Treaty of Rome. The CT sought, amongst other things, to redress the symbolic deficit of the Union's existing constitutional framework. It was arguably the most ambitious manifestation of the EU's identity politics to that point. Dieter Grimm (2005: 207), interrogating the logic behind 'integration by constitution', questioned whether the text even deserved to be called by that name. As he noted, 'it is in the constitution that a society determines the form and content of its political unity', while, CT notwithstanding, '[t]he basic legal order of the European Union ... has neither originated in a decision made by its citizens, nor is it attributed to them'. The second half of Chapter 2 will consider the fallout from the CT's failure, including the subsequent ratification of the Lisbon Treaty, the first EU treaty that did not appreciably advance supranational integration, despite including, *verbatim*, most of the text of the CT.[9] The LT's significance lay precisely in its circumspection. Its retreat from the CT's high watermark of political and legal supranationalism and greater recognition of the place of sovereign member states was potentially a turning point for the integration project, albeit one whose significance has been dimmed by subsequent events, particularly the euro crisis.

The shift from CT to LT highlighted a growing ambivalence towards the concept of 'ever closer union' amongst European publics, political parties and even some governments. This was evident, to some extent, in France and the Netherlands, where the Constitution was defeated in popular referenda (though in both cases the negative vote was driven by many factors, not all EU-related). It could also be seen in the traditionally eurosceptical UK, where former Prime Minister Gordon Brown's decision not to hold a referendum on the LT fuelled concerns about the loss of British sovereignty, which were exploited to great effect by the UK Independence Party (UKIP), amongst other factions. Indeed, UKIP, which advocates Britain's withdrawal from the EU, is far from the only manifestation of political euroscepticism in Britain. Many Conservative parliamentarians are openly critical of European integration, and party policy includes using the euro crisis as an opportunity to 'renegotiate' EU membership and holding an 'in–out' referendum by 2017 (Cameron 2013). Even in the heart of Europe, the idea of ever closer union has lost ground. From a constitutional point of view, this may be illustrated in relation to traditionally pro-European Germany. Chapter 3 analyses that country's jurisprudential landmarks on European integration, including the Constitutional Court's assessment of the Maastricht and Lisbon Treaties and the euro rescue measures. Although it has consistently ruled in favour of the European treaties put before it, the Court has not done so unreservedly, strongly hinting that legal and political integration may soon reach its limits.

There are several reasons for making Germany the focus of this study. From a legal point of view, the German Constitutional Court (GCC) has been highly vocal on the subject of European integration for a long period of time. As such, the GCC is a fitting national counterpart to the ECJ in terms of its judicial activism and privileged and influential position within the political system. The analysis of the GCC's jurisprudence also provides a salutary reminder that the ECJ's vision of European constitutional law as self-contained, self-sustaining and supreme is incomplete. Politically, Germany is today the EU's 'reluctant hegemon' and, despite its troubled history, the state most capable of influencing the Union's future, a fact that the euro crisis has brought into stark relief (Paterson 2011).[10] The rest of the continent looks to Germany for leadership, vision and the financial firepower to secure the eurozone. So far these expectations have been only partially met and it does not appear likely that the German government elected in 2013 will drastically change course. Political will is not the only consideration here; the opinion of the GCC – a traditional outlet for euroscepticism in Germany – will influence the country's EU policies as well. Thus, Chapter 3 will further explicate the book's key themes, including the uses and limits of law as an integrationist tool, the complex interplay between national and supranational actors that shapes EU constitutionalism, and the impact of integration on traditionally nation-state-centric concepts such as sovereignty and representative democracy.

Chapter 4 analyses the EU's democracy and legitimacy deficits. These distinct, though interrelated, phenomena are negative consequences of the Union's institutional design that predate the twin crises but have been exacerbated by them. It is when considering the difficulty of replicating representative democracy (or coming up with a viable alternative) within the framework of EU governance that one is able to appreciate how legal integration became a victim of its own success. The integration-through-law model is self-limiting because legal integration cannot advance too far ahead of political integration without destabilising the polity. This principle may be applied to the ill-fated Constitutional Treaty. Substantively, the CT did not add all that much to the Union's existing uncodified constitutionalism, certainly nothing that could not have been incorporated via an ordinary reform treaty (in fact, this is what eventually happened in the form of the LT). The point of the enterprise, however, was to bring politics up to speed with law; to 'europeanise' national peoples as decades of legal integration had already europeanised national polities. Yet, the CT, as a legal instrument, was unable to do this. Not only the fact of its defeat, but also the manner in which it was replaced – by a reform treaty negotiated by national leaders behind closed doors and packaged so as to avoid referenda – confirmed the EU's status as an elite-driven project.

Finally, Chapter 5 focuses squarely on the euro crisis – the second of the twin crises of EU constitutionalism and the first test of the post-Lisbon institutional structure. Whereas the CT's failure was primarily a symbolic setback with legal consequences, the challenge of preventing a disorderly collapse of Europe's currency union was a genuine state of emergency. As such, it exposed even more clearly what the CT's defeat foreshadowed – the limits of law as an integrationist instrument. European Council-led efforts to secure the solvency of heavily indebted sovereigns have illustrated the predominance of politics – albeit, a form of intergovernmental, executive-centred politics – by jettisoning legality as well as legitimacy in the name of expediency. EU leaders' convoluted reinterpretation of the Maastricht Treaty's 'no-bailout clause' (Article 125 TFEU) in an attempt to reconcile it with rescue packages for Greece, Ireland and Portugal is one example of this behaviour. Another example is the ECB's decision to buy government bonds on secondary markets, potentially in breach of its charter.[11]

Giandomenico Majone (2011: 6) described Europe's monetary union as a synecdoche, a part that may be used to study the whole. The crisis of the eurozone plays a similar role in the context of this book. The crisis poses an acute challenge to the EU's continued existence that brings into sharp relief the reconfiguration of the Union's constitutional order triggered by the treaty reforms of 1980s and 1990s. Some longstanding features of EU constitutionalism have been strengthened, such as the use of technocratic, non-majoritarian tools and modes of governance to further the integrationist cause. However, the specific means have changed: instead of ever closer union via law, promoted by activist, politicised courts (Chapter 1), we have integration via administrative measures and fiscal conditionality, propped up by the ECB (Chapter 5).

EU constitutionalism is perpetually unsettled. It has always been marked by competing forces of centralisation and diffusion. The euro crisis response measures taken so far are unsustainable because they combine the *weaknesses* of both, rather than their strengths. Measures such as the ESM, the Fiscal Compact and, more broadly, an excessive reliance on the European Council for agenda setting and policymaking reflect a turn towards a peculiar type of centralised intergovernmentalism that Jürgen Habermas (2012: 12) described as 'executive federalism'. This is not intergovernmentalism in the sense of a re-nationalisation or repatriation of powers, but rather intergovernmentalism in the sense of European-level decision-making dominated by the national executives of the most powerful member states, primarily Germany.

One corollary of the elevation of executive institutions is the marginalisation of parliaments and, consequently, electorates; ironically at a time when European policies are more politically salient than they have ever been. In terms of its engagement with citizens, the Union has regressed from a failed attempt at democratisation via politicisation (the CT) to an unintended politicisation without democratisation (the euro crisis). Other paths are possible, though they may require a winding back of the EU's supranational competences and a reassessment of what European integration can realistically achieve. The LT signalled a more sustainable, pluralistic form of constitutionalism based on 'parallel and overlapping spheres' (Cooper 2010) and any future revision of the treaties would do well to return to that model. However, at present – *contra* the 'crisis as opportunity' school of thought (see, for example, Beck 2009, 2012; Habermas 2011, 2012; Menasse 2012) – events in the eurozone are actually damaging the fabric of EU constitutionalism and, hence, the integration project as a whole.

Notes

1 As Jo Shaw (1996: 240) put it, '[D]isintegration should not be viewed as a negative, destructive or malign concept or process, but as one which accommodates processes of decentralization or non-centralization, which themselves highlight weaknesses in the integration process as it has been hitherto conceived'.

2 Walter Hallstein, the first President of the European Commission, made a similar point when he described the then-European Economic Community (EEC) as 'a remarkable legal phenomenon'. Unique in Europe's history, the post-war project to unify the continent had been based not on force, but on law. Thus, Hallstein (1972: 30) concluded, the EEC 'is a creation of the law; it is a source of law; and it is a legal system'. This notion of law as both instrument and object of integration does not only pertain to the Community's formative period, but is also an apt characterisation of the dynamics of EU governance up until the present day.

3 Though intended to free the EU from traditional, and thus constraining, categories of polity, this method of understanding the Union as a 'political and legal community of its citizens' (Busch and Ehs 2008: 6) is limiting in one, crucial respect. As long as EU citizenship remains derivative of national citizenship (under Article 20 TEU), it cannot, conceptually, afford the European polity the legal autonomy from the member states that it *de facto* exercises, and which the ECJ *de jure* claims. To realise more fully the Kelsenian ideal of *Rechtsgemeinschaft*, European citizenship would need to be detached from nationality and extended to all lawful residents of the Union (Busch and Ehs 2008: 21–22).

4 Kelsen's legal monism is distinct from the idea of *constitutional* monism, which holds that 'the sole centres or units of constitutional authorities are states' (Walker 2002: 337). Nevertheless, as will be clear from Chapter 1, the conception of constitutionalism on which I rely is also a pluralistic one (necessarily so, since I apply it to the non-state EU).

5 According to Alec Stone Sweet (2010: 31), the constitutionalisation of the treaties 'radically enhanced judicial authority within national systems, positioning national judges to become important policymakers at both the EU and national levels'.

6 In this vein, the ECJ has been described as 'the most progressive [European institution] in terms of its innovativeness and *anticipation* of the political will' (Safferling 2007: 684, emphasis added). Moreover, despite legal interpretation and adjudication being the Court's ostensible remit, 'development of the law is generally accepted as one of the main aims of European jurisprudence' (Safferling 2007: n.47). The elevation of the ECJ to the role of 'engine of integration' harks back to the EU's origins in the aftermath of the Second World War, and the idea of a European mission to secure peace and prosperity, which Weiler (2011) termed 'political messianism'.

7 Cf. R. Daniel Kelemen (2012), who argued that the judicialisation of European politics has not undermined democracy, but merely changed its character.

8 In Germany, '*alternativlos*' (no alternative), a favourite catch-cry of Chancellor Angela Merkel, was voted '*das Unwort des Jahres*' in 2010 (this is an annual competition to identify the ugliest and most undesirable word from public language). Merkel's use of the term to foreclose debate on a number of major policy decisions, including management of the eurozone, marginalised voters and left them frustrated (Göbel 2011). It was also disingenuous. What is lacking in European policy debates, not only in Germany but throughout the EU, is not alternatives, but the ability and willingness to fully discuss all options and involve citizens in the decision-making process. In early 2013, a new political party was created in Germany precisely in reaction to this politics of no alternative. *Alternative für Deutschland* (Alternative for Germany), which secured 4.7% of the vote in Germany's September 2013 election (just short of the 5% threshold needed to enter parliament), advocated dismemberment of the currency union as a major plank of its policy platform.

9 Though relatively minor in scale, I will argue that the differences between the LT and CT were significant in terms of the vision they set out for the European integration project.

10 Timothy Garton Ash (2012) wrote of a 'European Germany' reluctantly leading a 'German Europe'.

11 In fact, the changing role of the ECB is emblematic of the crisis-driven reconfiguration of EU constitutionalism away from a heavy reliance on law, towards reliance on new forms of (potentially extra-legal) administrative governance. See Chapter 5 for an elaboration of this argument.

References

Alter, K. (2001) *Establishing the Supremacy of European Law: The Making of an International Rule of Law in Europe* (Oxford: Oxford University Press).

Beck, U. (2009) 'This Economic Crisis Cries Out to Be Transformed into the Founding of a New Europe'. *The Guardian*, 13 April.

——(2012) *Das deutsche Europa* (Berlin: Suhrkamp Verlag).

Bickerton, C. (2012) *European Integration: From Nation-States to Member States* (Oxford: Oxford University Press).

Busch, J. and Ehs, T. (2008) 'Kelsen's Concept of Legal Community and the European Union'. *International Constitutional Law (ICL) – Working Paper 01/2008*, pp. 1–25.

Cameron, D. (2013) 'David Cameron's EU Speech – Full Text'. *The Guardian*, 23 January.

Cooper, I. (2010) 'Mapping the Overlapping Spheres: European Constitutionalism after the Treaty of Lisbon'. *ARENA Centre for European Studies Seminar Paper*, pp. 1–32.

Curtin, D. (1993) 'The Constitutional Structure of the Union: A Europe of Bits and Pieces'. *Common Market Law Review*, Vol. 30, No. 1, pp. 17–69.

De Witte, B. (2009) 'The Lisbon Treaty and National Constitutions: More or Less Europeanisation?' In Closa, C. (ed.) *The Lisbon Treaty and National Constitutions: Europeanisation and Democratic Implications* (Oslo: ARENA Report No 3/09).

Della Sala, V. (2012) 'Understanding the Crisis: Did EU Studies Get It Wrong?' *Paper presented at the 6th ECPR SGEU Pan-European Conference on EU Politics*, Tampere, Finland, 13–15 September.

Everson, M. (1998) 'Beyond the *Bundesverfassungsgericht*: On the Necessary Cunning of Constitutional Reasoning'. *European Law Journal*, Vol. 4, No. 4, pp. 389–410.

Everson, M. and Joerges, C. (2012) 'Reconfiguring the Politics–Law Relationship in the Integration Project through Conflicts-Law Constitutionalism'. *European Law Journal*, Vol. 18, No. 5, pp. 644–66.

Garton Ash, T. (2012) 'Angela Merkel Needs All the Help She Can Get'. *The Guardian*, 8 February.

Göbel, H. (2011) 'Merkels Verdrusswort'. *Frankfurter Allgemeine Zeitung*, 18 January.

Grimm, D. (2005) 'Integration by Constitution'. *International Journal of Constitutional Law*, Vol. 3, No. 2–3, pp. 193–210.

——(2009) 'Defending Sovereign Statehood against Transforming the European Union into a State'. *European Constitutional Law Review*, Vol. 5, No. 3, pp. 353–73.

Habermas, J. (2011) 'Europe's Post-Democratic Era'. *The Guardian*, 10 November.

——(2012) *The Crisis of the European Union: A Response* (Cambridge: Polity).

Hallstein, W. (1972) *The Making of Europe* (London: George Allen & Unwin).

Haltern, U. (2004) 'Integration through Law'. In Wiener, A. and Diez, T. (eds) *European Integration Theory* (Oxford: Oxford University Press).

Heisbourg, F. (2013) *La Fin du Rêve Européen* (Paris: Stock).

Hooghe, L. and Marks, G. (2009) 'A Postfunctionalist Theory of European Integration: From Permissive Consensus to Constraining Dissensus'. *British Journal of Political Science*, Vol. 39, No. 1, pp. 1–23.

Joerges, C. (2012a) 'Europe's Economic Constitution in Crisis'. *ZenTra Working Papers in Transnational Studies*, No. 06/2012, pp. 1–28.

——(2012b) 'Recht und Politik in der Krise Europas: Die Wirkungsgeschichte einer verunglückten Konfiguration'. *Merkur*, Vol. 66, No. 11, pp. 1013–24.

Kelemen, R. D. (2012) 'Eurolegalism and Democracy'. *Journal of Common Market Studies*, Vol. 50, No. S1, pp. 55–71.

Kelsen, H. (1989) *Pure Theory of Law* (Gloucester, MA: Peter Smith).

Laffan, B., O'Donnell, R. and Smith, M. (2000) *Europe's Experimental Union: Rethinking Integration* (London: Routledge).

MacCormick, N. (1995) 'The Maastricht-Urteil: Sovereignty Now'. *European Law Journal*, Vol. 1, No. 3, pp. 259–66.

——(1998) 'Risking Constitutional Collision in Europe?' *Oxford Journal of Legal Studies*, Vol. 18, No. 3, pp. 517–32.

——(1999) *Questioning Sovereignty* (Oxford: Oxford University Press).

Majone, G. (2009) *Europe as the Would-Be World Power: The EU at Fifty* (Cambridge: Cambridge University Press).

——(2011) 'Monetary Union and the Politicization of Europe'. *Keynote Speech at the Euroacademia International Conference: 'The European Union and the Politicization of Europe'*, Vienna, 8–10 December.

——(2012) 'Rethinking European Integration after the Debt Crisis'. *UCL: The European Institute, Working Paper No. 3/2012,* June.

Marsh, D. (2013) *Europe's Deadlock* (New Haven, CT: Yale University Press).

Menasse, R. (2012) *Der europäische Landbote: Die Wut der Bürger und der Friede Europas* (Vienna: Zsolnay).

Paterson, W. (2011) 'The Reluctant Hegemon? Germany Moves Centre Stage in the European Union'. *Journal of Common Market Studies,* Vol. 49, Annual Review, pp. 57–75.

Phelan, W. (2010) 'Political Self-Control and European Constitution: The Assumption of National Political Loyalty to European Obligations as the Solution to the *Lex Posterior* Problem of EC Law in the National Legal Orders'. *European Law Journal,* Vol. 16, No. 3, pp. 253–72.

Ragazzoni, D. (2011) 'Identity vs. Representation: What Makes "The People"? Rethinking Democratic Citizenship through (and beyond) Carl Schmitt and Hans Kelsen'. *Perspectives on Federalism,* Vol. 3, No. 2, pp. 1–30.

Safferling, C. J. M. (2007) 'A World of Peace under the Rule of Law: The View from Europe'. *Washington University Global Studies Law Review,* Vol. 6, pp. 675–87.

Scharpf, F. (2011) 'Monetary Union, Fiscal Crisis and the Preemption of Democracy'. *LSE 'Europe in Question' Discussion Paper Series (LEQS) Paper No. 36, Annual Lecture May 2011,* pp. 1–50.

Schilling, T. (1996) 'The Autonomy of the Community Legal Order: An Analysis of Possible Foundations'. *Harvard International Law Journal,* Vol. 37, No. 2, pp. 389–410.

Schmidt, V. A. (2006) *Democracy in Europe: The EU and National Polities* (Oxford: Oxford University Press).

——(2009) 'Re-Envisioning the European Union: Identity, Democracy, Economy'. *Journal of Common Market Studies,* Vol. 47, Annual Review, pp. 17–42.

Schmitt, C. (2005) *Political Theology: Four Chapters on the Concept of Sovereignty* (Chicago, IL: University of Chicago Press).

Shaw, J. (1996) 'European Union Legal Studies in Crisis? Towards a New Dynamic'. *Oxford Journal of Legal Studies,* Vol. 16, No. 2, pp. 231–53.

Stein, E. (1981) 'Lawyers, Judges and the Making of a Transnational Constitution'. *American Journal of International Law,* Vol. 75, No. 1, pp. 1–27.

Steinbach, A. (2010) 'The Lisbon Judgment of the German Federal Constitutional Court – New Guidance on the Limits of European Integration'. *German Law Journal,* Vol. 11, No. 4, pp. 367–90.

Stone Sweet, A. (2010) 'The European Court of Justice and the Judicialization of EU Governance'. *Living Reviews in European Governance,* Vol. 5, No. 2, pp. 1–50.

Vinx, L. (2011) 'Kelsen's Legal Monism and the Future of the European Constitution'. *Paper presented at the 6th ECPR General Conference,* Reykjavik, Iceland, 25–27 August.

Walker, N. (2002) 'The Idea of Constitutional Pluralism'. *Modern Law Review,* Vol. 65, No. 3, pp. 317–59.

——(2009) 'Reframing EU Constitutionalism'. In Dunoff, J. L. and Trachtman, J. P. (eds) *Ruling the World? Constitutionalism, International Law, and Global Governance* (Cambridge: Cambridge University Press).

Weiler, J. H. H. (1981) 'The Community System: The Dual Character of Supranationalism'. *Yearbook of European Law,* Vol. 1, No. 1, pp. 267–306.

——(1991) 'The Transformation of Europe'. *The Yale Law Journal,* Vol. 100, No. 8, pp. 2403–83.

——(1994) 'A Quiet Revolution: The European Court of Justice and Its Interlocutors'. *Comparative Political Studies*, Vol. 26, No. 4, pp. 510–34.

——(1997) 'The Reformation of European Constitutionalism'. *Journal of Common Market Studies*, Vol. 35, No. 1, pp. 97–131.

——(1999) *The Constitution of Europe: 'Do the New Clothes Have an Emperor?' and Other Essays on European Integration* (Cambridge: Cambridge University Press).

——(2011) 'The Political and Legal Culture of European Integration: An Exploratory Essay'. *International Journal of Constitutional Law*, Vol. 9, No. 3–4, pp. 678–94.

Wiener, A. (2011) 'Through Uncharted Waters of Constitutional Quality: Navigating between Modern Statehood and International Organisation'. In Wiener, A. and Neyer, J. (eds) *Political Theory of the European Union* (Oxford: Oxford University Press).

Zielonka, J. (2006) *Europe as Empire: The Nature of the Enlarged European Union* (Oxford: Oxford University Press).

Zimmerman, H. and Dür, A. (2012) 'Introduction: Key Controversies in European Integration'. In Zimmerman, H. and Dür, A. (eds) *Key Controversies in European Integration* (Basingstoke: Palgrave Macmillan).

1 A 'quiet revolution'?

The self-limiting success of the EU's uncodified constitution

Introduction: constitutionalism in the EU and its limits

The notion of EU constitutionalism is as difficult to grasp as the nature of the European Union itself. It is in a permanent state of flux – shaped by myriad treaty reforms, judicial pronouncements, legislative changes and administrative decisions at both the national and European levels. There have been larger shocks to the system as well. The Constitutional Treaty's derailment in 2005 forced a re-evaluation of the aims of the integration project, the nature of EU constitutionalism, and the proper relationship between the EU and its member states (Bellamy 2006; de Witte 2009). The results of that re-evaluation were embodied in the 2009 Lisbon Treaty (LT), which offered a vision of a more limited, more flexible, and, therefore, more viable EU. Whereas the Constitutional Treaty (CT) had expressed federalist aspirations, the LT charted a path for a Europe of nation state democracies, governed by a constitutional framework that recognised the equality and autonomy of the member state and supranational legal orders (Cooper 2010).

However, the LT had barely come into force before the constitutional settlement it brokered was threatened by another significant shock, the euro crisis, which first came to light in Greece in early 2010 and proceeded to unfold in financial markets, real economies and political systems across Europe. Many of the euro rescue initiatives – including the European Stability Mechanism (ESM), the Fiscal Compact and the proposed banking union – rely on a level of supranational and transnational co-ordination that exceeds the EU's institutional capacity for democratic governance. This places decision makers in danger of repeating some of the mistakes that doomed the CT, including underestimating public dissatisfaction with 'Brussels' institutions that many perceive as ineffective and alien (Majone 2012: 12–14). In order to successfully navigate the EU's latest, and perhaps most serious, existential challenge, its leaders must heed the lessons of a turbulent decade of European-level constitutional reform. This means resisting the mantra of 'more Europe' as the only way forward, and instead reinforcing the Lisbon Treaty's constitutional balance between centralisation and diffusion.

Determining what the CT's rejection by voters and abandonment by political elites meant for EU constitutionalism is one of the issues I consider in this and the following chapter. In other words, how has the failure of formal constitutionalisation impacted on the EU's informal (that is, uncodified) functional constitution? How has it affected relationships amongst EU institutions, member states and citizens? Perhaps most importantly, what can an analysis of the EU's perennially unsettled constitutionalism tell us about the future of the integration project?

My characterisation of the EU's legal system as a *de facto* constitution is not an endorsement of the federalist narrative of European integration, whereby it is presumed that the Union is moving towards a European federal state. Merely accepting that the EU's legal order has gone from international to constitutional does not settle issues such as the scope of supremacy and does not mean that one would resolve disputes over the distribution of powers in favour of the supranational level. Indeed, the scope of the EU's jurisdiction is very much constrained by national doctrines on the origins of EU legal authority and interpretative principles such as conferral, subsidiarity and proportionality (Dashwood 2004). Accordingly, my adoption of a constitutional analytical framework does not imply any particular end point, or *finalité*, for the European project. Rather, it examines the relationship between the Union, its member states and European citizens through what I argue is its most important dimension, in a manner that contemplates the potential for partial disintegration, or de-centralisation, as well as further integration, or centralisation.

What is constitutionalism?

Constitution and *constitutionalism* are contested concepts even within their 'natural cradle' of the Westphalian nation state (Blokker 2011). Their application to the European Union is, thus, fraught with disagreement and misunderstanding. As a starting point, Joseph Raz (1998: 153) has drawn a distinction between 'thin' and 'thick' understandings of constitutionalism. In its thin sense, a constitution is simply the law that establishes, empowers and regulates the main organs and levels of government and their relationships with each other. In this vein, Michel Rosenfeld (1992: 497) articulated the minimum tasks required of a constitution as 'imposing limits on the powers of government, adherence to the rule of law, and the protection of fundamental rights'. At an even more stripped back level, Hans Kelsen – prioritising the formal over the substantive – defined a polity's constitution as its *Grundnorm* (basic norm). In other words, for Kelsen, a constitution is simply that which regulates the creation of general legal norms (Kelsen 1989: 221–24; Busch and Ehs 2008: 7–8).[1]

Yet, there is much more to the symbolic and functional role of modern constitutions than such minimal definitions suggest. Constitutions carry certain connotations about the nature and qualities of the polities and citizens they represent. They are important markers of identity and expressions of popular sovereignty. Therefore, we need to elucidate those characteristics that distinguish constitutions from ordinary laws.

The thick sense of constitutionalism is difficult to define at any level of specificity, as its understanding differs across legal cultures and times. Raz has noted seven key features on which a definition may be centred. First, a constitution is *constitutive* of the legal and political system, its institutions, and their powers and inter-relationships (this criterion is encompassed by the thin definition). Second, a constitution provides, or at least aspires to provide, *stability and continuity* in the legal and political system and its guiding principles. Third, constitutions generally adopt a *canonical* formulation in that they are codified, often in one document. Fourth, constitutions are *superior law* and, as such, take precedence over conflicting ordinary legislation. Fifth, constitutions are *justiciable*, meaning that there are judicial processes by which they may be interpreted, and the compatibility of other legal acts with the constitution may be tested. Sixth, constitutions are subject to an above average level of *entrenchment*, so that amendments, while possible, are relatively rare and difficult to accomplish. Seventh, constitutions express the *guiding principles* and common beliefs of the polity they represent. These may include, for example, democracy, and basic political and civil rights. The combination and relative weight of these elements vary from case to case, but they may all be taken as indicative of the existence of a thick constitution (Raz 1998: 153–54).

Adopting the idea of a constitution as described in its thick sense, this book uses the term *constitutionalism* descriptively. Thus, '[t]he inquiry is as to the extent to which a particular legal system does or does not possess the features associated with a constitution' (Craig 2001: 127). It follows then that *constitutionalisation* describes the process by which an entity moves towards the attainment of those features. In the context of EU legal scholarship, the terms *constitutionalism* and *constitutionalisation* refer to the transformation of the EU from an international to a constitutional legal order (Weiler 1991, 1999). That is to say, the evolution of the Community's legal system from one based on, and governed by, the laws of international treaties, to a self-contained and self-governing constitutional order not dependent on either international or national law for its existence and authority (at least in the view of supranational jurisprudence).

Informal and formal constitutionalism in the EU

There are two broad strands of EU constitutionalism with which this book is concerned. The first may be termed *informal*, or uncodified, constitutionalism. It refers to the treaty-based, judicially constructed constitution that is the subject of this chapter. The second may be termed *formal*, or codified, constitutionalism and it refers to the EU's unsuccessful attempt to adopt an officially designated, 'capital C' constitution in the mid-2000s.

Both informal constitutionalism and formal constitutionalism are well-documented phenomena.[2] Thomas Christiansen and Christine Reh (2009: 14), for example, mapped the constitutionalisation of the EU (and its predecessor organisations) over time according to its level of explicitness. From very low levels in the 1970s and 1980s, when legal innovations were largely driven by the ECJ and hence not politicised, explicit constitutionalism reached its zenith with the 2004 CT. The abandonment of that text, in the face of negative referenda results in France and the Netherlands in mid-2005, prompted both scholarly and official claims that EU treaty reform had been 'de-constitutionalised' (Reh 2009). However, in a legal sense, this term is a misnomer. In fact, the process that culminated in the ratification of a new, more modestly styled reform treaty – the Lisbon Treaty – was not a rejection of constitutionalism *per se*, but rather a return to the EU's standard *modus operandi* of informal or uncodified constitutionalism (Moravcsik 2006). Moreover, the post-CT reduction in the level of 'explicitness' of EU constitutionalism ought not to be regarded as regressive. Implicit constitutionalism has served the integration project well in the past and can continue to do so as long as supranational political ambitions are muted.

Thus, as it is understood in this book, *informal constitutionalism* refers to the solid and coherent legal framework that has grown around the foundations of the EU's primary law.[3] Importantly, the descriptor 'informal' should not be confused with 'insubstantial' – the corpus of EU law is extensive and its impact on the member states' legal orders is profound. I characterise this type of constitutionalism as informal because for several decades there was little acknowledgment or even awareness, outside of legal circles, that the European Community was being constitutionalised. One of the clearest manifestations of the process's implicit nature is the very fact that it took place in the absence of a document explicitly labelled as a 'constitution'. Informal constitutionalisation was driven from the outset by the ECJ through its expansive interpretation of the Treaty of Rome. Although the story is well known, it is worth briefly recapitulating.

Post-war European integration was initiated through an international treaty and the EU's primary legal texts still take that form. Nevertheless, the EU has been undergoing a process of constitutionalisation almost since its inception as the European Economic Community (EEC) in 1958.[4] In fact, some of the ECJ's most famous and consequential judgements were handed down in the early 1960s. One of the most remarkable things about these radical, federalising legal developments is that they coincided with political crisis and economic stagnation. In June 1965, French President Charles De Gaulle withdrew French representation from the Council of Ministers in an incident that became known as the 'Empty Chair Crisis'. De Gaulle, a staunch opponent of supranationalism, was protesting the Commission's push to extend the use of Qualified Majority Voting (QMV) in the Council. He was particularly concerned to prevent the possibility of a coalition of liberal states reforming the protectionist Common Agricultural Policy (CAP). More broadly, though, De Gaulle's protest was about protecting and projecting his own vision of Europe – that is, as a purely intergovernmental venture and a vehicle for securing French national interests.

Eventually De Gaulle's vision prevailed over that of Commission President Walter Hallstein, who had wanted to increase the Commission's powers and strengthen the Community's supranational character. Under the Luxembourg Compromise, an informal agreement reached in January 1966, it was decided that a decision would not be taken on the basis of QMV if any member state felt that vital national interests were at stake. In practice, this meant that consensus and unanimity became the norm in Council decision making, thus restoring intergovernmental control in the Community's most important legislative body. This state of affairs did not change significantly until the re-introduction of QMV via the Single European Act (SEA) in 1987 (Dinan 2012: 32–34).

At the end of the 1960s, then, the member states appeared very much in control of the integration process, with the supranational institutions – i.e. the Commission and Parliament – reduced to supporting roles. The following decade was also a difficult one for the European Community, both economically and politically. The poor international economic situation, particularly following the 1973 oil crisis, adversely affected Community members and the nascent common market as a whole. Low economic growth and high unemployment and inflation were the hallmarks of a period referred to as 'Eurosclerosis', in which the Community appeared to be stagnating: losing its relevance within Europe and externally, and incapable of responding to economic challenges (Whitman 2005: 679). Politically and institutionally, the Community experienced both setbacks and achievements. Britain, Ireland and Denmark joined in 1973. However, the successful completion of the Community's first enlargement was somewhat marred by the difficulty of the process, especially in regards to Britain, which had had two previous accession attempts vetoed by De Gaulle's France. That inauspicious start to British–European Community relations was compounded by the insistence of Britain's new Labour government on renegotiating the country's accession terms almost immediately after joining (Dinan 2012: 35–36).

Nevertheless, the perception of malaise was misleading in one very important respect – legal integration, championed by the ECJ, continued apace. In 1981, Eric Stein famously observed that:

> Tucked away in the fairyland Duchy of Luxembourg and blessed, until recently, with benign neglect by the powers that be and the mass media, the Court of Justice of the European Communities has fashioned a constitutional framework for a federal-type structure in Europe.
>
> (Stein 1981: 1)

Similarly, in the early 1990s, Anne-Marie Burley and Walter Mattli (1993: 43) noted that the process of integration through law corresponded 'remarkably closely to the original neofunctionalist model', despite that model having been discredited in the political and economic realms. In other words, legal integration evinced a pattern whereby supranational regulation and the corresponding thickening of transnational ties in one area spilt over into other, related areas. The doctrines of supremacy and direct effect, which Alec Stone Sweet (2010: 29) described as the 'big bang' of European legal integration, were critical to this process.

Though not explicitly addressed in the Treaty of Rome, the ECJ proclaimed the supremacy of Community laws over national laws in areas of supranational competence in the 1964 case, *Costa v ENEL*.[5] The Court held that, by ratifying the Treaty of Rome, member states had permanently limited their sovereign rights, including the right to pass domestic legislation incompatible with Community law. The Court described the Treaty of Rome as an 'independent source of law', which imbued Community legislation with a 'special and original nature' not susceptible to amendment or repeal by the legislative acts of member states. The ECJ reiterated and strengthened its position on supremacy in the 1970 case, *Internationale Handelsgesellschaft*, in which it held that Community law took precedence even over conflicting national constitutional law.[6] These rulings on supremacy reinforced the constitutional reading of the Treaty of Rome adopted by the Court in 1963 in *Van Gend en Loos*, in which it proclaimed the direct effect of certain Community measures within the member states.[7] That case is also notable for its teleological perspective on integration: the ECJ considered that the 'objective of the EEC Treaty' – which it defined as the establishment of a common market – necessarily implied the conferral of rights and obligations upon member states' citizens, as well as the member states themselves, as 'part of their legal heritage'.

The line of reasoning employed in *Van Gend en Loos* and *Costa* was significant because it meant that the EU's legal authority – according to the ECJ, at least – did not derive from the member states, but rather was independent and self-sustaining. For the Court, that legal autonomy flowed from the Union's founding treaties, which it described as Europe's 'constitutional charter'.[8] Critically, the ECJ was able to oversee the implementation of its legal worldview in the member states, despite lacking an extensive European-level administration with coercive enforcement powers. Through their widespread acceptance of direct effect and supremacy (in substance, if not always reasoning), as well as their frequent use of the preliminary reference procedure, national courts became the primary enforcers, and thus legitimisers, of European law (Stone Sweet 2010: 29–31). The ECJ's success in propagating a supranational legal order, via the co-option of member state courts, was no less than a 'quiet revolution' (Weiler 1994).

Weiler's 'quiet revolution' epithet also captures the fact that this process occurred largely out of the public view, and certainly out of the realm of contested politics. During the early period of European integration, while the ECJ was driving the constitutionalisation of the treaties, supranational competences were quite limited and the legislative and executive activities of Community institutions rather removed from the daily lives of most Europeans. Popular ignorance and apathy, particularly prior to the introduction of direct European Parliamentary elections in 1979, were silent but vital components of Community governance. Only certain economic groups, such as the agricultural sector and transnational business, with strong vested interests in the CAP and common market provisions, actively followed and participated in Community-level policy-making. The judicially inspired constitutionalisation of the EU was very much in line with the Monnet method of 'integration by stealth' (Majone 2009a: 12).

To summarise, then, *informal constitutionalism* denotes an incremental legal process with profound political consequences. It was a process that successfully established the contemporary EU as a *sui generis* polity, somewhere between international organisation and federal state, but fundamentally as a community of law (Weiler 1999: 10–101). Yet, it was also a process that, by consistently favouring legalisation over politicisation, helped to cement the democratic deficit that still plagues the EU today.

There is a second sense in which one may invoke the spectre of a 'European Constitution'. This sense refers to the explicit, or *formal constitutionalisation* project that encompassed the attempted adoption of the CT in the early to mid 2000s. The rise and fall of this constitutional project will be discussed in Chapter 2, but even at a glance some contrasts may be drawn with the first, informal conception of EU constitutionalism. Unlike the 'quiet revolution' described above, the CT project was overtly focused on winning the hearts and minds of Europe's citizens for the cause of 'ever closer union'. To this end, the Constitution was debated and drafted through an open and consultative process, of which the 2002–03 European Convention was the showpiece, rather than proceeding via the closed negotiations and deliberations that had characterised previous rounds of legal reform (Piris 2010: 14–17). The democratic spirit imbued in the text's creation (at least in theory) extended to the method of its ratification, with several member states opting to put the Constitution to a popular vote. In short, the CT was a political project pursued by legal means, and – in further contrast to informal constitutionalism – it was unsuccessful.

Several years later, the common currency – a political project pursued by legal and economic means – may also be failing, but with much more serious consequences. If politicisation means stimulating public debate on EU-level policy decisions and, more generally, the future of European integration, then the euro has achieved this to an even greater extent than the CT did. However, increased politicisation has not produced the committed, pro-integration mass of European citizens for which EU leaders had hoped. Instead, the financial crisis is causing a popular backlash in both debtor and creditor countries.[9] Attempts to resolve the crisis through a singular and unrelenting faith in 'more Europe' – a reflection of what Giandomenico Majone (2011: 1) termed the EU's 'political culture of total optimism' – will fail for reasons similar to those that brought about the CT's demise. That is, any European-level push to achieve greater fiscal integration will upset the constitutional equilibrium that, for the most part, has allowed 28 economically, politically, socially and culturally diverse national governments and peoples to coexist with each other and with the Union's supranational institutions. Just as a one-size-fits-all Constitution could not overcome the 'constraining dissensus' (Hooghe and Marks 2009) of popular opinion, enforced austerity through supranational oversight is more likely to provoke conflict than convergence among disenfranchised citizens and national parliaments. Whereas the CT's failure revealed the *symbolic* deficiencies of European constitutionalism, the euro crisis is exposing the *functional* shortcomings of post-Maastricht EU governance. The following section analyses the EU's functional-symbolic constitutional dichotomy in more detail.

Functional and symbolic constitutionalism in the EU

Modern constitutions have both a functional dimension and a symbolic dimension. James Tully (2002: 205) put it slightly differently when he distinguished between two principles that govern the 'legitimacy of contemporary forms of political association'; the principle of constitutionalism (or the rule of law) and the principle of democracy (or popular sovereignty).[10] Tully's first principle describes well the imperatives of functional constitutionalism. It requires that:

> [T]he exercise of political power in the whole and in every part of any *constitutionally* legitimate system of political, social and economic cooperation should be exercised in accordance with and through a general system of principles, rules and procedures, including procedures for amending any principle, rule or procedure.
>
> (Tully 2002: 205, emphasis in original)

Thus, the functional, or instrumental, constitution is depoliticised and somewhat impersonal. Its focus is on legality, or the rule of law. On the other hand, the symbolic dimension of a constitution is more substantive and is geared towards political ends. These ends include identity formation, the promotion of unity in pluralistic polities, the articulation of political and cultural values, the expression of the community's aspirations, and the representation of the community as a sovereign people (Blokker 2010: 1–3; Priban 2007: 20).

The complementarity of the two dimensions and the importance of both to a well-balanced constitution have long been recognised. Walter Bagehot (1928: 8–9) made the observation that a successful constitution needed both its 'dignified parts' and its 'efficient parts'. He wrote of the nineteenth-century English Constitution that 'its dignified parts are very complicated and somewhat imposing, very old and rather venerable; while its efficient part ... is decidedly simple and rather modern'.[11] Together the two parts formed a coherent whole, a framework that facilitated the administration of government, whilst also commanding the respect and loyalty of the general public. Bagehot regarded this favourable combination as the great accomplishment of the English Constitution. By contrast, one of the most striking features of EU constitutionalism is the strict separation between its functional and symbolic dimensions. The EU's informal constitutionalism evolved entirely along functional/instrumental lines to meet functional/instrumental ends. As constitutionalisation was not politicised, little thought was given to the constitution as symbol, as representation of the sovereign people (or peoples) of Europe. The principle of democratic self-government – that is, the legal fiction of the people constituting themselves – was eschewed in favour of legality as the overriding value of the EU's functional constitution. Through this process the founding treaties, as construed by the ECJ, established a 'remarkable transnational legal regime in which politics [was] framed and constrained by judicially enforceable law' (Kumm 2006: 505).

Notwithstanding its functional successes, this approach to constitutionalisation also has its drawbacks. The preponderance of depoliticised, judicialised modes of governance was both informed by, and left its imprint on, the culture of the Community. One of the more problematic legacies of this fact is the Union's enduring technocratic bent, that is, its relative subordination of partisan politics to supposedly value-neutral administration. Since '[d]emocracy without politics is an oxymoron', the Union's 'political deficit' is also at the heart of its democratic deficit, and both have become ever more glaring as the scope of integration has expanded (Weiler 2011: 680). The project of explicit constitutionalisation was driven precisely by the desire to politicise European integration and secure a mandate for the further expansion of EU activities. The symbolic dimension was front and centre throughout the drafting of the CT and the public relations campaign that followed its signing. Some of the most heated debates over the Constitution concerned emotionally charged, identity based questions of political, cultural and historical beliefs, values and aspirations with little functional value (Closa 2005: 426–27). These included the proper place of God and Christianity in the text, the recognition that ought to be accorded to Union symbols such as the flag and anthem, and whether the new representative for foreign policy should, in fact, be called a 'Foreign Minister'.[12]

Part of the problem with the CT was that it tried to be everything to everyone. It was symbolically potent enough for Ulrike Liebert (2010: 71) to describe it as 'one of the most ambitious ideas' in the quest to establish a democratic EU polity. Yet, the Treaty did little to change the complex institutional structures that prevent meaningful engagement and participation by European citizens (Kumm 2008: 127–30). In fact, the lack of substantial institutional reform allowed the then UK Foreign Secretary, Jack Straw, to reassure Britons that the EU Constitution was not unlike that of a golf club.[13] Of course, Straw was being somewhat disingenuous in his comparison. His comments sought to present the CT in a functional/instrumental sense as merely cleaning up and simplifying the EU's complex legal framework. However, legal consolidation was never an end in itself, but rather a by-product of the process of giving the EU a formal Constitution. Straw's efforts were also in vain as the British people remained sceptical of the CT and overly preoccupied with its invocation of state-like motifs.

Thus, despite its functional coherence, the symbolic dimension of EU constitutionalism remained rather weak following the CT's failure. Proponents of ever-closer integration tend to regard the EU's symbolic deficiency as a serious problem because it calls into question the legitimacy of EU legal authority, which in turn limits the democratically tolerable scope of the Union's legislative and executive activities. Mattias Kumm (2006: 509) framed the key debate as being whether the Union has a constitution in 'the strong normative sense of constituting a new legal and political authority that limits the authority of national constitutions'. However, my view is that the EU does not need a constitution in the strong normative sense. Functional European constitutionalism, supported by the constitutional tolerance of the member states, is sufficient to support the EU as a legally pluralistic, non-hierarchical union of nation states. Although the possibility of recreating democratic politics at the supranational level has been much theorised (see, e.g., Hix, 2008; Eriksen, 2010), the legal and political framework of the nation state still provides distinct advantages for the practice of democracy, and these advantages ought not to be hollowed out by excessive transfers of national competences to the EU.

Therefore, the various conceptions of EU constitutionalism presented here are intertwined. The unsuccessful project of formal, symbolic constitutionalisation was nevertheless an important addition to the Union's informal, functional constitutional patchwork; albeit one that counterbalanced the semi-federal legal order established by the ECJ. It is critical to the EU's long-term stability that that balance not be lost amid the clamour for economic and fiscal union as the solution to a dysfunctional monetary union.

Can constitutionalism beyond the state happen?

The relationship between constitutionalism and the modern nation state has significant ramifications for how the European Union is, and ought to be, conceptualised as a legal and political entity. This book is predicated on the view that it is both possible and desirable to use the language of constitutionalism and constitutionalisation to describe the evolution of the EU. Certainly, the breadth and depth of law's reach and its influence in shaping the integration project support Antje Wiener's (2011: 213–16) assertion that the EU is navigating previously uncharted waters of constitutional quality between sovereign state and treaty-based organisation. Moreover, in the second half of the twentieth century and into the twenty-first, the EU has been a pioneer in a global trend. Other international organisations, such as the World Trade Organization (WTO) and United Nations (UN), also have become increasingly 'constitutionalised'. That is to say, they are governed by an increasingly thick set of rules encompassing treaty provisions, conventions and practices, and – critically – judicially generated and enforceable norms (Dunoff and Trachtman 2009).[14] Empirically, then, there is a strong case to be made that constitutionalism beyond the state is an established feature of contemporary international relations.

Nevertheless, for that school of thought that sees constitutionalism as irrevocably linked to the modern state as incubator and guarantor, to even contemplate a *European Constitution*, or *European constitutionalism*, is nonsensical (Walker 2009: 6–12). Tully (1995: 9) captured some of the essence of the statist position when he noted that the idea of modern constitutionalism 'presuppose[s] the uniformity of a nation state with a centralised and unitary system of legal and political institutions'. There are, indeed, a number of 'institutionalised and mythical links' between statehood and modern constitutionalism, which have accumulated through their long association (Wiener 2008: 23). These links give meaning to the notion of a constitution, and cannot be completely disregarded even if the development of non-state organisations, such as the EU, WTO and UN, provides good empirical grounds for decoupling contemporary understandings of constitutionalism from the political category of 'nation state'. It is still the case, for example, that certain constitutional functions, such as the symbolic task of being authorised by, and representative of, the sovereign people, are especially reliant on the unity and mutual identification engendered by nationally based 'imagined communities' (Anderson 1991: 5–7). In fact, the principle of democracy (or popular sovereignty) is the second of Tully's two tenets of constitutional legitimacy, the first of which was discussed in the previous section. Tully's second principle stipulates that:

> Although the people or peoples who comprise a political association are subject to the constitutional system, they, or their entrusted representatives, must also impose the general system on themselves in order to be sovereign and free, and thus for the association to be *democratically* legitimate.
>
> (Tully 2002: 205, emphasis in original)

It is precisely those legitimacy-generating functions contained within Tully's principle of democracy that EU constitutionalism lacks. As much as the EU's uncodified constitution fulfils the institutional, governance and rule of law requirements of a foundational legal settlement, its connection to Europeans is conspicuously absent. This, in turn, has negatively affected political theoretical perceptions of the potential for the EU's constitutionalisation. Continental European debates tended to follow what Kumm (2006: 509) termed the 'emphatic republican tradition' by requiring that a constitution be attributable to 'we the people', that is, the *pouvoir constituant,* which is the ultimate source of legitimate constitutional authority. Accordingly, the inability of EU institutions and the EU's supranational legal order to represent a sovereign European people lent credence to the view that the EU did not and could not have a constitution, at least not in the strong sense (Kumm 2006: 509–11). Such thinking is at the core of the 'no *demos* thesis' espoused by some European legal scholars (Grimm 1995; Craig 2001: 136–39). Dieter Grimm (1995: 294–99), for example, contended that the EU would only be suitable for a democratic constitution if and when national identities were supplanted by a supranational sense of belonging to a European political community.

One does not have to accept the no *demos* thesis *in toto* in order to realise that the absence of a self-identifying European political community places very real limits on the integration project. The eurozone crisis brought this issue into sharp focus: Europe's faltering currency union could be secured and strengthened by the completion of economic and fiscal union (encompassing, for example, institutionalised fiscal transfers and a central budgetary authority), but such solutions are not politically feasible due to their unpopularity with national electorates. The gap between what is economically necessary and what is politically possible (at least whilst trying to retain some semblance of democratic propriety) has left European leaders to 'muddle through' with a series of half-measures. As Christian Joerges (2012: 1016) put it, Economic and Monetary Union (EMU) has been operating at a hurried pace since the spring of 2010, with European leaders producing ever more daring regulatory mechanisms in a piecemeal, rather than holistic, manner. The crisis has also led to a rise in nationalist sentiments and the re-emergence of the kind of ugly national stereotypes that European integration was intended to banish.[15] All of these factors indicate the weakness of the ties that bind Europeans.

The perceived importance of 'instil[ling] in European citizens the feeling of belonging to one Community' preceded the euro crisis by at least a couple of decades (Clark 1997: 800). The range of cultural activities and initiatives sponsored by the EU testifies to the fact that its officials take the issue of fostering a common European identity seriously.[16] The difficulty for the EU is in defining such a community, and the appropriate criteria of belonging to it. Any racially or ethnically based criteria obviously would be unsuitable to a liberal democratic and highly diverse polity. A wholly legalistic understanding of belonging to a European community (e.g. along Kelsenian lines) would be too weak to bind peoples who already have strong alternative political/ national identities. The EU institutions, particularly the Commission, have pursued alternative modes of belonging based on civic values (e.g. commitment to common laws and rights) and shared aspirations (e.g. commitment to a common future). However, these too have proved problematic, as the example of Habermasian constitutional patriotism in Chapter 2 will demonstrate.

The formal constitutionalisation project launched in the early 2000s was intended to go some way towards developing a popular pro-European mindset. The CT was envisaged as providing the connection between a well-established supranational legal and political order and its ostensible subjects. It was to be Europe's 'Madisonian solution', appealing directly to Europeans in their capacity as Union citizens, rather than relying solely on indirect legitimation via the mediation of the member states (Majone 2005: 23–27; 2009b: 8–9). There were many reasons for the CT's failure, but its hubristic and overreaching attempt to codify European identity must be considered an important contributing factor.[17]

Thus, even if one accepts that the EU's legal structure has been constitutionalised via the informal process described earlier, its democratic and representative gaps indicate serious political difficulties that are unlikely to be encountered by golf clubs, Jack Straw's thoughts on constitutionalism notwithstanding. However, it does not follow from the EU's shortcomings as a democratically legitimate polity that it is not capable of supporting a constitution *at all*. An insistence that all constitutional legitimacy must derive from the act of a *pouvoir constituant* is unnecessarily statist, and misleading even when applied to the Westphalian nation state. It greatly simplifies the processes by which national constitutions were created and it is unhelpful in analysing the EU's legal framework (Kumm 2006: 518–21). At the same time, however, there is also a danger of stretching the concept of constitutionalism too far by dismissing entirely the legitimising link between a legal order's subjects and the legal order itself. Scholars and practitioners of European integration should not be overawed by the EU's *sui generis* nature to the point where its democratic shortcomings are excused or ignored (Shore 2006).

Neil Walker (2002: 333–35) also articulated the fear that constitutionalism – disconnected from its Westphalian context and set the task of describing a vast array of post-state political and social developments – has been 'debased' as a conceptual currency. Nevertheless, he argued for the continued value and utility of a renewed constitutional pluralism that recognises the importance of states as sites of legal and political authority, whilst also being open to constitutionalism beyond the state. The notion of renewal is important here. In order to retain its analytical power, constitutional pluralism must build on the concept's historical and ideational background, even when applied to vastly different circumstances, such as the politico-legal character of the EU:

> Constitutional pluralism ... recognises that the European order inaugurated by the Treaty of Rome has developed beyond the traditional confines of inter-*national* law and now makes its own independent constitutional claims, and that these claims exist alongside the continuing claims of states. The relationship between the orders, that is to say, is now horizontal rather than vertical – heterarchical rather than hierarchical.
>
> (Walker 2002: 337, emphasis in original)

In line with Walker's thinking, the premise of this book is that the language of constitutionalism can be usefully applied to a non-state entity such as the European Union in order to explain its unique legal character – that is, the degree to which it has a coherent and effective supranational legal order, and the way in which that legal order interacts with those of the member states in an overarching European legal system. Borrowing from Ingolf Pernice (1999,

2009), EU constitutionalism is not only pluralistic, but also multilevel. Pernice used the term '*Verfassungsverbund*' (which he translated into English as 'multilevel constitutionalism') to describe the EU's novel legal constellation:

> Multilevel constitutionalism is a theoretical approach to conceptualize the "constitution" of this system as an interactive process of establishing, organizing, sharing, and limiting powers – a process that involves national constitutions and the supranational constitutional framework as two interdependent elements of one legal system.
>
> (Pernice 2009: 352–53)

This concept is highly valuable because it goes beyond the ECJ's monistic narrative of EU constitutionalism as a top-down phenomenon, which is merely received and implemented by national actors as agents of a supranational system.[18] Instead, 'multilevel constitutionalism' describes a process that is both contested (between national and European spheres) and limited in ways that do not apply to state-based understandings of constitutionalism.

In summary, then, the lack of a sovereign European people is much more relevant to the question of *what sort of constitution* the EU has, and should aspire to have, than the question of whether it has a constitution at all. The no *demos* thesis exposes the folly of explicit constitutionalisation in the absence of political union – and the futility of trying to construct the latter through the former – but it does not preclude the sort of judicially constructed, limited constitutionalism that has, in fact, flourished in the EU (Kumm 2006). What it does do is imply limits. If there is no sovereign European people capable of endorsing a democratic constitution (and there may never be one), then the core functions and competences of government ought to remain at the national level. A constitutional settlement that recognises and respects these limits is both possible and desirable for the long-term stability and viability of the EU. On the other hand, the EU's attempt at formal constitutionalisation was unnecessary and unviable because of its reliance on those symbolic aspects of constitutionalism that are much better suited to the context of the nation state. Similar criticisms may be levelled at the EU's attempt at monetary union, given its reliance on the (unfounded) assumption that a common currency would promote fiscal convergence amongst a large and diverse group of nation states. The consequences of that act of faith are not yet clear, but they will involve yet another reconfiguration of EU constitutionalism.

Integration through (judge-made) law

There are, then, good grounds for asserting that the EU has a constitution, at least in a functional sense, even though it lacks statehood (Kumm 2006: 508–9). Many of the characteristics identified by Raz are indeed present. The Union's founding treaties perform the institutional structuring and regulation required of a thin constitution. As well as being *constitutive*, EU primary law also provides *stability and continuity* to the integration project, so that the Union can trace its institutional history from 1958 despite having undergone major legal reforms, a considerable expansion in membership, and even name changes since then. Treaty norms are also *superior law* and, accordingly, take precedence over secondary EU legislation. Moreover, owing to the supremacy doctrine, EU legal norms prevail over conflicting member state legislation, including national constitutions. It should be noted, though, that there are caveats to the ECJ's position on supremacy, which has never been fully accepted by national courts (de Witte 2009: 28–30).

Several other of Raz's criteria are applicable to the EU as well. The treaties create rights and obligations that are directly effective and, thus, *justiciable* before the European Court of Justice. The Court's arrogation of the exclusive right of judicial review of the treaties, combined with extensive use of the preliminary reference procedure, have also helped to ensure the uniform interpretation and implementation of treaty norms. Though subject to some degree of 'judicial amendment' (as is any constitution over which a supreme court has the power of judicial review), the actual treaty texts are strongly *entrenched*, at least formally. This is because any changes need to be agreed upon and ratified by all member states, which makes the process of treaty amendment difficult and time-consuming and, hence, rare. Finally, the treaties espouse the *guiding principles* and common values of the Union in several places, including in the preamble and Article 2 of the TEU.[19] Following the Lisbon Treaty, the TEU also incorporates (by reference) the Charter of Fundamental Rights, though human rights have been part of the EU's uncodified constitution since the 1970s, when the ECJ found them to be 'an integral part of the general principles of EC law' (Haltern 2004: 185).[20]

Thus, even without a 'canonical' formulation, judicially driven constitutionalisation established a coherent, effective, and largely supreme legal framework for the European Union. This, in turn, enabled the ECJ to present a law-and-rights-based alternative to the legitimacy via the 'we the people' argument outlined earlier. The EU's legitimacy, in the Court's conception, was based on its constitutional legality. It flowed from the idea of Europe as a legal community bound together by common laws, institutions and a post-war commitment to peace, prosperity and human rights. The principle of democratic self-government, which underpins theories of legitimacy based on the constitution-making authority of a sovereign people, or *pouvoir constituant*, did not factor into such a view (Kumm 2006: 513–15). Instead, it was Kelsenian in the sense of regarding the citizenry as *pouvoir constitué*; that is, as being constituted *by* its subjection to common laws (Ragazzoni 2011: 20).

Importantly, under the ECJ's approach, individuals – rather than human communities – were the beneficiaries of the rights prescribed in the treaties. The doctrine of direct effect meant that private citizens and other legal persons became agents in the enforcement of European legal norms as they were empowered to pursue their rights through national and European courts

(Kelemen 2012: 58–59). Accordingly, the absence of a collective *demos* became less problematic. This was a legitimisation strategy that relied heavily on outputs, including political and economic rights, rather than democratic inputs. However, the global financial crisis showed that EU leaders and institutions could not count on winning the hearts and minds of European citizens by 'delivering the (economic) goods'. Moreover, since the European-level economic constitution was separated from national-level social and labour constitutions, European integration has tended to promote market-related 'goods', the benefits of which are unevenly distributed. In other words, as the ECJ has historically focused on fleshing out the 'four freedoms' of the common market (free movement of goods, services, capital, and people), the weight of its case law is skewed towards the goal of economic liberalisation (Scharpf 2009). Hence, many citizens, particularly in older member states, fear that the ECJ's (and EU's) promotion of individual rights is harming the collective rights that underpin national welfare states. This, in turn, feeds perceptions of EU law and EU decision making as an illegitimate imposition (Scharpf 2009; Joerges 2010: 18–20, 40–49). Such perceptions were a significant factor in the French CT referendum debate, where the 'No' campaign's attack on the CT as the 'handmaiden of an ultraliberal Europe' converged with opposition towards the liberalisation of services as proposed in the Bolkestein directive (Hainsworth 2006: 103–4).

In some respects, then, it is relevant to ask whether constitutionalisation has been *too* successful. That is, whether the exponential growth in the scope and 'substantive penetration' of Community law (Burley and Mattli 1993: 43) has led EU institutions, including the ECJ, to take decisions that exceed their bases of legitimacy or their ability to act efficiently, thus alienating citizens and jeopardising many of the gains of five decades of integration. These questions are taken up again in Chapter 4 in the context of the EU's national and supranational democratic deficits. The next section analyses in more detail the characteristics and ramifications of the judicialisation of EU governance.

The judicialisation of politics and its impact on European integration

The court-led development of European integration was part of a global phenomenon towards the judicialisation of politics that characterised late twentieth- and early twenty-first-century 'new constitutionalism' (Hirschl 2008). This included the judicialisation of 'mega-politics', which Ran Hirschl (2008: 98) described as the 'core political controversies that define the boundaries of the collective or cut through the heart of entire nations'. Mega politics could include, for example, matters concerning electoral processes, restorative justice, regime legitimacy and collective-identity formation. There are both upsides and downsides to the judicialisation of such issues. On the one hand, strong and independent judicial organs are an essential part of any liberal democratic institutional framework, especially insofar as they facilitate the realisation of democracy-enhancing values such as transparency, accountability, access to justice and individual rights (Kelemen 2012: 65). However, the transformation of fundamentally political questions into justiciable controversies can also be problematic from a democratic standpoint, as it pushes the boundaries of the legitimate application of judicial review over the actions of democratically elected legislatures by unelected courts.

Hirschl grouped explanations for the judicialisation of politics into four categories: functionalist, rights-centred, institutionalist, and court-centred. Functionalist approaches emphasised the growing complexity of the welfare state and the concomitant proliferation of administrative and regulatory agencies, which needed to be monitored by independent courts or tribunals with review powers. Rights-based approaches focused on the increased global salience of human rights issues, thus introducing an element of bottom-up judicialisation, as individuals, movements and interest groups turned to courts to vindicate their rights. Institutionalist accounts of judicialisation pointed to the growth in democracy around the world as an explanatory factor. This was because the basic structural features of democracy – including the separation of powers, acceptance of the rule of law, and the existence of independent courts with judicial review powers – were also the preconditions of judicialisation. This is especially true for democratic polities with federal structures, because of the extra layers of checks and balances that such structures require. Finally, court-centred explanations identified courts and judges, themselves, as the agents of judicialisation, at least partly in furtherance of their own institutional interests. To this matrix of factors, Hirschl added political culture, emphasising the importance of courts as political actors that interact with, and are supported by, other sectors of the political elite (Hirschl 2008: 95–98).

The preponderance of judicialised modes of governance was, then, not solely a European phenomenon, but such modes were particularly well entrenched at the supranational level in Europe.[21] R. Daniel Kelemen (2012) termed the EU's tendency to advance political goals through legal means 'Eurolegalism'. Echoing Hirschl's description of global developments, Kelemen described how 'the judicialization of politics in Europe has led courts to become involved in nearly every sort of major political and policy dispute imaginable' (Kelemen 2012: 59). Indeed, all of the explanations discussed by Hirschl shed some light on the judicialisation of European politics. For example, the functionalist approach fits with the complexity of European governance, whereby the EU's model of diffused *political* power – horizontal diffusion amongst Union institutions and vertical diffusion between the Union institutions and the member states – facilitated the *judicial* resolution of policy disputes instead. In addition, the economic liberalisation imperative that drove the creation of the single internal market proved conducive to judicial regulation and oversight (Scharpf 2009: 13–19). Hence, liberalisation resulted over time in traditional national approaches to regulation being replaced by EU regulatory modes that tended to be 'more formal, inflexible and juridified' (Kelemen 2012: 57).

Rights-based approaches are also relevant to an analysis of European judicialisation, since fundamental rights have been an integral part of European constitutionalism for several decades, first through the ECJ's jurisprudence and later through the Charter of Fundamental Rights. In a range of policy areas, from anti-discrimination law to the four freedoms of the single market, Community law was made real and its reach extended throughout the member states by private parties asserting their legal rights in national courts. Furthermore, the structural features described by institutionalist theories as supporting the judicialisation of a polity were present in the multi-level, multi-sphere EU, where the ECJ as 'apex court' was the only institution capable of imposing uniformity. The court-centric approach also offers analytical insights into supranational European judicialisation, given the eagerness with which the ECJ exploited and expanded upon its treaty-based mandate (Pech 2008: 51–52). Finally, the political environment of integration also facilitated judicialisation, as the ECJ had the support both of supranational elites, keen to pursue 'ever closer union', and (at least implicitly) national elites, keen to ensure the adherence of their fellow member states to hard-won legislative bargains (Weiler 1994: 526–27).

The phenomenon of Eurolegalism is reflected in the power dynamics between the EU's legislative branch – split between the Council and the Parliament – and its judicial branch – the ECJ. Striking the right balance between branches of government is one of the main constitutional challenges for any liberal democratic polity. If the legislature is preponderant, it may create a 'tyranny of the majority', thereby jeopardising individual liberties. On the other hand, concentrating excessive power in the hands of an unelected and unrepresentative judicial elite is undemocratic. As described above, the EU's institutional structure favoured the judicial branch from the outset and the ECJ, for its part, seized the ample opportunities provided to it to extend judicial power even further (Kelemen 2012: 58). As with other forms of technocracy, or non-majoritarian rule, 'rule by judges' is not value neutral. Courts have a greater tendency than legislatures to serve privileged minorities and vested interests at the expense of collective interests (Bellamy 2008; Kelemen 2012: 63).[22] Thus, the excessive empowerment of courts in Europe, along with the progressive *disempowerment* of national parliaments (without the restoration of commensurate parliamentary powers at the European level) have contributed to the Union's democratic deficit.

Of course, charges of illegitimate judicial activism and usurpation of legislative and executive prerogatives are levelled at national supreme courts too, especially in states in which the court holds the final power of judicial review (Hirschl 2008: 97). However, in a national context the fallout is limited by the fact that courts are embedded in the legal, political and social structures of the state. National supreme courts may be criticised as unrepresentative and out-of-touch when they hand down unpopular decisions (especially those that overturn the policies of democratically elected governments) but they cannot be regarded as 'foreign', nor their decisions as 'imposed'. The same cannot be said for the ECJ, which is not similarly embedded and, hence, is not as receptive to feedback from the other organs of government and from public opinion, and is not accorded the same level of institutional respect as its national counterparts. The ECJ is not the only EU institution whose legitimacy suffers from a lack of embeddedness. As I will argue in Chapter 5, this is also a problem for the European Central Bank (ECB), which has significant consequences for its ability to manage the euro crisis (Majone 2012: 14).

Queries on the ECJ's legitimacy are not just about perceptions of its embeddedness and responsiveness. As noted above, the EU's legal framework is entrenched in a manner that indicates the existence of a thick constitution (Raz 1998: 153–54). This means that many areas of what would – in a domestic context – be considered ordinary law are granted a 'constitutional character' by virtue of their mention in the treaties (for example, competition law and anti-discrimination law). Whereas it is relatively easy for a national legislature to overcome an unfavourable judicial ruling on an ordinary law by redrafting it to better reflect the legislature's intentions, this is not the case at the European level. In some ways, therefore, EU law is *too* entrenched and the hurdles for amendment via political means are too high – unanimous member state ratification in the case of treaty changes and a Commission proposal, plus European Parliament (EP) approval, plus at least a qualified majority in the Council in the case of secondary laws. These hurdles enhance the power of the EU's 'judicial legislation' and give it a peculiar air of finality. In comparison to the institutional balance of power typical of nation states, 'ECJ interpretations of European law are much more immune to attempts at political correction than is true of judicial legislation at the national level' (Scharpf 2009: 10). This is another way in which Eurolegalism contributes to the EU's democratic deficit.

Not only does Eurolegalism overtax the ECJ's legitimacy base, it also overburdens the law as such. This manifests itself in what Damian Chalmers (2009: 1) described as 'the cumbersomeness of EU law', that is, 'the added significance or resonance attributed to a provision simply by virtue of it having an "EU" tag'. Chalmers (2009: 2) argued that this cumbersomeness could only be understood by reference to 'the claims EU law makes about itself'. In order to justify the existence of its institutional machinery, which it must do on an ongoing basis, EU law is compelled to promise goods that would be otherwise unattainable by other levels of government or other forms of transnational cooperation. The overinflated and even unrealisable claims that EU law makes about its potential to better the lives of European citizens are also partly an attempt to make up for the lack of strong affective ties between the EU and those citizens (Chalmers 2009: 9–10). In this regard, framing policies as rights has the potential to boost the EU's legitimacy by showing 'that it is serving the interests of European citizens' (Kelemen 2012: 58). However, this strategy also carries a considerable risk of backfiring. For its reliance on a politics of betterment, which Chalmers terms a 'European *eudaimonia*', 'leads to an escalation of expectations of government and of the citizen that will not only never be met but can also generate perceptions of breakdown or crisis' (Chalmers 2009: 8). Thus, in times of weak growth and economic tumult, the EU's seeming impotence is exacerbated by the unrealistic standards it has set itself.

Despite the drawbacks of an excessive reliance on law and courts, there were good historical reasons for privileging juridified modes of governance in the European Union. Weiler (2011: 687) described the founders' 'pronounced reliance on the law and legal institutions' as 'not only an audacious but also a prudentially wise choice'. Many post-war West European societies were quite receptive to Eurolegalism, as its rise coincided with a re-evaluation of ideal modes of democratic governance at the national level. Unfettered parliamentary democracy had been widely discredited in continental Europe by the experience of fascist parties seizing power through democratic processes and then using their power to destroy liberty and democracy. Judicialisation, which entailed constraining popular sovereignty and its most important manifestation, the directly elected parliament, was largely a reaction to the disastrous failure of inter-war democratic models. The shift towards checking the power of majoritarian institutions was particularly evident in states such as Germany, Italy and Austria, which had had the worst experiences of those institutions' manipulation by malevolent forces (Müller 2011: 146–49). The governments of these states responded, after 1945, by creating strong and independent constitutional courts charged with protecting individual human rights and given extensive powers of judicial review (Stone Sweet, 2000). A related trend – prompted by the growth and ever-greater complexity of the welfare state (Kaube 2010) – was the increasing delegation of administrative tasks to unelected bodies. This practice, too, tended to bolster the power of the judicial branch of government, as it was ultimately courts rather than parliaments to which bureaucracies were held accountable via administrative judicial review (Müller 2012: 40–42). Broadly, then, West European politics after the Second World War was characterised by a shift from a democratic model heavily centred on representative institutions, to liberal, constitutional democracies, or, as Jan-Werner Müller (2011: 125–30) termed them, 'self-disciplined democracies'.[23]

Developments in the constitutional practices of West European states were complemented by events at the European level. An early example of elite-driven integration overseen by non-majoritarian institutions was the European Coal and Steel Community (ECSC). This organisation was envisaged by the Schuman Declaration of 9 May 1950, and created by the Treaty of Paris in 1952. Under the ECSC's system of governance, authority over member states' coal and steel sectors was ceded to a supranational High Authority, forerunner of the European Commission. This body consisted of unelected technocrats accountable to national executives as represented in the Council of Ministers. Though the ECSC featured an Assembly comprised of national parliamentarians, its powers were weak and its membership nominated rather than elected. Following the entry into force of the Treaty of Rome on

1 January 1958, the ECSC became one of the three 'European Communities' (along with the European Economic Community (EEC) and the European Atomic Energy Community (EURATOM)). At this point, the Assembly became a common institution of all three communities. However, it remained marginal to the process of European integration, even after renaming itself the 'European Parliament' in 1962 (Scully 2010: 163–65; Urwin 2010: 16–25).

Like the institutional changes that occurred at the national level, the belated and incremental empowerment of the European Parliament may be partly explained by the post-war aversion of continental European elites to the excesses of majoritarian democracy. An elected legislature was not essential to an enterprise that was primarily about constraining peoples and preventing their backsliding into authoritarianism (Auer 2010: 137–38). Such an approach to European integration was understandable given the political context of Europe in the late 1940s and 1950s, but the implications for the EU today are profound. The indirectly representative institutional structures that marked the Community at its inception are increasingly frustrating attempts to promote further and closer integration. Simply put, '[d]emocracy was not part of the original DNA of European integration' (Weiler 2011: 694), and its absence will not be remedied by any amount of tinkering at the margins.

Therefore, the effects of the judicialisation of European integration are paradoxical. On the one hand, a heavy reliance on legal integration allowed the European project to take root and thrive; growing from a six-member common market to a 28-member Union with extensive clout beyond the internal regulation of goods, services, capital and labour mobility. On the other hand, the very success of supranational judicialisation made the EU's technocratic nature increasingly problematic as its reach was extended to ever more 'mega political' issues. That the corollary to the judicialisation of politics is the politicisation of courts may seem obvious, but it bears explicit mention because it foreshadows another dimension of the EU's democratic deficit that is becoming more significant. The EU's reliance on legal regulations and judicially enforceable rights points towards a more general preference for empowering and politicising non-majoritarian institutions. In this connection, one notable outcome of the euro crisis has been the increasing tendency of the formally independent and notionally apolitical ECB to take what are, in fact, highly political decisions, for example, in relation to the purchase of eurozone sovereign debt.

Overcoming this paradox at the heart of EU constitutionalism will require either a radical overhaul of the Union's institutional structure and processes – giving it a level of democratic legitimacy commensurate to its competences (see, for example, Hix 2008) – or a scaling back of the range and degree of powers held at the supranational level, thereby bolstering the nation state's position as democratic mainstay. This debate turns partly on the issue of how the EU relates to its citizens, and how it *ought* to do so; an issue that may be illuminated by a comparison with state-based federations.

Locating people and place: a comparison between EU and federal constitutionalism

The EU's confederal, or even federal-like, constitutional framework has inspired comparisons with established federal states such as the United States of America, Canada, Germany and Switzerland (for a summary of these debates, see Aroney 2009). Since it is in the legal realm that the EU most closely resembles a federal state, it is unsurprising that there are many analogies between the roles of the US Supreme Court and the ECJ in promoting the integration and centralisation of their respective polities. In terms of its constitutional significance, *Van Gend en Loos*, which established the doctrine of direct effect, has been compared to the landmark US case *Marbury v Madison* (1803), in which the Supreme Court established the principle of constitutional judicial review of legislative actions:

> Despite a limited textual basis and against the interpretation of key political actors, both the European Court of Justice and the US Supreme Court asserted the supreme authority of their respective founding texts and established themselves as the final judicial authority with respect to their interpretation and the validity of legislation derived from them.
>
> (Pech 2008: 51–52)

Although the ECJ has taken on a role comparable to that of a state-based constitutional court, the 'founding texts' over which it presides are international treaties, rather than a federal Constitution. As noted earlier, the fact that there is no 'European people' is sometimes used to argue the impossibility of having a European constitution (Kumm 2006: 506). It follows that the problem of the European *demos* (or lack thereof) is linked to debates on the treaty/constitution dichotomy. For scholars who adhere to the no *demos* thesis (and hence hold the symbolic dimension of a constitution to be at least as important as its functional dimension), the EU is fundamentally different from a federal state because its founding documents were, and remain, international treaties (Aroney 2009: 10). This distinction between a treaty-based polity and a constitutional polity is supposedly reflected in the mode of adoption of key foundational texts. Thus, whereas the Treaty of Rome and all subsequent EU treaties were signed and ratified by independent, sovereign states, the US Constitution of 1788 is regarded as the act of a single American *demos* – 'we, the people' constituting themselves as a federal union.

While there are real and critical differences between the EU and integrative federations, such as the United States of America, the treaty/constitution dichotomy is misleading because it understates the similarities between European *legal* integration and equivalent processes in federal states (Aroney 2009). The form that a text takes, in and of itself, does not determine the nature of that text. A text that takes the form of a treaty between states is not precluded from giving rise to a transnational constitution. Whether it does so or not is a question of interpretation (Kumm 2006: 517). The history of some of the world's most successful national constitutions gives the lie to the idea that a constitution must be authorised by a pre-existing national people in order to be legitimate. The 1901 Australian Constitution, for example, was approved in referenda held separately in each colony, but only became law (i.e. gained its authoritative force) after being passed as an Act of the British Parliament.

To cite a European example, the German Basic Law was drafted in the context of Germany's defeat in the Second World War and its subsequent partition. At the time of its promulgation in 1949, West Germany was not fully sovereign, and the text was subject to the approval of the western allied powers (Tipton 2003: 506). Nevertheless, it came to occupy a central place – functionally and symbolically – in the West German state, becoming a touchstone of common identity, and even patriotism, in a polity in which national affective ties had been so thoroughly discredited by the experience of Nazism (Grimm 2005: 202–203). It is possible, therefore, for constitutions to accrue legitimacy over time as important markers of national (or potentially supranational) identity, even if they did not originate from the deliberative act of a self-aware *pouvoir constituant*.

The United States of America itself provides an example of the ability of constitutions to transcend their origins. Giandomenico Majone (2005, 2009b) has described the fiction of the 'Madisonian solution', employed in the US case in an attempt to overcome state resistance to federation by appealing over their heads directly to the American people. Notably, the US Constitution still had to be ratified on a state-by-state basis by specially elected conventions. There were no popular referenda or nationwide approval mechanisms of any sort. In other words, even if there were such a thing as 'the American people', they were not consulted on the Constitution in that capacity. The more plausible conclusion to draw is that 'the American people' were constituted *through* the process of federation, rather than being a pre-existing and independent agency capable of constituting the USA (Grimm 2009: 54–60). Thus, ratification of the US Constitution was not substantively all that different to treaty ratification processes used in the EU.

Still, there are qualitative differences in the potential for *demos* creation between the USA, which was deliberately constitutionalised as a federal state, and the EU, a non-state entity that was constitutionalised 'by stealth', largely by the ECJ. Jürgen Habermas (2012: 16–17) argued that much scepticism towards the idea of transnational democracy was based on a confusion of popular and state sovereignty – two concepts that are only associated as a result of a 'contingent historical constellation'. Thus, he wrote of the possibility, and indeed necessity, of decoupling those two concepts as a first step towards 'an uncoupling of the democratic procedure from the nation state' (Habermas 2012: 14). However, there is little sign of a transnational public sphere emerging in Europe that would be capable of exercising popular sovereignty. The Constitutional Treaty may have been the EU's attempt at a 'Madisonian solution', but it was rejected, and its failure is indicative of the challenges the

EU faces in winning the hearts and minds of Europeans.[24] As Jean-Claude Piris noted, '[t]he use of words such as "laws", "minister", "flag" or "anthem" and, above all, of the word "constitution" did have a powerful political effect'. However, it was not the *positive* effect for which the CT's drafters had hoped. Instead, the use of such loaded terms 'provoked a psychological shock which proved to be politically much larger than the legal nature and substantive content of the Constitutional Treaty', and which contributed to its rejection (Piris 2010: 23).

The EU's sovereign nation states have long histories and a diverse range of political, economic and social structures, all of which complicate the task of achieving the degree of unity and coordination required of even a loose federation. In the USA, on the other hand, factors such as a common language, an overwhelmingly common (British) legal and cultural heritage and the experience of having fought a war of independence together, contributed greatly to the task of nation building and identity formation. Even then, it was only after a bloody civil war – fought almost eighty years after federation – that the Union was truly cemented. The American federalists in 1788–89 also had the benefit of operating in a 'constitutional moment', unlike their European counterparts in the 2000s, when the EU attempted to adopt its formal constitution. Though not an absolute pre-requisite, the presence of a constitutional moment – that is, a historical juncture in which a general consensus exists on the need for, and desirability of, transformative legal and political change – can be significant 'for a constitution's integrative and identity-building force' (Grimm 2005: 200; see also Ackerman 1989).

Another factor distinguishing the EU from state-based federations is the relative weakness of its 'federal' or 'supranational' institutions. After all, the US Constitution did give the American polity a strong national Congress and President. The EU, on the other hand, does not have a true central government at all. Alexander Hamilton's (1787) robust critique of the inefficacy of 'government over governments' ('the political monster of an *imperium in imperio*') is instructive. Hamilton's views were informed by the economic, political and security weaknesses of the American confederation, which he blamed on the coercive incapacity of the national government and its resultant dependence on the states; each with its own level of ability and willingness to enforce national law.

The experience of the eurozone illustrates the pitfalls of pushing for state-like levels of integration in one area without an overarching federal structure in place. The creation of a currency union without the centralised oversight and administration of a federal treasury and without effective enforcement mechanisms meant that individual national governments were able to pursue very different fiscal policies for too long without sanction. This undermined the effectiveness of the ECB's common monetary policy over a number of years, and eventually precipitated a full-blown crisis that threatened the integrity of the eurozone as a whole. Legislative measures originally put in place in order to maintain states' macroeconomic and budgetary discipline, including the Stability and Growth Pact (SGP), first adopted in 1997 and reformed in 2005, proved too easily violable (Louis 2010: 978–80). Indeed, the SGP, which relied on monitoring and peer pressure amongst the Eurogroup, was described as being akin to having 'a fire code without a fire brigade' (Paul de Grauwe, quoted in Louis 2010: 980).[25]

The euro crisis has prompted changes to the EU's governance structures, starting with more centralised economic coordination and oversight for eurozone members (plus non-euro states that wish to participate). However, it is still highly doubtful whether these measures will prove sufficient. That is, it is doubtful whether imposing further layers of *'governance* over governments' can induce those governments to follow common European-level policies, potentially to the great detriment of their respective national interests.

Concluding remarks: the competing narratives of EU constitutionalism and their legal and political consequences

It is difficult to overstate the complexity of EU constitutionalism, or its importance to the European integration project. This book focuses on two distinct, but mutually interacting, subcategories of the broader constitutional concept. On the one hand, informal constitutionalism – evolutionary, legalistic, and judicially driven – a sturdy foundation for a common market, but not symbolically potent enough to support political union. On the other hand, formal constitutionalism as represented by the Constitutional Treaty – a symbolically loaded and politically ambitious attempt to bridge the gap between EU institutions and European citizens.

The study of EU constitutionalism, then, is the study of the relationship between law and politics in Europe. At the heart of this relationship is the place of Europe's people, or peoples. How best are we to conceive of the legal and political role of Europeans in the integration project: as the subjects and beneficiaries of EU laws and rights, or also as their authors? As a loose association of national publics, whose connection to the Union is mediated through national representatives, or as a European public sphere, capable of legitimising the institutional arrangements of EU governance? In both cases the first option appears to describe more closely the reality of the situation. The success of the EU's informal, functional constitutionalism demonstrates that legality can be extended beyond the nation state. However, there is only so much political integration that can be achieved through legal means. This fact is amply illustrated by the euro crisis, the resolution of which is seriously hampered by a lack of unity and solidarity amongst the peoples and states of Europe. The failure of the CT demonstrated just as clearly that conferring democratic legitimacy on a non-state entity is much more difficult than endowing it with a constitutionalised legal framework. It is the troubled history of that project to which I now turn.

Notes

1 Kelsen's concept of constitution was linked to his understanding of legal order as hierarchy:

> The legal order is not a system of coordinated norms of equal level, but a hierarchy of different levels of legal norms. Its unity is brought about by the connection that results from the fact that the validity of a norm created according to another norm, rests on that other norm, whose creation in turn, is determined by a third one. This is a regression that ultimately ends up in the presupposed basic norm.
>
> (Kelsen 1989: 221–22)

2 For an overview see Paul Craig (2001). Joseph Weiler (2005) neatly captured the complex interplay between informal and formal constitutionalism with his analysis of the huge significance attached to the very word, 'constitution'.

3 The EU's primary law consists of the two founding treaties, the Treaty on European Union (TEU) and the Treaty on the Functioning of the European Union (TFEU), as most recently amended by the Lisbon Treaty. According to Article 1(2) TFEU, 'This Treaty and the Treaty on European Union constitute the Treaties on which the Union is founded. These two Treaties, which have the same legal value, shall be referred to as "the Treaties"'. Any references to the TEU or TFEU in this book are to the post-Lisbon Treaty consolidated versions, unless otherwise indicated.

4 The European Union (EU) was created by the 1992 Maastricht Treaty. The European Economic Community (EEC), or simply, the European Community (EC), as it came to be known, was only one of the EU's three pillars. Under the terms of the 2009 Lisbon Treaty, the EU succeeded the EC and assumed its own legal personality. For the sake of convenience, references in the book will be to the EU and EU law, unless the specific context indicates otherwise.

5 *Costa v ENEL* [1964] ECR 585 (Case 6/64).

6 *Internationale Handelsgesellschaft* [1970] ECR 1125 (Case 11/70).

7 *Van Gend en Loos v Nederlandse Administratie der Belastingen* [1963] ECR 1 (Case 26/62).

8 *Parti Ecologiste 'Les Verts' v European Parliament* [1986] ECR 1339 (Case 294/83).

9 In a number of countries 'political entrepreneurs' are seizing on widespread anti-EU sentiments to differentiate themselves from mainstream, pro-EU political parties (Majone 2011: 1–3).

10 It should be noted that in this book *constitutionalism* is used in a much broader sense, in accordance with Raz's thick definition of the concept. Therefore, it cannot be simply equated with the rule of law, though adherence to the rule of law is an element of thick constitutionalism.

11 The EU's most significant attempt to constitutionalise its 'dignified parts' failed in 2005. The Constitutional Treaty's defeat revealed that the task of identifying, let alone propagating, appropriate common symbols is a serious challenge for the EU given the historical, political and cultural diversity of its constituent states. Moreover, the EU's governance structures, ideally the 'efficient parts', are actually very complex and little understood by European citizens.

12 These debates, some of the most colourful in the EU's history, also provide a valuable insight into the conflicts at the heart of the integration project. For an argument in favour of the recognition of Christianity in some form in the CT, see Joseph Weiler (2004: 36–65).

13 The Foreign Secretary argued that, '[t]he point about having a constitution is that it's a clearly understood word describing the basic rules for the operation of an

institution, whether it's a golf club, a political party or in this case a European Union' (*The Guardian*, 2002).

14 See the contributions in Jeffrey L. Dunoff and Joel P. Trachtman (eds) (2009) for a discussion of constitutionalisation beyond the state in general as well as specific institutional case studies.

15 In an interview with *Der Spiegel*, Jean-Claude Juncker, former head of the Eurogroup, bemoaned the fact that, contrary to the original intention of monetary union, 'far too many Europeans are returning to a regional and national mindset'. He went on to draw parallels between Europe in 2013 and Europe in 1913, cautioning against complacency and warning that '[t]he demons [of nationalism and war] haven't been banished' (*Spiegel Online*, 2013).

16 See, for example, the 'Culture' webpage of the Directorate-General of Education and Culture, http://ec.europa.eu/culture/index_en.htm (Accessed: 24 March 2014).

17 As Albrecht Sonntag (2011: 120) observed, 'it turned out to be highly counterproductive to raise unrealistic expectations by solemnly naming a new treaty, whose major purpose was to adapt the functioning of the institutions to the new scope of the Union, a "Constitution"', arguing further that Europeans were not ready to accept an 'ultimate, definitive settlement', which is what the term, 'Constitution', implies.

18 For an insightful discussion of monistic versus pluralistic conceptions of EU constitutionalism, and cogent arguments in favour of the latter, see the 2008 symposium held at the European University Institute (EUI) with Julio Baquero Cruz, Mattias Kumm, Miguel Poiares Maduro, and Neil Walker (Avbelj and Komarek 2008).

19 Article 2 TEU states:

> The Union is founded on the values of respect for human dignity, freedom, democracy, equality, the rule of law and respect for human rights, including the rights of persons belonging to minorities. These values are common to the Member States in a society in which pluralism, non-discrimination, tolerance, justice, solidarity and equality between women and men prevail.

20 The ECJ's human rights jurisprudence was not just about representing common European values. It was also a practical measure undertaken to safeguard the integrity of the supremacy doctrine in the face of national legal challenges (Hartley 2010: 143–51). See Chapter 3 for a discussion of this issue in the context of the German Constitutional Court's EU jurisprudence.

21 Alec Stone Sweet (2010: 5) described the judicialisation of EU governance as 'one of the most complex and dramatic examples of judicialization' in world history.

22 Richard Bellamy (2008: 19) argued, contrary to the supposed benefits of rights-based judicial review, that 'the check this procedure imposes on majoritarian decision-making risks undermining political equality, distorts the agenda away from the public interest, and entrenches the privileges of dominant minorities and the domination of unprivileged ones'.

23 As on other issues, the United Kingdom is the odd one out. It does not have a written constitution (or, at least, not one codified in a single document) and it was only relatively recently (largely as a result of EU membership) that the doctrine of parliamentary sovereignty has been challenged by developments in the judicial branch, including enhanced powers of judicial review.

24 See Paul Statham and Hans-Jörg Trenz (2012), especially Chapter 3, for an analysis of the CT's impact on the transnationalisation of national public spheres in France, Germany and the UK, which finds that these spheres were only weakly Europeanised insofar as European-level developments, or developments in other member states (e.g. the French referendum), were 'domesticated' in national debates.

25 Again, Alexander Hamilton's warning that the pull of 'common interests' was insufficient to guarantee the cooperation and compliance of the independent states of the confederation is relevant:

> In our case, the concurrence of thirteen distinct sovereign wills is requisite, under the Confederation, to the complete execution of every important measure that proceeds from the Union. It has happened as was to have been foreseen. The measures of the Union have not been executed; the delinquencies of the States have, step by step, matured themselves to an extreme, which has, at length, arrested all the wheels of the national government, and brought them to an awful stand ... The greater deficiencies of some States furnished the pretext of example and the temptation of interest to the complying, or to the least delinquent States. Why should we do more in proportion than those who are embarked with us in the same political voyage? Why should we consent to bear more than our proper share of the common burden? ... Each State, yielding to the persuasive voice of immediate interest or convenience, has successively withdrawn its support, till the frail and tottering edifice seems ready to fall upon our heads, and to crush us beneath its ruins.
>
> (Hamilton 1787)

References

Ackerman, B. (1989) 'Constitutional Politics/Constitutional Law'. *The Yale Law Journal*, Vol. 99, No. 3, pp. 453–547.

Anderson, B. (1991) *Imagined Communities: Reflections on the Origin and Spread of Nationalism* (London and New York: Verso).

Aroney, N. (2009) 'Federal Constitutionalism/European Constitutionalism in Comparative Perspective'. *The Federal Trust European Essay*, No. 45, pp. 1–30.

Auer, S. (2010) 'The European Union's Politics of Identity and the Legacy of 1989'. *Humanities Research*, Vol. XVI, No. 3, pp. 135–49.

Avbelj, M. and Komarek, J. (eds) (2008) 'Four Visions of Constitutional Pluralism'. *European University Institute (EUI) Working Papers LAW 2008/21*, pp. 1–37.

Bagehot, W. (1928) *The English Constitution*, 2nd edn. (London: Oxford University Press).

Bellamy, R. (2006) 'The European Constitution is Dead, Long Live European Constitutionalism'. *Constellations*, Vol. 13, No. 2, pp. 181–89.

——(2008) 'The Democratic Constitution: Why Europeans Should Avoid American Style Constitutional Judicial Review'. *European Political Science*, Vol. 7, No. 1, pp. 9–20.

Blokker, P. (2010) 'Democratic Ethics, Constitutional Dimensions, and Constitutionalisms'. In Febbrajo, A. and Sadurski, W. (eds) *Central Eastern Europe after Transition: Towards a New Socio-Legal Semantics* (Aldershot: Ashgate).

——(2011) 'Constitutional Anomie in Post-Westphalian Europe'. *Paper presented at the 6th ECPR General Conference*, Reykjavik, Iceland, 25–27 August.

Burley, A. and Mattli, W. (1993) 'Europe before the Court: A Political Theory of Legal Integration'. *International Organization*, Vol. 47, No. 1, pp. 41–76.

Busch, J. and Ehs, T. (2008) 'Kelsen's Concept of Legal Community and the European Union'. *ICL – Working Paper 01/2008*, pp. 1–25.

Chalmers, D. (2009) 'Gauging the Cumbersomeness of EU Law'. *LEQS Paper No. 2 May 2009*, pp. 1–37.

Christiansen, T. and Reh, C. (2009) *Constitutionalizing the European Union* (Basingstoke: Palgrave Macmillan).

Clark, C. (1997) 'Forging Identity: Beethoven's "Ode" as European Anthem'. *Critical Inquiry*, Vol. 23, No. 4, pp. 789–807.

Closa, C. (2005) 'Deliberative Constitutional Politics and the Turn towards a Norms-Based Legitimacy of the EU Constitution'. *European Law Journal*, Vol. 11, No. 4, pp. 411–31.

Cooper, I. (2010) 'Mapping the Overlapping Spheres: European Constitutionalism after the Treaty of Lisbon'. *ARENA Centre for European Studies Seminar Paper*, pp. 1–32.

Craig, P. (2001) 'Constitutions, Constitutionalism, and the European Union'. *European Law Journal*, Vol. 7, No. 2, pp. 125–50.

Dashwood, A. (2004) 'The Relationship between the Member States and the European Union/European Community'. *Common Market Law Review*, Vol. 41, No. 2, pp. 355–81.

De Witte, B. (2009) 'The Lisbon Treaty and National Constitutions: More or Less Europeanisation?' In Closa, C. (ed.) *The Lisbon Treaty and National Constitutions: Europeanisation and Democratic Implications* (Oslo: ARENA Report No 3/09).

Dinan, D. (2012) 'How Did We Get Here?' In Bomberg, E., Peterson, J. and Corbett, R. (eds) *The European Union: How Does it Work?* (Oxford: Oxford University Press).

Dunoff, J. L. and Trachtman, J. P. (2009) 'A Functional Approach to International Constitutionalization'. In Dunoff, J. L. and Trachtman, J. P. (eds) *Ruling the World? Constitutionalism, International Law, and Global Governance* (Cambridge: Cambridge University Press).

Dunoff, J. L. and Trachtman, J. P. (eds) (2009) *Ruling the World? Constitutionalism, International Law, and Global Governance* (Cambridge: Cambridge University Press).

Eriksen, E. (2010) 'What Democracy for Europe?' In Eriksen, E. and Fossum, J. (eds) *What Democracy for Europe?* (RECON Report No 11).

Grimm, D. (1995) 'Does Europe Need a Constitution?' *European Law Journal*, Vol. 1, No. 3, pp. 282–302.

——(2005) 'Integration by Constitution'. *International Journal of Constitutional Law*, Vol. 3, No. 2–3, pp. 193–210.

——(2009) *Souveränität. Herkunft und Zukunft eines Schlüsselbegriffs* (Berlin: Berlin University Press).

Habermas, J. (2012) *The Crisis of the European Union: A Response* (Cambridge: Polity).

Hainsworth, P. (2006) 'France Says No: The 29 May 2005 Referendum on the European Constitution'. *Parliamentary Affairs*, Vol. 59, No. 1, pp. 98–117.

Haltern, U. (2004) 'Integration through Law'. In Wiener, A. and Diez, T. (eds) *European Integration Theory* (Oxford: Oxford University Press).

Hamilton, A. (1787) 'The Federalist No. 15: The Insufficiency of the Present Con-federation to Preserve the Union'. *The Federalist Papers*, available at www.constitution.org/fed/federa15.htm (Accessed: 25 March 2014).

Hartley, T. C. (2010) *The Foundations of European Law* (Oxford: Oxford University Press).

Hirschl, R. (2008) 'The Judicialization of Mega-Politics and the Rise of Political Courts'. *Annual Review of Political Science*, Vol. 11, pp. 93–118.

Hix, S. (2008) *What's Wrong with the European Union and How to Fix It* (Cambridge: Polity).

Hooghe, L. and Marks, G. (2009) 'A Postfunctionalist Theory of European Integration: From Permissive Consensus to Constraining Dissensus'. *British Journal of Political Science*, Vol. 39, No. 1, pp. 1–23.

Joerges, C. (2010) 'Unity in Diversity as Europe's Vocation and Conflicts Law as Europe's Constitutional Form'. *LEQS Paper No. 28 December 2010*, pp. 1–66.

——(2012) 'Recht und Politik in der Krise Europas: Die Wirkungsgeschichte einer verunglückten Konfiguration'. *Merkur*, Vol. 66, No. 11, pp. 1013–24.

Kaube, J. (2010) 'Vater Staat und seine Erwachsenen. Die Politik des Lebensstandards als Maß aller Dinge'. *Merkur*, Vol. 64, No. 9–10, pp. 996–1004.

Kelemen, R. D. (2012) 'Eurolegalism and Democracy'. *Journal of Common Market Studies*, Vol. 50, No. S1, pp. 55–71.

Kelsen, H. (1989) *Pure Theory of Law* (Gloucester, MA: Peter Smith).

Kumm, M. (2006) 'Beyond Golf Clubs and the Judicialization of Politics: Why Europe has a Constitution Properly So Called'. *The American Journal of Constitutional Law*, Vol. 54, Fall, pp. 505–30.

——(2008) 'Why Europeans Will Not Embrace Constitutional Patriotism'. *International Journal of Constitutional Law*, Vol. 6, No. 1, pp. 117–36.

Liebert, U. (2010) 'Contentious European Democracy'. In Lacroix, J. and Nicolaidis, K. (eds) *European Stories, Intellectual Debates on Europe in National Contexts* (Oxford: Oxford University Press).

Louis, J.-V. (2010) 'The No-Bailout Clause and Rescue Packages'. *Common Market Law Review*, Vol. 47, No. 4, pp. 971–86.

Majone, G. (2005) *Dilemmas of European Integration: The Ambiguities and Pitfalls of Integration by Stealth* (Oxford: Oxford University Press).

——(2009a) *Europe as the Would-Be World Power: The EU at Fifty* (Cambridge: Cambridge University Press).

——(2009b) 'The "Referendum Threat", the Rationally Ignorant Voter, and the Political Culture of the EU'. *RECON Online Working Paper 2009/04*.

——(2011) 'Monetary Union and the Politicization of Europe'. *Keynote speech at the Euroacademia International Conference: 'The European Union and the Politicization of Europe'*, Vienna, 8–10 December.

——(2012) 'Rethinking European Integration after the Debt Crisis'. *UCL: The European Institute, Working Paper No. 3/2012*, June.

Moravcsik, A. (2006) 'What Can We Learn from the Collapse of the European Constitutional Project?' *Politische Vierteljahresschrift*, Vol. 47, No. 2, pp. 219–41.

Müller, J.-W. (2011) *Contesting Democracy: Political Ideas in Twentieth Century Europe* (New Haven, CT: Yale University Press).

——(2012) 'Beyond Militant Democracy?' *New Left Review*, Vol. 73, Jan–Feb, pp. 39–47.

Pech, L. (2008) 'The Fabulous Destiny of the EC Treaty: From Treaty to Constitution to Treaty Again?' *Irish Journal of European Law*, Vol. 15, No. 1–2, pp. 49–78.

Pernice, I. (1999) 'Multilevel Constitutionalism and the Treaty of Amsterdam: European Constitution-Making Revisited?' *Common Market Law Review*, Vol. 36, No. 4, pp. 703–50.

——(2009) 'The Treaty of Lisbon: Multilevel Constitutionalism in Action'. *Columbia Journal of International Law*, Vol. 15, No. 3, pp. 349–407.

Piris, J.-C. (2010) *The Lisbon Treaty: A Legal and Political Analysis* (Cambridge: Cambridge University Press).

Priban, J. (2007) *Legal Symbolism: On Law, Time and European Identity* (Hampshire: Aldershot).

Ragazzoni, D. (2011) 'Identity vs. Representation: What Makes "The People"? Rethinking Democratic Citizenship through (and beyond) Carl Schmitt and Hans Kelsen'. *Perspectives on Federalism*, Vol. 3, No. 2, pp. 1–30.

Raz, J. (1998) 'On the Authority and Interpretation of Constitutions: Some Preliminaries'. In Alexander, L. (ed.) *Constitutionalism: Philosophical Foundations* (Cambridge: Cambridge University Press).

Reh, C. (2009) 'The Lisbon Treaty: De-Constitutionalizing the European Union?' *Journal of Common Market Studies*, Vol. 47, No. 3, pp. 625–50.

Rosenfeld, M. (1992) 'Modern Constitutionalism as Interplay between Identity and Diversity'. *Cardozo Law Review*, Vol. 14, No. 3–4, pp. 497–531.

Scharpf, F. (2009) 'The Double Asymmetry of European Integration. Or: Why the EU Cannot Be a Social Market Economy'. *Max-Planck-Institut für Gesellschaftsforschung, MPIfG Working Paper 09/12*, November.

Scully, R. (2010) 'The European Parliament'. In Cini, M. and Perez-Solorzano Borragan, N. (eds) *European Union Politics* (Oxford: Oxford University Press).

Shore, C. (2006) '"Government without Statehood"? Anthropological Perspectives on Governance and Sovereignty in the European Union'. *European Law Journal*, Vol. 12, No. 6, pp. 709–24.

Sonntag, A. (2011) 'False Expectations: The Counterproductive Side Effects of the EU's Use of Political Symbols'. In Cerutti, F. and Lucarelli, S. (eds) *The Search for a European Identity* (London: Routledge).

Spiegel Online (2013) 'Jean-Claude Juncker Interview: "The Demons Haven't Been Banished"'. 11 March.

Statham, P. and Trenz, H.-J. (2012) *The Politicization of Europe: Contesting the Constitution in the Mass Media* (Oxford: Routledge).

Stein, E. (1981) 'Lawyers, Judges and the Making of a Transnational Constitution'. *American Journal of International Law*, Vol. 75, No. 1, pp. 1–27.

Stone Sweet, A. (2000) *Governing with Judges: Constitutional Politics in Europe* (Oxford: Oxford University Press).

——(2010) 'The European Court of Justice and the Judicialization of EU Governance'. *Living Reviews in European Governance*, Vol. 5, No. 2, pp. 1–50.

The Guardian (2002) 'Straw Calls for EU Constitution'. 27 August.

Tipton, F. B. (2003) *A History of Modern Germany since 1815* (Berkeley and Los Angeles: University of California Press).

Tully, J. (1995) *Strange Multiplicity: Constitutionalism in an Age of Diversity* (Cambridge: Cambridge University Press).

——(2002) 'The Unfreedom of the Moderns in Comparison to Their Ideals of Constitutional Democracy'. *Modern Law Review*, Vol. 65, No. 2, pp. 204–28.

Urwin, D. W. (2010) 'The European Community: From 1945 to 1985'. In Cini, M. and Perez-Solorzano Borragan, N. (eds) *European Union Politics* (Oxford: Oxford University Press).

Walker, N. (2002) 'The Idea of Constitutional Pluralism'. *Modern Law Review*, Vol. 65, No. 3, pp. 317–59.

——(2009) 'Multilevel Constitutionalism: Looking Beyond the German Debate'. *LEQS Paper No. 8*, June, pp. 1–30.

Weiler, J. H. H. (1991) 'The Transformation of Europe'. *The Yale Law Journal*, Vol. 100, No. 8, pp. 2403–83.

——(1994) 'A Quiet Revolution: The European Court of Justice and Its Interlocutors'. *Comparative Political Studies*, Vol. 26, No. 4, pp. 510–34.

——(1999) *The Constitution of Europe: 'Do the New Clothes Have an Emperor?' And Other Essays on European Integration* (Cambridge: Cambridge University Press).

——(2004) *Ein christliches Europa* (Salzburg: Verlag Anton Pustet).

——(2005) 'On the Power of the Word: Europe's Constitutional Iconography'. *International Journal of Constitutional Law*, Vol. 3, No. 2–3, pp. 173–92.

——(2011) 'The Political and Legal Culture of European Integration: An Exploratory Essay'. *International Journal of Constitutional Law*, Vol. 9, No. 3–4, pp. 678–94.

Whitman, R. (2005) 'No and After: Options for Europe'. *International Affairs*, Vol. 81, No. 4, pp. 673–87.

Wiener, A. (2008) *The Invisible Constitution of Politics. Contested Norms and International Encounters* (Cambridge: Cambridge University Press).

——(2011) 'Through Uncharted Waters of Constitutional Quality: Navigating between Modern Statehood and International Organisation'. In Wiener, A. and Neyer, J. (eds) *Political Theory of the European Union* (Oxford: Oxford University Press).

2 Constructing and reconstructing the Constitution for Europe

Introduction: the end of the 'permissive consensus' and the search for solidarity in a formal European Constitution

The European integration project underwent a number of upheavals between the 1980s and the early 2000s. The reintroduction of QMV, the significant post-Cold War enlargement and the Maastricht Treaty's launch of a more overtly political EU all affected the nature of the integration project as well as perceptions of it. Liesbet Hooghe and Gary Marks (2009) documented the shift from 'permissive consensus' to 'constraining dissensus' that occurred in the post-Maastricht period, focusing on growing unease amongst European publics. Since national elites remained broadly in favour of further integration, the EU's increased prominence in citizens' daily lives tended to widen the cleavage between elites and masses. It also contributed to higher levels of euroscepticism in many member states (Auer 2010a).

By the early twenty-first century, concerns over the EU's weak base of popular legitimacy, amongst other things, prompted an initiative to adopt a formal constitution. It was not *legally* necessary since the EU already possessed an effective, though uncodified, functional constitution. However, a 'capital C', Constitution for Europe was regarded by many EU scholars and practitioners as politically and symbolically desirable. Attempts to foster a common EU-European identity had been made in the past but the CT was to be the grandest gesture yet, a triumphant capping of the many achievements of European integration. To this end, the Constitution's framers drew on German philosopher Jürgen Habermas's concept of constitutional patriotism to design a document that would infuse the EU's well-established legal order with the symbolism it had hitherto lacked.

Yet, despite the coherence and normative strength of the EU's *de facto* constitution, the turn to explicit constitutionalisation was spectacularly unsuccessful. In fact, the CT's failure triggered a process of so-called 'de-constitutionalisation' that culminated in the entry into force of the Lisbon Treaty in December 2009. The content of the two treaties was almost identical. However, the differences, particularly as they related to expressions of an incipient European identity, were also striking. I argue that the Constitution's failure demonstrated the limits of law's capacity to achieve political goals and, hence, the limits of European integration as a political project. Following the setback of the CT's defeat, the EU did not return to the constitutional *status quo ante*, but rather, supranational Europe ceded ground to a union of nation states. The Constitution's rejection reinforced not only the vitality of uncodified European constitutionalism (Moravcsik 2006, 2008), but also its malleability. As the euro crisis also demonstrates, bold political initiatives can backfire, thereby undermining the gains of piecemeal integration that were hard-won over decades.

This chapter discusses the constitutionalisation project from multiple angles – legal, symbolic/identity-based, and values-based – in order to draw a more comprehensive picture of Europe's integration. This is in keeping with Brigid Laffan's useful conceptualisation of the EU as a construction based on three pillars – regulative, normative, and cognitive (that is, encompassing symbols and frames of meaning). While the regulatory pillar often seems the most prominent, due to the centrality of law to European integration, to ignore the other pillars would offer only a 'partial picture' of an extremely complex entity (Laffan 2001: 714). Thus, I begin by examining constitutional patriotism as a European identity-building mechanism. I will then analyse the EU's formal constitutionalisation project in terms of both its aspirations and the consequences of its failure. Although constitutional patriotism featured prominently in the CT, it was largely erased from its supposedly 'de-constitutionalised' successor.[1] This raises questions about what the European Union is and what it is becoming. I argue that the separation of the symbols and rhetoric of constitutional patriotism from EU treaty reform coincided with, and reinforced, a trend away from the legal supranationalism that characterised the 'Community method'. The question of what will replace it – especially pressing in light of the euro crisis – will be analysed in subsequent chapters.[2]

Constitutional patriotism for Europe? Connecting the universal to the particular

Constitutional patriotism is a 'post-national, universalist form of democratic political allegiance', first developed by Dolf Sternberger in the context of post-war West Germany and later applied to the EU as a political entity beyond both nation *and* state (Müller 2006: 278–79). Sternberger sought to separate patriotism from nationalism, arguing that patriotism was a civic tradition that could be traced back to Aristotle, and thus pre-dated the nation. His ideas were developed further by Jürgen Habermas, who advocated constitutional patriotism as a civic-minded and democratic means of identity building. For Habermas, the focus is less on the state and more on the public sphere of free and equal citizens engaging in open-ended communication (Habermas 1995: 270–71; Turner 2004: 297). Emphasising the public sphere obviates the need to confine constitutional patriotism to state-bound communities. Instead, collective identities are constructed around respect for universal liberal values (such as democracy, human rights and the rule of law), which are then interpreted according to the particular history and 'form of life' of the community in question (Habermas 2001a: 107).

Despite its post-national pretensions, constitutional patriotism has been described as 'essentially an attempt to provide a European alternative to the national principle' (Shore 2006: 719). However, in contrast to theories of nation building, Habermas's constitutional patriotism does not place much emphasis on the role of culture in identity formation. Instead, he relies heavily on a socio-economic conception of European identity as a commitment to the social-democratic welfare state (Habermas 2001b: 9–12). In fact, for Habermas, it is the undermining of national welfare and social rights protections by the forces of globalisation that necessitates the expansion of supranational political institutions. He posits that, given the challenges to the nation state posed by globalisation and multiculturalism, constitutional patriotism could take the place of nationalism in turning 'subjects' into 'citizens' bound together in the public sphere (Habermas 1998: 106–7, 118; Murphy 2005: 146). On this view, democratic citizenship can only realise its integrative potential – that is, foster solidarity amongst strangers – if it guarantees a certain material standard of living, in addition to the civil liberties usually associated with citizenship of a liberal constitutional polity (Habermas 1998: 118–19).

Habermas's ideas on constitutional patriotism were reflected in the political realm by former German foreign minister, Joschka Fischer. In a well-known speech on the future of Europe delivered at Humboldt University in May 2000, Fischer called for the creation of a 'United States of Europe' in order to give the EU a global political standing befitting its economic weight. Both Fischer and Habermas envisaged this federal entity emerging out of the closer integration of a postulated 'core Europe' (Fischer 2000; Habermas and Derrida 2003). The scope of this European vanguard was never clearly defined, though it was suggested that it would naturally coalesce around the eurozone (Fischer 2011b). In fact, some have argued that the euro crisis is hastening the emergence of a leaner and tighter currency union as 'the avant-garde of Europeanisation' (Beck 2011). However, this proposition is highly debatable, not least because even within so-called 'core Europe' political leaders and electorates do not necessarily want the same thing. It is precisely this lack of consensus on political objectives amongst EU leaders that explains why and how the Union's uncodified constitutionalism served it so well in the past. It also explains why it was a mistake to push too far towards the codification of political goals and aspirations in the Constitutional Treaty.

Despite the mixed fortunes of grand European projects since his 2000 speech, Fischer has maintained his views. Although its nations are a reality, he has argued that Europe must move beyond the outdated Westphalian model of sovereign statehood in order to maintain control over its destiny and compete with the global players of the twenty-first century (Fischer 2011a). Accordingly, both Habermas and Fischer have argued that what Europe needs, now more than ever, is *more* EU. In their view, actors such as

Germany's Constitutional Court – still preoccupied with state sovereignty – and the famously vision-less German government, led by Chancellor Angela Merkel, are short sighted and are damaging the legacy of Germany's post-war, pro-integration statesmen (Scally 2011). I will return to the inadequacies of the 'more-Europe-as-the-solution' school of thought in Chapter 5. Suffice it to state here that it relies too heavily on a normative 'ought' that is increasingly contradicted by the empirical 'is'. EU leaders, by and large, have responded to the challenges facing Europe with new forms of executive-dominated intergovernmentalism, which, in turn, are straining rather than consolidating transnational solidarity.

There are, then, various shortcomings in the idea of harnessing constitutional patriotism for the EU. Habermas's focus on the social policy dimension of identity construction underestimates the importance of culture and looks for shared values along the very fault line (socio-economic ideology) that typically characterises domestic political systems. It is not self-evident, either, that the further development of European-level social and welfare policies would promote the formation of a post-national identity in Europe. EU encroachments in this field have largely occurred through 'competence creep', a process that involves, for example, the use of general internal market provisions to pass legislation that is only peripherally connected to the common market and whose main purpose concerns an area of competence usually reserved for member states. As a result, EU-level social policy interventions often lack the transparency and inclusiveness of their national-level counterparts, and as such may leave citizens feeling alienated from, and disempowered by, the European polity (Murphy 2005; Scharpf 2009). Moreover, the goal of establishing an EU-wide 'European social model' is being made more difficult by high levels of public debt and unfavourable demographic trends in many EU states.

The role of historical memory in the application of constitutional patriotism to the EU is also problematic. It reveals the German origins of the concept, whereby the achievements of post-war West Germany – democracy, the rule of law, economic stability, and the welfare state – were always understood through the historical experience of Nazism (Müller 2006: 286–89). Habermas (2001b: 21) transposes this view to the European level in arguing that the 'common core of European identity' consists in 'the character of the painful learning process it has gone through, as much as its results'. He refers further to the 'lasting memory of nationalist excess and moral abyss', against which the post-war achievements of the EU may be set. However, this transposition does not work as well as Habermas suggests. The German Basic Law was able to gain the symbolic significance and popular reverence it did in Germany because of the unique set of circumstances pertaining at the time of its adoption. As Dieter Grimm (2005: 202–3) argued, '[w]here other nation-states found a sound basis for integration and identity, postwar Germany faced a vacuum'. Neither nation, nor history, nor culture could provide a unifying bond and so the Basic Law stepped into the breach.

There is no comparable breach at the European level into which a new form of identification and belonging may step.

Thus, the conceptualisation of European identity implied by constitutional patriotism relies on historical experiences that are *not* common to all EU states. It is a distinctly West European interpretation of what it means to be European. The countries of Central and Eastern Europe had a significantly different experience of nationalism and a very different post-war history. The lessons these nations drew from their own painful learning processes (first Nazi and then Soviet domination) are not the same as those drawn in the 'core' of Europe (Turner 2004: 302–5; Auer 2010b: 183–84).[3] Therefore, it is not clear that there is enough commonality between the EU's diverse member states and peoples to forge a robust, constitutional patriotism-inspired, European identity. This is borne out by the fate of the CT.

Not quite Philadelphia: framing the Constitution for Europe

Proponents of formal constitutionalisation framed the project in different ways. Fischer linked it to the issue of *finalité* (that is, the projected end point of integration), which he conceived as a European federation (Fischer 2000). Other advocates were less ambitious, focusing on the need to streamline institutions and processes, increase the EU's efficiency and provide citizens with greater transparency. For many EU scholars and practitioners, perturbed by growing popular resistance to political integration, the constitutional project was about addressing the Union's democracy and legitimacy deficits (Skach 2005: 150–53). It was thought that the process of debate, drafting and ratification, as much as the result, would 'be healthy for the democratic and civil ethos and praxis of the polity' (Weiler 2000: 2).

However, this was not a universal view. Andrew Moravcsik (2002, 2006) strongly argued that, as a technocratic organisation limited by numerous checks and balances and indirectly controlled by national governments, the EU did not lack either democracy or legitimacy. Explicit constitutionalisation was, therefore, unnecessary and imprudent. Whilst I agree with Moravcsik's assessment of the constitutional project's merits, I do not accept his characterisation of the EU as a mere regulatory body.[4] Moreover, while the CT's failure greatly undermined visions of a federal Europe, it did not simply confirm the stability of the EU's *de facto* constitution (cf. Moravcsik 2006: 221–22). Instead, it exposed divisions – amongst the nations of Europe and between publics and elites – that called into question the achievability of ever-closer union.

The popular disenchantment reflected in the negative outcome of the constitutional project was at odds with the drafting process, which sought to involve the public to an extent unknown during previous rounds of treaty reform. Following the Laeken Declaration of 15 December 2001, a Convention on the Future of Europe was established to consider options for reform. It was the Convention, itself, led by former French president Valéry Giscard d'Estaing, that decided to take on the task of drafting a Constitution, 'believing [that] the merging of the various treaties into a single, more coherent document offered the best solution to the various issues it had been asked to consider' (Bellamy and Schönlau 2003: 7). The initial decision to appoint a Convention, rather than acting through an Inter-Governmental Conference (IGC), was taken in the hope that it would avoid partisan bickering and foster an open debate focused on European interests. Previous IGCs, on the other hand, had tended to be dominated by national concerns and treated as opportunities for domestic political point scoring by national governments. Such negative impressions were certainly strengthened by the Nice IGC, which was widely criticised for its lack of transparency and its inefficiency, and which produced a Treaty that many regarded as unsatisfactory (Dimitrakopoulos 2008: 326–27).

The Convention met between February 2002 and July 2003. In keeping with the break from previous practice, its organisers made a conscious effort to make its proceedings inclusive and accessible, at least in appearance. A wide spectrum of delegates participated, including representatives of national governments, national parliaments, EU institutions, the European Parliament, NGOs and other civil society organisations. Moreover, Giscard d'Estaing had delegates sit in alphabetical order, rather than in political or national blocs and 'overt references to ideology or national interest were seen as breaches of Convention etiquette' (Bellamy and Schönlau 2003: 7). The Convention's proceedings were also disseminated through the Internet and other media (Rosenfeld 2003: 375–76).

Still, in some ways, the Convention on the Future of Europe was not as open and consultative as it appeared. Many of the NGOs that participated in the Convention's deliberations were directly funded by EU institutions or projects. The independence of such groups, as well as the degree to which they were truly representative of ordinary Europeans was, thus, questionable. Cris Shore (2006: 716) noted this tendency to use communication with well-connected NGOs – effectively insiders – as a proxy for communication with ordinary citizens, concluding that, '[w]hat the Commission calls "dialogue with civil society" others would describe as an act of ventriloquism'. More-over, the Convention's agenda was controlled rather tightly by Giscard d'Estaing in his capacity as President. His order that decisions on proposals and amendments be made by consensus, rather than by voting, with the Pre-sident himself defining 'consensus', was particularly contentious (Tsebelis and Proksch 2007: 177–78).

Such shortcomings notwithstanding, the Convention was a bold and ambi-tious statement of the EU's constitutional intent. Although it was not called a 'Constitutional Convention', allusions were made to the American Constitu-tional Convention of 1787. Giscard d'Estaing referred to the European Conven-tion's work as 'our Philadelphia', and even described himself as Europe's Jefferson (Sciolino 2003; Müller 2008: 148).[5] Yet, this ambition was tempered by uncertainty. The confusion over whether the CT was a treaty or a constitution proper – its official designation was 'Treaty establishing a Constitution for Europe' – indicated an 'ambivalence over the Union's course of development' that belied the grandiose rhetoric (von Bogdandy 2005: 304). In any event, the Convention's draft was presented to the European Council in July 2003, following which an IGC was convened to prepare the final version. The end product was adopted by the European Council in June 2004 and signed in Rome in October of that year, in the same room as the original Treaty of Rome.

Constitutional patriotism in the Constitutional Treaty: can legally sanctioned symbolism be effective?

In addition to its pragmatic reform function, the CT sought to foster a sense of civic attachment and allegiance inspired by constitutional patriotism (Closa 2005). As Jan-Werner Müller (2008: 148) observed, some officials appeared animated by 'an almost superstitious belief in the magic of the very word "constitution", as if dignifying policy goals and the distribution of competences with all the symbolic paraphernalia of constitution-making would automatically generate citizen support'. The desire to create a sense of belonging amongst Europeans, and to 'bring the Union closer to its citizens' predated the CT. A raft of 'cultural actions' were launched by the European Commission in 1985, in response to the findings of the Adonnino Committee, under the banner of 'the People's Europe Campaign' (Shore 2006: 710–11). The campaign included the promulgation of a range of symbols, such as the EU flag and logo, anthem and 'Europe Day' holiday.[6] Other major initiatives with symbolic import, including European citizenship and a common currency, were institutionalised in the Maastricht Treaty. Even the EU's increased commitment to human rights was partly about promoting values that could inform a common European identity.

All of these initiatives featured prominently in the text of the proposed Constitution. The EU's commitment to the Charter of Fundamental Rights was established in Article I-9, and the Charter reproduced in full as Part II of the CT. European citizenship was proclaimed in Article I-10 CT. The following official symbols of the Union were listed in Article I-8: flag, anthem ('based on the "Ode to Joy" from the Ninth Symphony by Ludwig van Beethoven'), motto ('United in Diversity'), euro currency, and Europe Day holiday (celebrated on 9 May). In fact, Article I-8 is worth considering further because, as an attempt to codify the symbolic edifice of European identity, it illustrated neatly the problematic nature of the formal constitutional project. Despite their use by EU elites to promote identity building around a particular, federalist narrative of European integration, the meanings of these symbols are ambiguous and their unifying potential rather uncertain. For example, the euro, described in the text as '[t]he currency of the Union', is not shared by all member states. Furthermore, its symbolic and practical value as a promoter of pan-European solidarity has been severely tested by the eurozone crisis.[7]

Even seemingly well-established symbols are not what they appear to be. Europe's famous standard – the circle of twelve golden stars on a blue background – is a case in point. Although the European Council adopted it in 1985, in order to provide the (then) Community with an identifiable image, it is not technically a flag.[8] The adoption of a motif so strongly associated with statehood, which had long been advocated by the European Commission and Parliament, proved extremely controversial with some member states, particularly the United Kingdom. Thus, officially, the so-called 'flag' was, in fact, 'a Community "logo" – or "emblem" – that was eligible to be reproduced on rectangular pieces of fabric, among other objects' (Theiler 2005: 1). Its legal status remained unchanged until the ill-fated attempt to convert it into the constitutionally recognised flag of the European Union.

The anthem, too, is an awkward compromise between unifying aspirations and pragmatic political considerations. The finale of Beethoven's Ninth Symphony, incorporating Schiller's 'Ode to Joy', evokes Enlightenment ideals of peace, reason, progress and universal brotherhood. Thus, it seemed fitting that the EU's supranational institutions should want to harness such symbolism in promoting their cause of ever closer union (Clark 1997: 791–94). However, it would have been politically difficult for the European institutions to endorse Schiller's German language text, and so the anthem officially consists of the music without lyrics. Caryl Clark (1997: 801) described this European anthem as 'truly a bastard child of the Enlightenment: a song without words; hope without a text'. Moreover, the anthem's 'wordlessness speaks volumes about the still fragile underpinnings of the new Europe' (Clark 1997: 807).

Europe's multiple, messy layers of history and meaning are exposed even more starkly by Europe Day. This is celebrated on 9 May, the anniversary of the 1950 Schuman Declaration, which paved the way for the creation of the European Coal and Steel Community (ECSC) in 1951. By adopting this date as Europe Day, EU officials designated the Schuman Declaration as the starting point of post-war European integration. Furthermore, the commemoration of Schuman's speech 'manifest[ed] the vocation of the European Union to be the main institutional framework' for the pursuit of the project of peace, stability and prosperity that he outlined (Larat 2005: 275). Choosing the Schuman Declaration as the EU's equivalent of a national day thus established a narrative in which the contemporary Union embodied the wisdom and vision of the founding fathers, and its development represented 'the positive evolution of History' (Larat 2005: 276). The narrative instrumentalised the past in order to justify a particular – federalist – vision of the future. Constitutionalising the commemoration of Europe Day was an attempt to further cement this narrative and strengthen its symbolic value.

There are, however, historical factors that complicate Europe Day's symbolic utility. The Schuman Declaration denotes the beginning of an era of peace and unity that may be favourably juxtaposed to the era of war, destruction and division that preceded it. But it is challenged by an alternative post-war European history – one marked by ongoing division, where, in fact, West

European integration was partly predicated on the Cold War partition of the continent. Europe Day itself unwittingly captures this complexity, as 9 May is also the anniversary of the Soviet Union's victory over Nazi Germany in 1945. This is celebrated in Russia as Victory Day, but for Central and Eastern Europe, the end of the Second World War brought not only victory and liberation, but further defeat, occupation and oppression. It is this experience – rather than the Franco-German reconciliation signified by the Schuman Declaration – that defines the post-war period for the EU's newer member states, limiting their ability to connect with Europe Day as a unifying symbol (Malksoo 2009: 664–65, 671–72).

The CT's identity-building agenda was also expressed in its preamble. Like the Article I-8 symbols, the preamble was part of an effort to present Europe's past in a way that justified the push for further unity. More specifically, it was a striking example of the attempt to articulate the aspirations of European citizens as a political community, one of the aims of symbolic constitutionalism. The preamble proclaimed that European citizens' memory of past trauma – 'bitter experiences' – had compelled them to 'transcend ancient divisions and, united ever more closely, to forge a common destiny'. This formulation echoed the 'ever closer union' aspired to in the Treaty of Rome and Maastricht Treaty preambles. As such, the CT continued the narrative of European integration as 'an inevitable and progress-oriented process' (Larat 2005: 274–75, 281). It was also reminiscent of Habermas's claim that a common European identity could be forged by the catastrophes of Nazism and the Second World War (Habermas 2001b: 21).

As well as drawing on the past, the CT preamble extolled the Union's foundational values of human rights, democracy and the rule of law, linking them to the 'cultural, religious and humanist inheritance of Europe'. The EU itself was glowingly described as a 'special area of human hope'.[9] Re-conceptualising the EU as an 'area' could be regarded as an attempt to imbue it with state-like qualities. States are geographically bounded territories, whereas international organisations are not.[10] By linking this 'European area' to universal values emerging from a common past and being pursued by citizens firmly committed to a common future, the CT laid the foundations for a European constitutional patriotism.

The CT's rhetoric may have been grandiose, but it was also vague, and therein lay formal constitutionalisation's limits. In some cases ambiguity was the result of compromise; for example, Poland and the Vatican advocated strongly for a reference to Europe's Christian heritage while other member states, such as France and the UK, lobbied against such an inclusion. Ultimately, all had to settle for the somewhat bland reference to 'religious and humanist inheritance' (Phinnemore 2004: 4). Intimations about Europe's past – that critical link between the universal and the particular that gives constitutional patriotism its substance – were kept similarly opaque. We were not told which 'bitter experiences' Europeans had suffered and from which they intended to move on. This suggests that, despite the efforts of the CT's drafters, these experiences, their interpretations and lessons learnt were just too different to ground a common identity.

The failure of the Constitutional Treaty and its consequences for the integration project

A striking feature of the interactions between ordinary Europeans and the EU is that, when given the opportunity via referenda, the former have regularly rejected the latter.[11] That trend was evident with the CT, which, like all EU treaties, required unanimous ratification by the member states before it could enter into force. As with previous revisions of the EU's founding texts, it was up to each national government as to how to proceed with ratification, though in some cases national law dictated the choice. Ireland, for example, is obliged to hold referenda on all amendments to the EU treaties that 'go beyond measures necessitated by the obligations of membership' (Gilland 2002: 527), a requirement that has twice disrupted the plans of EU elites, following Irish rejections of the Nice and Lisbon Treaties. Unsurprisingly, given the CT's mission to legitimise and democratise the EU, several member state governments chose, or succumbed to political pressure, to ratify the text via popular referenda.

The ratification process proved to be the CT's undoing. Its popular reception was lacklustre at best and, at worst, downright hostile. That a reform project so explicitly aimed at capturing the public imagination and building affective ties should fail so ignominiously points to paradoxes at the heart of European integration. The fact that the negative referenda results occurred in two of the EU's founding member states was 'perceived as a political earthquake' (Piris 2010: 24), which was serious enough to halt the ratification process in other countries.

The CT's rejection laid bare contradictions that have long haunted the EU, such as the tension between elites and masses and that between democratic rhetoric and bureaucratic reality. The EU's poor track record with referenda is also, to an extent, a product of the lack of normal democratic politics at European level, which deprives citizens of regular opportunities to voice their preferences on supranational policies that affect their lives and to have those preferences reflected in substantive outcomes (Follesdal and Hix 2006). This transforms the very occasional popular referenda on specific treaties or issues into votes for or against the EU as a whole (Majone 2009b: 9–10). Giandomenico Majone (2009a: 8) aptly described the proposition faced by national leaders as 'referendum roulette' because of the considerable risk that electorates will not endorse the elite consensus that EU treaties represent.

A number of studies have analysed the dynamics of the CT's ratification process from various angles.[12] My focus, however, is on how the collapse of formal constitutionalisation affected the EU's pre-existing constitutional framework. With this in mind, it is possible to distinguish between a 'narrow' and a 'broad' sense of the CT's failure. Narrowly speaking, the Treaty was defeated in referenda in France (55% 'No') and the Netherlands (62% 'No') on 29 May and 1 June 2005 respectively, following which the ratification process was put on hold. The CT was then completely abandoned after the European Council summit of 17 and 18 June called for a 'period of reflection' before renegotiating a more modest reform treaty (Kurpas 2007: 2; Kaunert 2009: 467). Of course, there were many factors driving the 'No' campaign in both France and the Netherlands, including some that were purely domestic (such as the unpopularity of Jacques Chirac's government in France).[13] Thus, it cannot be concluded that French and Dutch voters rejected the constitutional concept in its entirety just because they rejected its embodiment in the CT (Walker 2006: 144–45). In fact, many 'No' voters in France may have considered themselves constitutional patriots of sorts – the sentiment of the pro-European 'No' was captured by the slogan '*Oui à l'Union; non à la Constitution*', which was common amongst left-wing opponents of the Treaty (Milner 2006: 257).

Still, it would be erroneous to attribute the CT's failure exclusively to a narrow set of circumstances. The constitutional project – from the 2001 Laeken Declaration to the 2004 Treaty Establishing a Constitution for Europe – also failed in a much broader sense. The CT, and the European constitutional patriotism that it embodied, simply did not speak to the European people(s). Both citizens and, to some extent, political elites across the EU were wary of the Treaty's implications for national sovereignty and parliamentary democracy. The very term 'Constitution' remained anathema in the United Kingdom – where the promised referendum almost certainly would have been defeated (Baines and Gill 2006: 464–65).[14] The immediate failure in France and the Netherlands allowed those governments that were sceptical from the outset (such as the British and some of the Central and Eastern European member states) to push an agenda of pragmatic treaty reform devoid of higher aspirations (de Witte 2009: 36–37). The thoroughness with which the defeated Treaty's symbolic and overtly constitutional rhetoric was removed further indicates the extent to which a common European identity failed to take hold in the imagination of Europeans.

Thus, the Lisbon Treaty quite deliberately abandoned the ambitious identity-building project of its predecessor, along with its constitutional form and trappings (Reh 2009: 644–47). Whereas the CT would have repealed and replaced all other EU treaties with a single text, the Lisbon Treaty, like Amsterdam and Nice before it, was an amending Treaty.[15] Article I-8 was dropped, as was Article I-6, which would have codified the ECJ's doctrine of EU legal supremacy. The Charter of Fundamental Rights was not directly incorporated into the text, which it would have been in the CT. Instead, it was made legally binding by reference under Article 6 TEU. In another cosmetic, but telling, change, the position of 'Foreign Minister', created by the CT, was retained, but renamed 'High Representative of the Union for Foreign Affairs and Security Policy'.

The Constitutional Treaty and Lisbon Treaty were, then, substantively very similar. So similar, in fact, that the LT's relatively low-key (and almost referendum-free) ratification caused considerable controversy amongst opponents of the former CT, who considered that the democratic will of the people was being ignored. This was, perhaps, most evident in Britain, where debates over the meaning of 'de-constitutionalised' and the applicability of that appellation to the LT took on a decidedly political significance. Then Prime Minister Tony Blair had promised to consult the British people on the CT in a popular referendum. However, the British vote never materialised, as the country froze its ratification process following the French and Dutch referenda. This turn of events was likely a relief to the British government, since perennially 'reluctant' Britain could not be held responsible for this particular failure. Nevertheless, Prime Minister Gordon Brown's decision to ratify the LT via a parliamentary vote became something of a rallying point for British eurosceptics, whose campaigns to preserve national sovereignty have increasingly revolved around the device of the popular referendum (Wellings 2010).

There is, indeed, merit to claims that the explicit 'de-constitutionalisation' process that accompanied the CT's transformation into the LT was undertaken with the intention of depoliticising the process, avoiding popular referenda and generally smoothing the way for ratification (Kurpas 2007; Kaunert 2009; Reh 2009). It was not only eurosceptics who argued that the Lisbon Treaty, though shorn of its symbolism, was just a constitution by another name. This view was also expressed by EU officials such as Valéry Giscard d'Estaing, who claimed that, 'all the earlier proposals will be in the new text, but will be hidden or disguised in some way'. Similar sentiments were voiced by other European leaders, including German Chancellor Angela Merkel, who stated that, '[t]he fundamentals of the constitution have been maintained in large part' (Halligan, Watts and Stares 2007).

Nevertheless, the apparently minor differences between the two treaties do have substantive consequences for the integration project. Most of the changes were symbolic, but political symbolism matters. It contributes to the construction of political reality and to the making of the polity itself. Albrecht Sonntag (2011: 117) elucidated the three main functions of political symbols as follows: firstly, symbols are 'consciously used tools of polity building and identity formation', which are propagated by elites in a top-down manner in order to legitimise a political entity. Secondly, symbols are 'transmitters of presumed common values and shared meanings', which also help to establish identity and distinguish in-groups from out-groups. Thirdly, symbols have a teleological dimension, that is, they 'represent high and noble purposes, aspirations, visions of the future' and 'raise expectations of finality'.

All three functions are relevant to the European integration project, which relies on symbolic outputs to build affective ties with its citizens, just as it relies on material outputs to build its credibility as an economic and political actor. The Constitution, itself, was a symbol; any treaty can implement institutional reforms, but the CT went beyond that to embody an idealised narrative of Europe's past and future, its values and aspirations. Its defeat symbolised the very *lack* of consensus on such grand EU-European narratives (Sonntag

2011: 120). Thus, with the Lisbon Treaty, the EU consciously stepped back from its promotion of a common European identity. That the Charter of Fundamental Rights was made legally binding by reference rather than by incorporation probably does not affect its legal status. The exclusion of Article I-8 on official EU symbols does not prevent the continued use of the flag or anthem, or the continued recognition of Europe Day. The general reversion of the LT to the traditional language of international treaties did not change the legal foundations of the Union.[16] Nevertheless, all of these 'minor' amendments demonstrate that the failure of the CT was a setback in terms of the creation of a coherent and self-identifying European people. In this respect, it was also a setback for the EU's political agenda.

It is in this sense that the Lisbon Treaty has been described as a 'smashed vase'. Although it contains most of the pieces of the original, it is not quite the same and furthermore, it 'records and recalls the drama' that preceded it (Claes and Eijsbouts 2008: 2). It is impossible to judge the LT on its own merits, as merely the next step in a line of reform treaties including Maastricht, Amsterdam and Nice. It was significantly coloured by the preceding failure, and so it is difficult to see it as anything other than a retreat from the federalist vision of Europe.

Did the Lisbon Treaty retreat from constitutionalism or advance it in another direction?

The abandonment of the formal constitutional project was the first of the twin crises of twenty-first-century EU constitutionalism. Its link to the second – the euro crisis – lies partly in how the shift from CT to LT affected the supranational-intergovernmental balance of the Union's treaty framework. The SEA and subsequent treaties may have brought back majority voting, but they did not banish intergovernmentalism. On the contrary, the Maastricht Treaty formalised a division between the supranational and intergovernmental strands of the EU's legal framework by introducing two new pillars that were to operate outside of the Community method. This 'Maastricht Compromise' was an update to Weiler's 'foundational equilibrium' – it enabled integration in new, politically sensitive fields, such as foreign affairs, justice and policing, by placing control firmly in the hands of the member state governments. Even though the Lisbon Treaty did away with the Maastricht pillars, it kept, and even entrenched further, this 'dual constitution' (Fabbrini 2013: 1004–5).

It was the institutions and decision-making processes of the *intergovernmental* strand of the dual constitution that were mobilised in response to the euro crisis. However, the post-Lisbon institutional structure proved inadequate to the task, leading to the rescue efforts moving outside of the established constitutional framework altogether. Thus, as I will argue in Chapter 5, the intergovernmentalism of the euro crisis – de-legalised, executive-driven, dominated by Germany and France – is *not* that envisaged by the Lisbon

Treaty. First, though, we may ask what sort of regime Lisbon inaugurated following the CT's defeat.

As already noted, the LT was described as a 'de-constitutionalised' version of its predecessor. This label was accurate in one sense, but inaccurate in another. Lisbon did, indeed, represent a retreat from the lofty political ambitions of the CT. EU leaders were quite explicit about the Treaty's de-constitutionalisation agenda, so defined. In setting out the mandate for the IGC tasked with preparing the new reform treaty, the European Council declared that, '[t]he constitutional concept, which consisted in repealing all existing treaties and replacing them by a single text called "Constitution", is abandoned' (European Council, 21/22 June 2007: 15). Thus, it is possible to speak of a political/symbolic de-constitutionalisation, encompassing the abandonment of constitutional patriotism, in the transition from CT to LT.

Yet, from a legal, or functional, perspective, the term is a misnomer. The LT was an important addition to the EU's rich constitutional patchwork of treaties and case law, aptly described by Deirdre Curtin (1993) as a 'Europe of bits and pieces'. Part of its significance lay in its reorientation of the integration project away from the federalism of the CT. As well as being shorn of the CT's constitutional rhetoric and form, the LT reinforced the position of member states as 'Masters of the Treaties', and more clearly demarcated their autonomous spheres of action (Cooper 2010). Unlike previous reform treaties, the Lisbon Treaty did not greatly expand the EU's legislative purview through the addition of new competences. Simon Hix (2008: 183) described Lisbon as 'probably the least significant treaty the EU has ever signed' for precisely that reason. However, in terms of its constitutional impact, the fact that the Lisbon Treaty did not greatly advance the EU's supranational sphere of influence was one of its most noteworthy characteristics.

To be sure, the Lisbon Treaty must be evaluated in the context of the decade-long explicit constitutionalisation project that preceded it. My contention, that the text confirmed the nature of the EU as a pluralistic and non-hierarchical association of nation states may be briefly illustrated by the way in which it dealt with the concept of supremacy.

'Re-uncodification' of the doctrine of supremacy

The European Union's shift away from constitutional patriotism at a symbolic level was matched by a retreat from supranationalism in the realm of politics and law (Cooper 2010: 1–3). The defeat of the CT reflected both trends. One difference between the Constitutional and Lisbon Treaties that went *beyond* style concerned the recognition accorded to the principle of EU legal supremacy. Whereas the CT would have codified supremacy in Article I-6, the LT dropped that provision. In its place, the European Council opted for a non-binding declaration (declaration no. 17), according to which it recalled the ECJ's 'well settled case law' on the issue (de Witte 2009: 36). Aside from the fact that the declaration was not binding, the member states' somewhat vague recollection of supremacy compared unfavourably to the proposed wording of Article I-6, which stated simply and much more definitively that: 'The Constitution and law adopted by the institutions of the Union in exercising competences conferred on it shall have primacy over the law of the member states'.

Therefore, we may ask whether the ECJ's case law is really so well settled. Prior to the CT, the member states had left the question of supremacy open, neither revoking nor confirming ECJ doctrine in their periodic treaty revisions. Given the difficulty of obtaining the unanimous support of national governments for a definitive position on such a sensitive issue, their inaction could not be interpreted as consent to the ECJ's version of supremacy lock, stock and barrel (Kumm and Comella 2005: 477–78). It was all the more notable, then, that when the issue of supremacy *was* explicitly raised, many national governments baulked. Again, the 'smashed vase' metaphor is relevant. By expressly omitting the codification of supremacy, the EU's member states threw doubt upon the validity of the principle, at least in its absolute form (that is, that all EU legal norms, correctly adopted, overrule all conflicting national legal norms), as articulated by the ECJ (Cooper 2010: 7).

The so-called 'national identity' clause is also relevant to the assessment of the strength of the supremacy doctrine. This provision first appeared in the Maastricht Treaty as the single, somewhat enigmatic sentence, '[t]he Union shall respect the national identities of its Member States'. It was elaborated by Article I-5 of the CT, which enjoined the Union to respect the 'fundamental structures, political and constitutional' of member states, as well as their 'essential State functions', including maintaining territorial integrity, law and order, and national security. Following the CT's defeat, Article I-5 was reproduced as Article 4(2) TEU, which kept the CT version's wording but further emphasised member state control over national security. The retention of that clause combined with the deletion of Article I-6 CT on supremacy could weaken the authority of EU law within domestic legal systems. Indeed, Mattias Kumm (2005: 303) interpreted Article I-5 CT as giving member states an EU law-based justification, albeit narrow, to set aside EU law in certain circumstances, such as 'when specific rule-like commitments pertaining to fundamental constitutional commitments are at stake'.

Therefore, the LT amendments to the codification of supremacy and constitutional identity could encourage national courts to view themselves as guardians of national constitutional values against 'European threats'. This is a role already played by Germany's Constitutional Court, and one that has added resonance in light of the Court's interventions in relation to the euro rescue measures.

Concluding remarks: the Constitution for Europe and the political limits of legal integration

The failure of the CT and the consequent ratification of the LT brought about a significant change in the EU's constitutional framework, and that change was to the detriment of European federalism. Although imperfect, the uncodified nature of European constitutionalism, that is, its 'common law character', actually facilitated the creation and development of a supranational legal order (Dashwood 2004: 379–80). The EU must operate with a certain degree of constructive ambiguity because the alternative – complete agreement on the objectives of integration amongst all member states – is not feasible. This is one of the key lessons of the aborted attempt at formal constitutionalisation.

This chapter focused on Jürgen Habermas's theories about the potential for turning Europeans into a united body of constitutional patriots, capable of democratically legitimating the EU. Despite the CT's failure, Habermas has continued to call for 'more Europe' in response to the challenges facing the 28-nation bloc (Habermas 2011a, 2011b, 2012). However, by doing so, he ignores the fact that the very projects that were meant to unite European citizens and promote their common identity are now straining transnational solidarity and producing a rise in nationalist and protectionist sentiments. Parallels may be drawn between the common currency and the CT. Both had some technical advantages (for example, reduced inter-state transaction costs and the consolidation of a complex treaty system, respectively), though not enough to outweigh the risks or to make reform necessary. Both were essentially undertaken for political reasons. One project failed and the future of the other is uncertain, yet in both cases the damage is not solely political. The euro, of course, is also proving extremely costly economically, and the defeat of the CT also altered the Union's unwritten constitution.

The latter point is well demonstrated by the history of the doctrine of supremacy. From the ECJ's first articulation of the doctrine in the *Costa* case in 1964, until its appearance in the CT, supremacy was uncodified. And it was in the shades of grey – between the lines of the black letter law of the treaties – that the 'quiet revolution' flourished (Weiler 1994). National courts were able to implement the substance of the ECJ's doctrine without endorsing its reasoning. Germany's Constitutional Court was even able to theorise the source of European legal authority in ways that contradicted the ECJ, without causing a legal or political crisis. That is the great advantage of constructive ambiguity – it accommodates theoretical tension in a manner that makes actual conflict much less likely (see, for example, Kumm 2005; Kumm and Comella 2005).

On the other hand, the attempted codification of supremacy in Article I-6 CT unnecessarily forced a conflict between a supranational, federal vision of Europe and a more state sovereignist vision. The situation may be compared to that of a child who wants to do something that he suspects he is not allowed to do. Should he ask his parents, thereby risking being denied their permission? Or should he simply act, but then risk being caught and punished? Prior to the CT, the ECJ took the second option. Major doctrines such as supremacy and direct effect were formulated without the prior agreement of member states through the Treaty of Rome. This strategy proved remarkably successful over several decades.

However, the end of the permissive consensus and the coterminous push for greater political supranationalism saw EU elites look beyond pre-existing symbols such as the flag, anthem and common citizenship, towards a European Constitution as the harbinger of the popular identification and attachment that had thus far eluded the integration project. Through the CT, EU elites, in effect, were asking the peoples of Europe for permission. Yet, the attempt to fix what was not broken – European constitutionalism – instead shattered the judicially constructed illusion of European federalism. Permission was denied. Notwithstanding the official, though non-binding, affirmation of the *status quo ante* on supremacy, the doctrine is now weaker and less certain. More significantly, this is true of the federalist cause as a whole.

Thus, a legal reform that was meant to serve as a 'political act of foundation', which would enable the pursuit of even more far-reaching political agendas (Habermas 2001b: 6–8), instead called into question the validity of European integration as a constitutional project. The CT's failure not only illustrated the impossibility of manufacturing European constitutional patriots, it also made it clear that further and closer integration is neither inevitable nor limitless.

Notes

1 The Committee charged with repackaging the CT's substantive reforms assured the June 2007 European Council that: 'the clauses of the Constitutional treaty which most specifically point[ed] to its constitutional character' had not been carried over into the new treaty (Action Committee for European Democracy, 2007).

2 In the context of EU-level responses to the euro crisis, one may speak of a shift from the Community method to a 'Union method', characterised by an inter-governmental crisis management style that is 'anything but promising' in terms of democratic governance (Joerges 2012: 14–16).

3 Central and East European representatives to the EU institutions have challenged the largely *West* European construction of European identity and post-war history. One example was the controversial push in the European Parliament, led by Polish and Baltic MEPs, to equate the crimes of Stalinism with those of Nazism, on the sixtieth anniversary of the end of the Second World War in 2005 (Malksoo 2009).

4 In particular, his assertion that the EU should not be politicised because it deals overwhelmingly with issues of low popular salience is no longer convincing, given the eurozone crisis (Moravcsik 2006: 223–26). In fact, growing doubt over the common currency's future has brought to the fore the issue of the limits of European integration.

5 As well as being somewhat overstated, this claim was also inaccurate: Thomas Jefferson was United States Ambassador to France at the time of the Philadelphia Convention, and therefore did not attend.

6 Cris Shore (2006: 711–12) noted that it was striking – and somewhat ironic, given the EU's post-national mission – that its 'culture-building initiatives' echoed 'many of the techniques and methods used by nationalist élites in the nineteenth and twentieth centuries to forge Europe's existing Nation States'.

7 Although EU leaders have argued the very opposite: European Council President, Herman van Rompuy, in a speech in Berlin in November 2010, described the euro as 'the great bringer of unity and stability', and, 'the most visible and palpable sign

of our common destiny' (Van Rompuy 2010). However, this rhetoric sounds hollow in light of the nasty national stereotypes that the eurozone crisis has provoked.

8 The flag/emblem, anthem and Europe Day were all officially adopted by the European Council in June 1985, on the recommendation of the *ad hoc* Committee on a People's Europe. It is no coincidence that this was around the time of the launch of the Single Market programme (Clark 1997: 800). The adoption of these symbols was a conscious attempt to infuse the political/institutional revitalisation of the integration project with a sense of European identity.

9 This phrase echoes the image of America as 'the city on the hill', which is common in discourses of American exceptionalism (Kumm 2008: 126). In doing so it illustrates the tension at the heart of the EU's constitutional project – while very ambitious in scope, it is couched in neutral, bureaucratised language that is unlikely to evoke much passion in European citizens.

10 Armin von Bogdandy (2005: 306) noted that the attempted 'shift in association of the European Union from an organization in Brussels to an area, in which Union citizens live' represented a significant step towards establishing a European identity.

11 Not including votes on accession, there have been seven unsuccessful referenda in EC/EU history: Denmark (1992: Maastricht Treaty), Denmark (2000: EMU), France (2005: Constitutional Treaty), Ireland (2001: Nice), Ireland (2008: Lisbon), the Netherlands (2005: Constitutional Treaty), and Sweden (2003: EMU).

12 See, for example, Ivaldi (2006); Laursen (2008); Lubbers (2008) and Statham and Trenz (2012).

13 The majority of 'No' votes in France came from the left and were prompted by social and welfare concerns (famously embodied in the 'Polish plumber'). However, right-wing euroscepticism and xenophobia also contributed significantly to the result, with CT opponents on the far right particularly exploiting the possibility of Turkish EU accession (Ivaldi 2006).

14 Over the fourteen-month period from April 2004 to June 2005, not one opinion poll showed a majority of people in the UK intending to vote for the Constitution (Baines and Gill 2006: 464–65).

15 See Sebastian Kurpas (2007) for a detailed overview of the main changes from the CT to the LT.

16 Article I-1 CT referred to 'the will of the citizens and States of Europe to build a common future … '. The Lisbon Treaty reverts to the traditional treaty language of 'the High Contracting Parties establish … '. This implicitly confirms that the EU is established entirely by agreement between national governments, rather than on the basis of popular sovereignty (which would indicate the presence of a European *demos*) (Cooper 2010: 6).

References

Action Committee for European Democracy (2007) 'A New Treaty and Supplementary Protocols', Explanatory Memorandum, Brussels, 4 June.

Auer, S. (2010a) '"New Europe": Between Cosmopolitan Dreams and Nationalist Nightmares'. *Journal of Common Market Studies*, Vol. 48, No. 5, pp. 1163–84.

——(2010b) 'Whose Europe is it Anyway? Habermas's New Europe and its Critics'. *Telos*, Vol. 152, pp. 181–91.

Baines, P. and Gill, M. (2006) 'The EU Constitution and the British Public: What the Polls Tell Us about the Campaign that Never Was'. *International Journal of Public Opinion Research*, Vol. 18, No. 4, pp. 463–73.

Beck, U. (2011) 'Europe's Crisis is an Opportunity for Democracy'. *The Guardian*, 28 November.

Bellamy, R. and Schönlau, J. (2003) 'The Good, the Bad and the Ugly: The Need for Constitutional Compromise and the Drafting of the EU Constitution'. *The Federal Trust for Education and Research*, Online Paper 33/03, November, pp. 1–12.

Claes, M. and Eijsbouts, W. T. (2008) 'The Difference'. *European Constitutional Law Review*, Vol. 4, No. 1, pp. 1–19.

Clark, C. (1997) 'Forging Identity: Beethoven's "Ode" as European Anthem'. *Critical Inquiry*, Vol. 23, No. 4, pp. 789–807.

Closa, C. (2005) 'Deliberative Constitutional Politics and the Turn towards a Norms-Based Legitimacy of the EU Constitution'. *European Law Journal*, Vol. 11, No. 4, pp. 411–31.

Cooper, I. (2010) 'Mapping the Overlapping Spheres: European Constitutionalism after the Treaty of Lisbon'. *ARENA Centre for European Studies Seminar Paper*, pp. 1–32.

Curtin, D. (1993) 'The Constitutional Structure of the Union: A Europe of Bits and Pieces'. *Common Market Law Review*, Vol. 30, No. 1, pp. 17–69.

Dashwood, A. (2004) 'The Relationship between the Member States and the European Union/European Community'. *Common Market Law Review*, Vol. 41, No. 2, pp. 355–81.

De Witte, B. (2009) 'The Lisbon Treaty and National Constitutions: More or Less Europeanisation?' In Closa, C. (ed.) *The Lisbon Treaty and National Constitutions: Europeanisation and Democratic Implications* (Oslo: ARENA Report No. 3/09).

Dimitrakopoulos, D. (2008) 'Norms, Strategies and Political Change: Explaining the Establishment of the Convention on the Future of Europe'. *European Journal of International Relations*, Vol. 14, No. 2, pp. 319–41.

European Council (2007) *Presidency Conclusions*, Brussels, 20 July, document 11177/1/07, Rev. 1.

Fabbrini, S. (2013) 'Intergovernmentalism and its Limits: Assessing the European Union's Answer to the Euro Crisis'. *Comparative Political Studies*, Vol. 46, No. 9, pp. 1003–29.

Fischer, J. (2000) 'From Confederacy to Federation – Thoughts on the Finality of European Integration'. *Speech given at Humboldt University*, Berlin, 12 May.

——(2011a) *Interview with Joschka Fischer*, conducted by Stefan Auer, Berlin, 4 July.

——(2011b) 'Merkel Wakes Up to New Euro Reality'. *The Australian*, 2 August.

Follesdal, A. and Hix, S. (2006) 'Why There Is a Democratic Deficit in the EU: A Response to Majone and Moravcsik'. *Journal of Common Market Studies*, Vol. 44, No. 3, pp. 533–62.

Gilland, K. (2002) 'Ireland's (First) Referendum on the Treaty of Nice'. *Journal of Common Market Studies*, Vol. 40, No. 3, pp. 527–35.

Grimm, D. (2005) 'Integration by Constitution'. *International Journal of Constitutional Law*, Vol. 3, No. 2–3, pp. 193–210.

Habermas, J. (1995) 'Citizenship and National Identity: Some Reflections on the Future of Europe'. In Beiner, R. (ed.) *Theorizing Citizenship* (Albany: State University of New York Press).

——(1998) 'The European Nation-State: On the Past and Future of Sovereignty and Citizenship'. In Cronin, C. and De Greif, P. (eds) *The Inclusion of the Other: Studies in Political Theory* (Cambridge, MA: MIT Press).

——(2001a) *The Postnational Constellation* (Cambridge, MA: MIT Press).

——(2001b) 'Why Europe Needs a Constitution'. *New Left Review*, Vol. 11, Sep–Oct, pp. 5–26.

——(2011a) 'Europe's Post-Democratic Era'. *The Guardian*, 10 November.

——(2011b) 'Merkels von Demoskopie geleiteter Opportunismus'. *Süddeutsche Zeitung*, 7 April.

——(2012) *The Crisis of the European Union: A Response* (Cambridge: Polity).

Habermas, J. and Derrida, J. (2003) 'February 15, or What Binds Europeans Together: A Plea for a Common Foreign Policy, Beginning in the Core of Europe'. *Constellations*, Vol. 10, No. 3, pp. 291–97.

Halligan, L., Watts, R. and Stares, J. (2007) 'New Treaty Is Just "Constitution in Disguise"'. *The Telegraph*, 1 July.

Hix, S. (2008) *What's Wrong with the European Union and How to Fix It* (Cambridge: Polity).

Hooghe, L. and Marks, G. (2009) 'A Postfunctionalist Theory of European Integration: From Permissive Consensus to Constraining Dissensus'. *British Journal of Political Science*, Vol. 39, No. 1, pp. 1–23.

Ivaldi, G. (2006) 'Beyond France's 2005 Referendum on the European Constitutional Treaty: Second-Order Model, Anti-Establishment Attitudes and the End of the Alternative European Utopia'. *West European Politics*, Vol. 29, No. 1, pp. 47–69.

Joerges, C. (2012) 'Europe's Economic Constitution in Crisis'. *ZenTra Working Papers in Transnational Studies*, No. 06/2012, pp. 1–28.

Kaunert, C. (2009) 'The Lisbon Treaty and the Constitutionalization of the EU'. *Journal of Contemporary European Research*, Vol. 5, No. 3, pp. 465–71.

Kumm, M. (2005) 'The Jurisprudence of Constitutional Conflict: Constitutional Supremacy in Europe before and after the Constitutional Treaty'. *European Law Journal*, Vol. 11, No. 3, pp. 262–307.

——(2008) 'Why Europeans Will Not Embrace Constitutional Patriotism'. *International Journal of Constitutional Law*, Vol. 6, No. 1, pp. 117–36.

Kumm, M. and Comella, V. F. (2005) 'The Primacy Clause of the Constitutional Treaty and the Future of Constitutional Conflict in the European Union'. *International Journal of Constitutional Law*, Vol. 3, No. 2–3, pp. 473–92.

Kurpas, S. (2007) 'The Treaty of Lisbon – How Much "Constitution" is Left? An Overview of the Main Changes'. *CEPS Policy Brief*, No. 147.

Laffan, B. (2001) 'The European Union Polity: A Union of Regulative, Normative and Cognitive Pillars'. *Journal of European Public Policy*, Vol. 8, No. 5, pp. 709–27.

Larat, F. (2005) 'Present-ing the Past: Political Narratives on European History and the Justification of EU Integration'. *German Law Journal*, Vol. 6, No. 2, pp. 274–90.

Laursen, F. (ed.) (2008) *The Rise and Fall of the EU's Constitutional Treaty* (Leiden: Martinus Nijhoff Publishers).

Lubbers, M. (2008) 'Regarding the Dutch "Nee" to the European Constitution: A Test of the Identity, Utilitarian and Political Approaches to Voting "No"'. *European Union Politics*, Vol. 9, No. 1, pp. 59–86.

Majone, G. (2009a) *Europe as the Would-Be World Power: The EU at Fifty* (Cambridge: Cambridge University Press).

——(2009b) 'The "Referendum Threat", the Rationally Ignorant Voter, and the Political Culture of the EU'. *RECON Online Working Paper 2009/04*, pp. 1–21.

Malksoo, M. (2009) 'The Memory Politics of Becoming European: The East European Subalterns and the Collective Memory of Europe'. *European Journal of International Relations*, Vol. 15, No. 4, pp. 653–80.

Milner, H. (2006) '"YES to the Europe I Want; NO to this One." Some Reflections on France's Rejection of the EU Constitution'. *Political Science & Politics*, Vol. 39, No. 2, pp. 257–60.

Moravcsik, A. (2002) 'In Defence of the "Democratic Deficit": Reassessing Legitimacy in the European Union'. *Journal of Common Market Studies*, Vol. 40, No. 4, pp. 603–24.

——(2006) 'What Can We Learn from the Collapse of the European Constitutional Project?' *Politische Vierteljahresschrift*, Vol. 47, No. 2, pp. 219–41.

——(2008) 'The European Constitutional Settlement'. *World Economy*, Vol. 31, No. 1, pp. 158–84.

Müller, J.-W. (2006) 'On the Origins of Constitutional Patriotism'. *Contemporary Political Theory*, Vol. 5, No. 3, pp. 278–96.

——(2008) '"Our Philadelphia"? On the Political and Intellectual History of the "European Constitution"'. *Journal of Modern European History*, Vol. 6, No. 1, pp. 137–54.

Murphy, M. (2005) 'Between Facts, Norms and a Post-National Constellation: Habermas, Law and European Social Policy'. *Journal of European Public Policy*, Vol. 12, No. 1, pp. 143–56.

Phinnemore, D. (2004) 'The Treaty Establishing a Constitution for Europe'. *Chatham House Briefing Note*, pp. 1–23.

Piris, J.-C. (2010) *The Lisbon Treaty: A Legal and Political Analysis* (Cambridge: Cambridge University Press).

Reh, C. (2009) 'The Lisbon Treaty: De-Constitutionalizing the European Union?' *Journal of Common Market Studies*, Vol. 47, No. 3, pp. 625–50.

Rosenfeld, M. (2003) 'The European Convention and Constitution Making in Philadelphia'. *International Journal of Constitutional Law*, Vol. 1, No. 2, pp. 373–78.

Scally, D. (2011) 'Philosopher's Stand against Creeping Nationalism'. *Irish Times*, 9 April.

Scharpf, F. (2009) 'The Double Asymmetry of European Integration. Or: Why the EU Cannot Be a Social Market Economy'. *Max-Planck-Institut für Gesellschaftsforschung, MPIfG Working Paper 09/12*, November, pp. 1–38.

Sciolino, E. (2003) 'United Europe's Jefferson? Giscard d'Estaing Smiles'. *New York Times*, 15 June.

Shore, C. (2006) '"Government without Statehood"? Anthropological Perspectives on Governance and Sovereignty in the European Union'. *European Law Journal*, Vol. 12, No. 6, pp. 709–24.

Skach, C. (2005) 'We, the Peoples? Constitutionalizing the European Union'. *Journal of Common Market Studies*, Vol. 43, No. 1, pp. 149–70.

Sonntag, A. (2011) 'False Expectations: The Counterproductive Side Effects of the EU's Use of Political Symbols'. In Cerutti, F. and Lucarelli, S. (eds) *The Search for a European Identity* (London: Routledge).

Statham, P. and Trenz, H.-J. (2012) *The Politicization of Europe: Contesting the Constitution in the Mass Media* (Oxford: Routledge).

Theiler, T. (2005) *Political Symbolism and European Integration* (Manchester: Manchester University Press).

Tsebelis, G. and Proksch, S.-O. (2007) 'The Art of Political Manipulation in the European Convention'. *Journal of Common Market Studies*, Vol. 45, No. 1, pp. 157–86.

Turner, C. (2004) 'Jürgen Habermas: European or German?' *European Journal of Political Theory*, Vol. 3, No. 3, pp. 293–314.

Van Rompuy, H. (2010) 'A Curtain Went Up – Ein Vorhang ging auf'. *Speech given at the Pergamon Museum*, Berlin, 9 November. Available at www.consilium.europa.eu/uedocs/cms_data/docs/pressdata/en/ec/117623.pdf (Accessed: 25 March 2014).

Von Bogdandy, A. (2005) 'The European Constitution and European Identity: Text and Subtext of the Treaty Establishing a Constitution for Europe'. *International Journal of Constitutional Law*, Vol. 3, No. 2–3, pp. 295–315.

Walker, N. (2006) 'A Constitutional Reckoning'. *Constellations*, Vol. 13, No. 2, pp. 140–50.

Weiler, J. H. H. (1994) 'A Quiet Revolution: The European Court of Justice and Its Interlocutors'. *Comparative Political Studies*, Vol. 26, No. 4, pp. 510–34.

——(2000) 'Epilogue: The Fischer Debate – The Dark Side'. In Joerges, C., Meny, Y. and Weiler, J. H. H. (eds) *What Kind of Constitution for What Kind of Polity?* Harvard Jean Monnet Working Paper No. 7/00, Symposium: Responses to Joschka Fischer.

Wellings, B. (2010) 'Losing the Peace: Euroscepticism and the Foundations of Contemporary English Nationalism'. *Nations and Nationalism*, Vol. 16, No. 3, pp. 488–505.

3 Contesting EU constitutionalism in Karlsruhe

Introduction: the German Constitutional Court and the limits of EU law

National courts may be the primary enforcers of EU law, but their views have often diverged, in significant ways, from those of the ECJ. Indeed, EU constitutionalism was formed, and is constantly being reformed, through the interaction between national and supranational legal systems. This chapter analyses the EU's overarching legal framework through the lens of German constitutional jurisprudence – one of the most important national perspectives for a number of reasons. Germany is the EU's most populous state and one of its six founding members. It is also one of the most economically powerful and politically influential states in the EU, a status further cemented by the euro crisis (Paterson 2011). Historically, the desire to firmly entrench post-war West Germany in Europe and Franco-German reconciliation were the driving forces behind European integration, and major events in German history are intertwined with the development of the European project. For example, the collapse of communism in 1989 and the reunification of Germany in 1990 presaged the EU's expansion into Central and Eastern Europe. These events also helped to instigate the push for political union, including the creation of EMU as a partial *quid pro quo* for German reunification (Marsh 2011).

Moreover, in the legal realm, German jurisprudence has played a uniquely significant role in the development of EU constitutionalism. Doctrines expounded by the *Bundesverfassungsgericht* (German Constitutional Court, or GCC) have made a real difference to European-level legal and political practices, for example, in relation to fundamental human rights protections (Hartley 2010: 143–51). Yet, the Court's relationship to the ECJ and its version of EU law has not always been comfortable. In this regard, the long-running dialogue between the two powerful courts reveals one of the paradoxes of Germany's relationship to the European project. While there was always a high degree of compatibility between German political interests and the integration strategies pursued by the EU institutions (Wessels 2003: 135), the GCC's attitude to legal integration has been much more ambivalent, to the point where it is sometimes described as a eurosceptical actor (Paterson 2011: 66–67). Actually, the opposing stances of Germany's political and judicial institutions are partly related. In post-war West Germany, the GCC soon became the primary means of expressing resistance to European integration, since political elites could not or would not articulate societal misgivings and objections to the process (Davies 2012: 6).

The GCC's outlook on European integration is chiefly informed by its reading of Germany's constitution, the Basic Law (*Grundgesetz*). As Bill Davies (2012: i) noted, 'the integrity of its national constitutional order' was a 'fundamental pillar of the postwar German identity', and it fell to the Court to reconcile that constitutional integrity with European integration. This is not a straightforward task. On the one hand, the Basic Law enshrines Germany's democratic statehood and the sovereignty and right to democratic representation of the German people (Article 20(1) and (2) of the Basic Law). So sacred are these rights that they are rendered inviolable by the so-called 'eternity clause' (*Ewigkeitsklausel*) in Article 79(3), which prohibits amendments to the principles laid down in Article 20. As the GCC has repeatedly warned, the process of European integration cannot be allowed to compromise these constitutional values, as would happen if too much of the German government's sovereign power was transferred to the EU, which lacks democratic legitimacy because of shortcomings in the European Parliament's representativeness (Grimm 2009: 362; Hoffmann 2009: 482–83). The Basic Law, therefore, places restrictions on Germany's involvement in an ever-closer union.

Yet, on the other hand, the same constitutional text evinces a pro-integration disposition ('*Europarechtsfreundlichkeit*'), primarily in Article 23(1), which compels German institutions to participate constructively in the development of the EU. Articles 24 and 25 also predispose Germany to international cooperation and permit the transfer of sovereign powers to international organisations. Those latter clauses reflect the context of the Basic Law's adoption in 1949. At that time, Konrad Adenauer, the first Chancellor of the Federal Republic of Germany (FRG), enthusiastically pursued a policy of *Westbindung* (establishing close links with the West) in order to facilitate the FRG's economic rehabilitation, stabilise its political system, and secure it against potential threats from the Soviet-dominated Eastern bloc, including the German Democratic Republic (GDR). Beyond those material rationales, embracing Europe was also essential to the creation of a new (West) German identity to replace racial and nationalistic forms of identification that were discredited after 1945. As Wolfgang Wessels (2003: 133–35) put it, 'West European unification loomed as some kind of *Ersatzvaterland*, or substitute fatherland' for a polity in search of new and sturdy moorings. At the time of the Basic Law's proclamation, the FRG was still under occupation by the Western Allies. This made it easier for political leaders to contemplate ceding sovereignty as the price the FRG had to pay for post-war reconstruction and acceptance by its neighbours.

Adenauer's chancellorship set the tone for the pro-integration consensus that marked subsequent generations of (West) German political elites. Moreover, that policy orientation was carried over from the Bonn Republic into the post-reunification Berlin Republic. The original text of Article 23 had established the Basic Law's application in the West German *Länder* and provided for its potential application to other parts of Germany upon their accession to the Federal Republic. This provision was used as the legal basis for the GDR's accession to the FRG in 1990, after which it was repealed. Then, in 1992, the Basic Law was amended again and the new Article 23 inserted in order to explicitly reaffirm reunited Germany's commitment to its European partners and to the EU itself (Hartley 2004: 157–58).

The contradictions in German constitutionalism have grounded a European integration jurisprudence that is confrontational – even hostile – in word, but accommodating in deed. The GCC's verdicts on integration-related matters are, to date, a series of conditional approvals wherein the Court indicates that the scope for integration *is* limited, but that those limits have not yet been breached. In its 1974 *Solange I*[1] judgment, for example, the Court checked the supremacy of Community law in the realm of fundamental rights. The Court went even further in its *Maastricht*[2] and *Lisbon*[3] decisions when it claimed for itself the authority to subject EU law to *ultra vires* review, in direct contradiction to ECJ jurisprudence. However, the GCC has not yet exercised this jurisdiction, and its euro rescue verdicts so far have maintained the 'yes, but' formula. Nevertheless, change is possible. Having signalled its disapproval of ECB interventions in secondary bond markets, Karlsruhe could be on course for an open confrontation with the EU system.

Reconciling sovereign statehood with European integration

The following sections will discuss specific GCC cases which, taken as a whole, offer a valuable insight into the contestation of norms between national and supranational legal orders. Contestation should not be regarded as a negative process – multilevel constitutionalism in the EU works *through* the dynamic of resistance and response, not in spite of it. It is through normative contestation that the aims of the integration project are refined and its limits tested. Thus, the case analyses will illuminate the multilevel dimension of key strands of EU constitutionalism, in particular, the phenomenon of judicialisation, the role of the *demos* in legitimating a polity, and the (conditional) nature of the EU's supranational legal authority.

As was noted in Chapter 1, judicialisation is a longstanding feature of European integration, partly by design of its founders and partly due to the ECJ's generous interpretation of its own powers. However, post-war judicialisation was not solely a supranational phenomenon. It was also a major feature of West German politics after 1945, where a strong and unwavering commitment to the *Rechtsstaat* (the 'rule of law state') was one of the foundational pillars of the young polity. The FRG's founders sought to learn from the failings of the Weimar Republic by creating a 'constrained democracy' in which the protection of basic rights was emphasised and majoritarian institutions were checked by law (Müller 2011: 6).

The German Constitutional Court was one of the linchpins of Germany's constrained democracy. Its authority rested not only on its prominent position in Germany's constitutional order, but also on its embeddedness within the German political system. This lent the GCC a solid legitimacy base that is not shared by the ECJ, which is not similarly embedded in the EU's system of 'governance without government'. In fact, the GCC has been consistently rated as one of Germany's most popular and trusted federal institutions. A 2012 study by the Allensbach Institute for Public Opinion Research found that 75% of respondents had a high or very high level of trust in the Court, placing it second only to the Basic Law (78%), and far above political institutions such as the *Bundestag* (39%) and the Federal Government (38%). In the same study, 68% of respondents were in favour of the Court deciding on Germany's participation in the euro rescue efforts, whilst only 17% thought that such matters should be left to politics alone (Köcher 2012).

One outcome of the GCC's self-perception of its role as guardian of the *Rechtsstaat* is the Court's preoccupation with the relationship between democracy and *demos*. A recurrent theme in the Court's integration-related jurisprudence is the extent to which a coherent 'people' is needed in order for a democratic system of government to be possible. Article 20(2) of the Basic Law stipulates that all state authority is derived from the people and is to be exercised through 'elections and other votes and through specific legislative, executive and judicial bodies'. At the federal level, popular sovereignty is chanelled through the *Bundestag*, whose members 'shall be elected in general, direct, free, equal and secret elections' (Article 38(1) Basic Law). Whenever the GCC has applied German constitutional standards of democratic representation to the European level, it has found the EU institutions, primarily the European Parliament, to be lacking (Doukas 2009; Grimm 2009).

Put simply, the Court does not consider the EP to be representative of a sovereign European people. In fact, the Court does not consider there to be a European *demos* at all. The GCC put these inadequacies front and centre in both the *Maastricht* and *Lisbon decisions*, a stance for which it was widely criticised. Joseph Weiler (1995: 223), for example, was scathing of what he regarded as the German Court's reliance on 'tired old ideas of an ethno-culturally homogenous *Volk* and the unholy Trinity of *Volk-Staat-Staatsangehöriger* as the exclusive basis for democratic authority and legitimate rule-making'. However, Europe's *demos* quandary cannot be disregarded so easily. As Navraj Singh Ghaleigh (2003: 53) argued, '[s]pecified appropriately, absent an "ethno-cultural framework", the requirement of homogeneity, ceases to become an objectionable democratic precondition, but instead reveals itself to be both a necessary and liberal feature of the self-governing polity'.

Thus, from the GCC's point of view, the absence of a democratically represented European people is a fundamental limitation on Germany's participation in the European integration process. Barring a radical overhaul of the Basic Law, a certain core of sovereign powers must be maintained at the national level and exercised through the national parliament. Indeed, the Court on more than one occasion has used its judgements to instruct the German parliament, in effect, to do its job.[4] The Court's jurisprudence on the centrality of the *demos* to a democratic polity, therefore, offers an important gloss on the EU's uncodified constitutionalism, which – legalistic, depoliticised and functional – took little account of the presence or absence of a self-identifying European people.

The EU's limitations, in the view of the GCC, extend beyond its lack of democratic legitimacy to the very nature of its constitution. In its *Maastricht decision*, the Court described the EU as a *Staatenverbund* (association of states). In addition, on various occasions the GCC has reiterated the fact that the EU is constituted by international treaties and that the member states are the 'Masters of the Treaties'. It follows that the legal authority EU institutions possess by virtue of the treaties has been delegated to them by the member states. The German Court has held, therefore, that no EU institution – including the ECJ – can have the ultimate say on the scope of its own powers; instead the competence to determine the competences of EU institutions must lie at the national level, with national constitutional courts (Kumm and Comella 2005: 475). This is the issue of *Kompetenz-Kompetenz*, to which I will return below.[5]

Thus, the GCC's jurisprudence exemplifies the view that EU law only applies in the domestic legal order because national law permits it to do so. Furthermore, that the validity of EU law is subject to the terms of its authorisation by national constitutional law, which can only be determined, in the final analysis, by the highest court within the national legal system. From this point of view, the ECJ's doctrine of supremacy, as expounded in *Costa v ENEL*, does not enjoy a constitutional level of security within member states, and it is certainly not valid by virtue of the EU legal system's own authority. The upshot is that EU legal norms *could* be overruled by contrary national legislation that is later in time, in keeping with the maxim *lex posterior derogat legi priori* (later laws overrule conflicting earlier laws) (Phelan 2007, 2010). However, as a matter of fact, the supremacy of EU law has been routinely observed throughout the EU, over many decades, including by the GCC.

William Phelan (2010) argued that 'political self-control', combined with courts' assumption that governments intend to honour their European obligations, is what actually ensures the effectiveness of the EU's supranational legal order. This may seem like a distinction without a difference – whether EU law is self-authorising, or whether it gains its authority from national law, the result (i.e. the functional supremacy of EU law) is the same. However, the distinction is important for our understanding of EU constitutionalism as a pluralistic enterprise, with multiple, 'distinct but interacting systems of law', rather than as a monistic enterprise with a clear hierarchy (MacCormick

1995: 264). Moreover, the distinction may prove decisive in times of crisis, during which the limits of European law are severely tested.

Phelan's argument is not only relevant to Germany; it may be illustrated also in relation to the UK. While it confronted many of the same dilemmas as other European jurisdictions, the UK also faced its own set of normative challenges in accepting the supremacy of EU law when it joined the European Community. This reflects Britain's own unique constitutional arrangements – it does not have a single, written constitution but rather an uncodified constitutionalism, rooted in several key pieces of legislation as well as the common law.[6] Over the centuries and, particularly, since the Glorious Revolution of 1688, parliamentary sovereignty has been the 'dominant characteristic' of the British constitution. According to this principle, Parliament has 'the right to make or unmake any law whatever; and, further, ... no person or body is recognised by the law of England as having a right to override or set aside the legislation of Parliament' (Dicey 1959: 39–40). Thus, prior to Community accession, British laws were not subject to judicial review by British courts, let alone supranational courts.

Since 1973, UK constitutionalism has evolved to accommodate the obligations of EU membership, but not to the extent of accepting the ECJ's claims about European legal authority. The application of EU law in the UK is governed by the *European Communities Act* (1972), section 2(1) of which provides for the direct effect of European norms. In fact, UK courts have confirmed that it is the *European Communities Act* alone that gives force to the EU treaties in the UK.[7] As Lord Justice Laws put it in 2003: 'there are no circumstances in which the jurisprudence of the Court of Justice can elevate Community law to a status within the corpus of English domestic law to which it could not aspire by any route of English law itself'.[8] These sentiments are echoed in section 18 of the *European Union Act* (2011), passed by the Cameron government in order to curtail future transfers of sovereign power to the EU and to confirm the primacy of the British parliament.

Similar reasoning applies in the Irish and Danish cases. Ireland's membership of the EU is based on its own *European Communities Act* (1972) as well as a constitutional amendment enacted at the time of accession. Ireland's High Court, in *Crotty v An Taoiseach*,[9] concluded that, while ratifying the Treaty of Rome and amending the Irish Constitution was enough to make Ireland a Community member, it was not enough to give Community law effect in Ireland. It was only through passage of the *European Communities Act* that the Treaty became part of the domestic law of Ireland and its obligations enforceable through the Irish courts. In Denmark, the application of EU law in the domestic legal order is based on the statute implementing the European treaties, as well as Article 20 of the Danish Constitution (which provides for the delegation of powers to 'international authorities'). The Danish Supreme Court confirmed in its decision on the Maastricht Treaty[10] that the extent of EU legal authority in Denmark is governed by the Constitution and not by EU institutions themselves (Phelan 2010: 257–62).[11]

Finally, since their accession, a number of constitutional courts in the Central and Eastern European member states have been writing their own 'chapter' in the '*Solange* story' (Sadurski 2012: 103). These courts, many of which are powerful actors within their domestic legal and political orders, have followed the pattern established in Germany and other older member states of challenging the ECJ's supremacy doctrine in the name of upholding national constitutional principles in the realm of democracy and human rights (Sadurski 2012: 99–104).

Fundamental rights as a source of contention between the ECJ and GCC

Thus, although the ECJ was the towering figure in the constitutionalisation of the EU, it never had the final word on the content and direction of that process. Instead, the ECJ's jurisprudence on the nature of the treaties and the Union they created has run in tandem with the GCC's jurisprudence (and that of other national courts) on the *constraints* placed on the supranational Union by national constitutional law. The ECJ and GCC have pursued a decades-long dialogue – neither entirely harmonious, nor entirely discordant – that exposes both the possibilities and limits of Europe's legal integration. In the 1960s and 1970s, the development of a European-level catalogue of 'constitutionalised' basic rights was a focal point for this dialogue.

Fundamental rights were not mentioned in the Treaty of Rome, leaving little primary material from which the ECJ could fashion European-level human rights protections. The Court's decision to do so anyway came about, to a large extent, in response to challenges to its supremacy doctrine from national courts, primarily the German and Italian Constitutional Courts (Kumm and Comella 2005: 474). During the 1960s, it was frequently argued before the German courts that Community laws that violated the fundamental rights guarantees of the Basic Law should be struck down as invalid. This line of reasoning was obviously incompatible with the ECJ's goal of ensuring the uniform application of Community norms in all member states, but the GCC showed considerable sympathy towards it. Thus, the ECJ was obliged to either find a way to protect human rights itself through Community law, or risk 'rebellion' by the GCC and other national courts dealing with similar cases (Hartley 2010: 143–44).

The ECJ first recognised fundamental rights as a part of Community law in the 1969 case, *Stauder v City of Ulm*.[12] It expanded on the new doctrine in *Internationale Handelsgesellschaft*,[13] holding that:

> Respect for fundamental rights forms an integral part of the *general principles of law* protected by the Court of Justice. The protection of such rights, whilst inspired by the constitutional traditions common to the Member States, must be ensured within the framework of the structure and objectives of the Community.
>
> (emphasis added)

Thus, the ECJ drew not on the treaties, nor on secondary Community legislation, but on the nebulous concept of 'the general principles of law' – divined from national constitutional doctrines – to justify its foray into the realm of fundamental rights. The Court's ulterior motive in *Internationale Handelsgesellschaft* was clear: to reiterate the doctrine of European legal supremacy, and thereby safeguard the integrity and coherence of European legal integration. To this end, in the same judgment the ECJ confirmed that Community legal measures took precedence over *all* national measures, even constitutional provisions – a direct rejection of the German line of argument (Hartley 2010: 145).

The GCC was initially unconvinced by the ECJ's efforts. In the 1974 case *Solange I*, the German Court insisted on its own right of judicial review of Community law in cases touching on the Basic Law's fundamental rights protections.[14] Moreover, in a rebuttal of the *Costa* doctrine, the GCC held that German constitutional rights protections would take precedence over conflicting Community norms unless and until comparable protections were established at the European level (Kumm and Comella 2005: 474). At the same time, the GCC did avoid open conflict with its European counterpart. *Solange I* was actually *Internationale Handelsgesellschaft*; the same case in which the ECJ expanded on its doctrines of supremacy and fundamental rights protections. On the facts of that case, the GCC agreed with the ECJ that the impugned measure did not breach any fundamental rights. This made it unnecessary for the GCC to exercise the jurisdiction that it had just claimed, so that the idea of a national-level constitutional right of judicial review of Community norms remained abstract. Still, the German Court's bold statements served as a warning that the ECJ's take on supremacy was not definitive, and that the authority of Community norms was contingent on their compliance with national constitutional requirements.

However, in an example of the give-and-take that has characterised interactions between the GCC and ECJ, the German Court backed away from its 'threat' to review the validity of Community acts twelve years later, in the *Solange II* case (van Ooyen 2011: 45–46).[15] In that decision, the GCC found that, since its *Solange I* verdict, the ECJ had established an effective fundamental rights jurisprudence, which afforded a substantially similar level of protection to that available to German citizens in the Basic Law. As long as that continued to be the case, the German Court declared that it would no longer subject Community norms to its own fundamental rights-based review (Doukas 2009: 868). This was not the end, though, of the GCC's challenge to the ECJ's self-claimed monopoly on the interpretation of European legal norms, as later cases made clear.

The Maastricht decision: integration so far and no farther

The Maastricht Treaty was a major step in a decade-long effort championed by then-Commission President Jacques Delors to kick-start the integration project after the 'Eurosclerosis' of the 1970s. Within member states, the Treaty was debated extensively in the media, amongst politicians and political parties and, in some cases, before the courts. National reactions to Maastricht ranged from positive, to lukewarm, to decidedly negative. The Treaty faced difficult ratification processes in a number of member states – being only narrowly approved by referendum in France and rejected at a first referendum in Denmark in June 1992.

Of all the national judicial responses to the Maastricht Treaty, the best known is the GCC's decision in *Brunner v The European Union Treaty*,[16] which evaluated the Maastricht Treaty's compatibility with the German Basic Law. Though the Court did not block Germany's ratification of the TEU, its acceptance of the Treaty was not unconditional, either. Having previously de-escalated its constitutional confrontation with the ECJ in *Solange II*, the GCC took the opportunity in its *Maastricht decision* to firmly restate its understanding of the limits placed on EU law by German law. Thus, the Court confirmed that Union acts that go beyond the scope of the treaties are invalid in Germany. It then went a step further in arrogating to itself the right to review acts of EU institutions to determine whether they exceed their conferred competences. If the GCC were to conduct such an *ultra vires* review, it would necessarily involve interpreting the treaties, since they are the source of Union competences. In this respect the German Court challenged the ECJ in a way that it did not do in *Solange I*, because the European Court claims the exclusive jurisdiction to interpret EU norms (Grimm 1997: 235–38; 2009: 357–58).

The GCC's reasoning was animated by political and constitutional considerations. The Court drew extensively on notions such as national sovereignty and democratic representation of peoples in order to circumscribe the potential for future supranational integration. It was widely criticised for this approach as parochial and outdated, but the *Maastricht decision* should not be so easily dismissed (Everson 1998: 391–92; Ghaleigh 2003: 49–51). It added texture, not only to the rich German jurisprudence on European integration, but also to EU constitutionalism itself. The German Court was called to reflect on the nature of the European polity and the difficult question of whence it drew its sovereignty. Was European law, as the ECJ claimed, autonomous and self-sustaining, drawing its legal authority from the EU's own sovereignty? Or, alternatively, was European legal authority still dependent on the transmitted sovereignty of the member states?

Prior to the *Maastricht decision*, scholarly debate tended to take the ECJ's supremacy doctrine, and its transformation of the EU into a *sui generis* entity with an autonomous legal order, as its starting point. The GCC, however, based its conception of the EU on its connection to the key concept of statehood – either the EU was a sovereign federal state in its own right, or it was constituted by sovereign states as a treaty-based organisation under international law. On the basis of that dichotomy, the Court defined the EU as an association of states (*Staatenverbund*), whose legal authority was delegated and circumscribed by the member states (Everson 1998: 392–93). This label, combined with the emphasis the Court placed on the role of a 'relatively homogenous' *demos* in sustaining a democratic polity, served to limit the possibilities for the political integration of Europe (Joerges 1996: 115).

Thus, the significance of the *Maastricht decision* lay partly in its re-examination of European legal orthodoxies. The Court's stubborn refusal to view the EU through a paradigm of 'uniqueness' drew indignation and even scorn. Michelle Everson (1998: 393) wrote critically of the GCC lacking the freedom 'from the constraints of inflexible doctrinal thought' that EU legal scholars and practitioners had developed by studying the 'real-world' evolution of European law into a constitutional system. Weiler (1995) condemned the Court's reliance on nationally based (and, he asserted, implicitly Schmittian and ethno-culturally homogenous) polities as the only possible site for democratic politics. It is, indeed, possible that Schmitt's theories influenced the Court's decision (Müller 2000: 1780; Ragazzoni 2011: fn.xlii). Even so, Weiler's condemnation is overstated. One need not endorse Schmitt's emphasis on the importance of an ethnically based *demos* in order to recognise that democratic representation relies on *some* form and degree of homogeneity, or commonness, amongst those represented (Ghaleigh 2003: 53). Moreover, the flexibility implied by the EU's 'uniqueness' paradigm is sometimes better described as a deliberate vagueness that brushes over its democratic shortcomings (Shore 2006).

For all the controversy it generated, the GCC did actually find that the TEU was consistent with the Basic Law, thus paving the way for German ratification. Indeed, as Christian Joerges (2012: 9–10) argued, what may be most consequential about the *Maastricht decision* is not the doubt the Court expressed about the potential for further supranational integration, but its *endorsement* of the Treaty and, above all, its endorsement of the euro. Not only did the GCC give its support to EMU as envisaged by the Maastricht Treaty – that is, as a legally structured and de-politicised currency union – it even made EMU's construction along such lines a precondition of German participation (Joerges 2012: 10). To this end, the Court stressed the importance of the concept of the EU as a 'stability community' ('*Stabilitätsgemeinschaft*'), secured in large part by the no-bailout clause. Thus, the GCC bought into the fallacy that something as inherently political as a currency union could be designed in a technocratic manner. Furthermore, that its success could be ensured, and any doubts about democratic legitimacy resolved, by the application of legal rules – rules establishing ECB independence, as well as (somewhat arbitrary) rules prohibiting excessive budget deficits and unsustainable levels of public debt (Joerges 2012: 10–11).

That this was a misjudgement on the part of the Court seems all the clearer in light of the euro crisis. By emphasising the role of strict legal criteria in the operation of monetary union, the GCC '[gave] its consent to an institutional configuration in which the law was to disempower politics' (Joerges 2012: n.41). The course of events since the euro's introduction (including multiple, unpunished violations of the Stability and Growth Pact and the serious mis-reporting of financial data in Greece) has given the lie to the notion that a currency union can be successfully run along purely legalistic, apolitical lines. Now, faced with the crisis-induced state of emergency, law has been found wanting and – in an ironic twist on its previous reliance on legality as a sub-stitute for legitimacy – the GCC was left with little choice but to approve of Germany's participation in the European Stability Mechanism (ESM), a pragmatic political measure of questionable legal validity and legitimacy.

The Lisbon decision: a restatement of the limits of European integration through law

The Lisbon Treaty was signed in the Portuguese capital on 13 December 2007, as EU leaders attempted to draw a line under the long and difficult treaty reform process that preceded it. The new reform treaty was welcomed by the major political parties in Germany and it was passed by both chambers of parliament in April and May 2008. However, as with previous EU treaties, there was some public disquiet over the transfer of sovereign powers from Germany to the supranational level. The GCC once again became the focal point for this dissent as a number of individuals lodged constitutional com-plaints against the LT. As a result, German ratification of the Treaty was delayed pending the GCC's verdict, which was delivered on 30 June 2009.

As with its previous decisions on European integration, the Court found the Lisbon Treaty to be compatible with the Basic Law, though it did require some amendments to the accompanying German legislation (Piris 2010: 344-46). The verdict restated key points from the *Maastricht decision*, evincing the same conviction that supranational integration is fundamentally limited by national constitutional principles that safeguard nation state-based repre-sentative democracy.[17] For the purposes of this summary, I will focus on a few specific aspects of the verdict that are relevant to understanding multilevel constitutionalism. These are: the GCC's confirmation of the EU's status as an international treaty-based organisation; the EU's structural democratic deficit and its implications for German participation in European integration; and the constitutional principles governing the application of EU law in Germany, including the German Court's review powers.

In the *Lisbon* verdict, the Court described the EU treaties as constituting a derivative legal order and confirmed again the status of member states as 'Masters of the Treaties' (*Herren der Verträge*) (Halberstam and Möllers 2009: 1241–42). The Court also rejected the possibility of the European Par-liament serving as the democratic legislature of a European people, conclud-ing instead that EU authority remained dependent on European *peoples* as constituted in the several member states and as represented by national par-liaments. Since the European Parliament was not up to the democratic stan-dards required by the Basic Law, the Court emphasised the necessity of leaving 'sufficient space' to the member states 'for the political formation of the economic, cultural and social living conditions'.[18] The GCC's approval of the LT was based on its assessment that the Treaty retained an appropriate balance between the EU's (low) level of democratic legitimacy and the extent of its conferred powers. The Court stressed the importance of maintaining this balance – were it to be lost, Germany may be obliged to withdraw its participation in the integration project (Piris 2010: 342–43, 352–54).[19]

The GCC also confirmed two constitutionally mandated grounds for reviewing the applicability of Union laws in Germany. These are, respectively, an 'identity review' and an '*ultra vires* review'. The first type of judicial review concerns issues of fundamental democracy, human rights and constitutional identity that were first raised in *Solange I*, namely that EU laws must not infringe the inviolable core content of the Basic Law. The second type of judicial review also follows from the idea that EU legal authority in Germany is derived from the Basic Law. In both the *Maastricht* and *Lisbon* decisions, the German Court stressed that EU institutions may exercise only those powers that are conferred upon them by the member states. Moreover, the GCC argued that the ECJ, as an EU institution itself, was capable of overstepping its competences and so could not have the final say on the jurisdictional boundaries of EU law. Therefore, insofar as the application of EU norms in Germany was concerned, the GCC claimed this right of competence-competence for itself (Grimm 1997: 236–37; Kumm and Comella 2005: 475).

The *Lisbon decision* was criticised by some as a negative, overly statist and legally incoherent attempt to protect German sovereignty from the EU bogeyman (see, for example, Bröhmer 2009; Halberstam and Möllers 2009; Selmayr 2009). However, the GCC's reasoning was not as out of step with the various currents of EU constitutionalism as many critics assumed. Indeed, it was congruent with what Ian Cooper described as the Lisbon Treaty's own attempt to preserve member states' autonomous spheres of competence. As Cooper (2010: 15) noted, '[f]or this to be sustainable, the area of Member State law outside the reach of EU law ... must be substantially large and not shrinking'. Thus, one may discern synergies between the process of treaty reform and the German Court's jurisprudence on that process. Just as constitutionally pluralist theories of the EU developed out of debates over the GCC's *Maastricht decision* (Baquero Cruz 2008), the constitutionally pluralist tendencies evident within the Lisbon Treaty are reinforced by the Court's evaluation of that text. In particular, the GCC's emphasis on conferral and its strengthening of the German parliament's role in the integration process reinforce the Lisbon Treaty's trend towards empowering national parliaments and delimiting national and EU legal orders as separate, though overlapping spheres.

In other words, rather than pursuing an anti-integration agenda, the Court regarded the limits it imposed as being entirely in keeping with Germany's obligations as an EU member state. Moreover, as its subsequent case law demonstrates, there is still considerable room for flexibility within the GCC's integration jurisprudence.

The Honeywell decision: a more conciliatory approach by the GCC

The difference of opinion between the European Court of Justice and the German Constitutional Court has so far remained rhetorical. The GCC illustrated its reluctance to openly breach the EU's judicially constructed edifice of legal supranationalism in the 2010 *Honeywell* case, which addressed the question of whether an overly activist jurisprudence of the ECJ could be regarded as an *ultra vires* act and, thus, liable to be declared void in Germany.[20] While the answer remained, technically, 'yes', the Court made clear that it would only set aside an ECJ ruling or other act of an EU institution in very narrow circumstances.

Honeywell concerned the compatibility of German legislation permitting the employment of older workers on short-term contracts with EU law, particularly Council Directive 2000/78/EC, which prohibited age discrimination in the workplace. In its 2005 *Mangold* decision, the ECJ, ruling on a preliminary reference from the German Federal Labour Court, had found that the German legislation did conflict with EU law and, hence, should be held invalid. The *Mangold* ruling was controversial for two reasons. Firstly, the ECJ applied the Directive even though the time for national authorities to transpose it into national law had not yet elapsed. In doing so, the Court relied upon and extended its previous jurisprudence that circumscribed member states' ability to pass legislation incompatible with progressive implementation of Directives not yet in force (Mahlmann 2010: 1407–8). Secondly, the ECJ went above and beyond the Directive to sustain its ruling, finding that the member states were also subject to a 'general principle of European Union law' that prohibited age-based discrimination in the workplace (Beyer-Katzenberger 2011: 518).

In the *Honeywell* proceedings that reached the GCC in 2010, the original plaintiff was also an older worker who challenged the legality of his fixed-term contract with an auto parts manufacturer. The Federal Labour Court relied on the ECJ's *Mangold* ruling to uphold the worker's complaint, whereupon the employer appealed to the GCC. The employer alleged, amongst other things, that *Mangold* involved so activist an interpretation of EU law as to create new law, thereby breaching the principle of conferral and constituting an *ultra vires* act. Therefore, the GCC was invited to hold the *Mangold* jurisprudence inapplicable in Germany in accordance with the *ultra vires* control it had claimed in the *Maastricht* and *Lisbon* decisions (Mahlmann 2010: 1408).

Although the GCC confirmed its competence-competence and right to review EU law in its verdict, it stated that it would exercise judicial restraint, only utilising these powers in coordination with the ECJ and in full mindfulness of the importance of the principle of uniform application of Union laws. In fact, quite a high threshold was set. The GCC held that the ECJ has 'a right to tolerance of error', and that it would not supplant Luxembourg's findings with its own in cases in which a legal rule was open to different interpretations, so long as the ECJ had complied with accepted standards of legal reasoning.[21]

Moreover, even in cases in which the ECJ departed from the usual standards of judicial interpretation, the GCC would not find the decision *ultra vires* unless it constituted a 'manifest breach leading to a shift in the structure of the competences between Member States and the Community' (Mahlmann 2010: 1410). The GCC held on the facts that the *Mangold* jurisprudence did not fundamentally alter the division of competences, and so there was no need to decide the question of whether the ECJ had followed accepted standards of legal reasoning (though the judges did express doubts about the soundness of the European Court's 'general principle of EU law' line of argument) (Beyer-Katzenberger 2011: 520–21). On that basis, the Court dismissed the employer's complaint and upheld the ECJ's *Mangold* jurisprudence.

Honeywell marked a significant de-escalation of the German Court's doctrinal conflict with the ECJ only a year after its rhetorically eurosceptic *Lisbon decision*. In fact, the GCC's verdict was criticised in some quarters as a missed opportunity to check the activist ECJ and the expansionary tendencies of EU law. Dieter Grimm (2010) argued that national sovereignty was endangered by the cumulative effect of ECJ activism and that the GCC needed to act early, rather than waiting for a case in which the ECJ egregiously overstepped the mark. In the same vein, the GCC's Justice Landau, who wrote a dissenting opinion, denounced what he regarded as a departure from the consensus reached in the *Lisbon decision*, without any good cause (van Ooyen 2011: 58).

Nevertheless, the fact that the GCC will only find the act of an EU institution *ultra vires* in narrow, highly circumscribed circumstances, does not mean that it could never happen. In fact, the Court laid the groundwork for an *ultra vires* finding against the ECB's Outright Monetary Transactions (OMT) programme in February 2014, when it referred the question of the scheme's legality to the ECJ for a preliminary reference. Far from abdicating its authority, the GCC's first ever preliminary referral fulfils one of the *Honeywell* criteria for finding a breach of competence by an EU institution; namely that the ECJ must be given a prior opportunity to clarify the potential breach. I will return to this case later in the chapter.

Thus, *Honeywell* illustrated well the complexity of the relationship between the GCC and the ECJ. On the one hand, the GCC acknowledged the pro-European integration predisposition of the German Basic Law. Yet, at the same time, it affirmed that European legal authority is not absolute, but rather is ultimately governed by the Basic Law, of which the GCC is guardian. As long as the member states are the 'Masters of the Treaties', the legal sovereignty of Union institutions will be subject to national constitutional checks. Whether, when and how those checks will come into operation remains uncertain, though the euro rescue measures are testing the limits of the GCC's ability to reconcile its own jurisprudence with EU governance.

The GCC and the euro rescue: framing the Court's role

In 2012, the GCC was called on to assess the Fiscal Compact (an intergovernmental treaty that tightens fiscal rules for eurozone members) and the European Stability Mechanism (ESM, the permanent eurozone bailout fund) for their compatibility with German constitutional law.[22] The two treaties were ratified by parliament on 29 July 2012, but not signed into law by the President because of the legal challenge. Some 37,000 plaintiffs, including ordinary citizens, academics, and parliamentarians from far left party, *Die Linke*, asked the Court to issue a preliminary injunction preventing the President's signature pending the final determination of their claims (*Spiegel Online*, 2012).

At issue was whether or not the German government's participation in these European undertakings was consistent with the constitutional protection of German democratic statehood (enshrined in Art. 20(1) and (2) of the Basic Law, and further entrenched by the 'eternity clause' in Art. 79(3)). Questions were raised as to whether the provisions of the Fiscal Compact, including its grant of national budgetary oversight powers to the European Commission, so infringed on the economic competences of the German parliament as to be unconstitutional. Doubts were also raised about the democratic accountability of the ESM, which was to be established 'among the euro-area Member States as an intergovernmental organisation under public international law', for the purposes of 'mobilis[ing] funding and provid[ing] financial assistance, under strict conditionality, to the benefit of euro-area Member States' (European Council, 24/25 March 2011: 22).

Once again, the GCC was not the only national court that had to grapple with the constitutionality of these measures. Challenges were also brought in Estonia, France and Ireland. The Irish Supreme Court, while holding that the ESM Treaty did not involve an impermissible transfer of sovereignty, still referred the question of the Treaty's compatibility with EU law to the ECJ for a preliminary ruling.[23] Nevertheless, the German legal challenge merits special consideration. It was made all the more pertinent by the GCC's previous declarations that fundamental fiscal decisions relating to revenue and expenditure were a part of the hardcore of national competences, without which democratic government would not be possible.[24] Moreover, in the context of the euro crisis, Germany has come to be seen as Europe's 'paymaster' – the ESM (to which Germany is the largest contributor) could not have come into force without German support, and that support hinged on the Court's blessing.[25]

The case generated intense scrutiny in Germany and beyond. One slice of the public debate that highlighted the issues at stake for Germany and the EU was a series of opinion pieces by influential figures published in the *Frankfurter Allgemeine Zeitung*, one of Germany's premier daily newspapers, in the lead up to the decision. The contributions ranged from the suggestion that the currency union had failed and should be abandoned completely unless the EU was to be converted into a fully fledged federal state (Sarrazin 2012); to the claim that a bold commitment to deeper, more social-democratic integration was needed to save the euro and secure Europe's place in a shifting global order (Bofinger, Habermas and Nida-Rümelin 2012).

Of particular interest from the legal point of view were two contributions that embodied two distinct approaches to the EU's predicament. Former

German Constitutional Court judge, Paul Kirchhof (2012b), stressed the need to follow established rules, even at great economic cost. His critique of the ESM and Fiscal Compact thus focused on the extent to which they fudged the provisions of the Maastricht Treaty.[26] On the other hand, Mattias Kumm (2012), in a variation of the 'crisis as opportunity' motif, went beyond the problems of legal inconsistency raised by Kirchhof to see an opportunity for Germany's governing institutions to realise their constitutionally based obligation to foster and direct European integration. I will look at both arguments in more detail.

Kirchhof (2012b) asserted that the international treaty-based responses to the euro crisis were damaging European unity by undermining its constitutional stability. He argued further that initiatives such as the ESM and Fiscal Compact were having a corrosive effect on democratic legitimacy in both creditor nations, where citizens were deceived about the potential extent of their liability for other countries' debts, and debtor nations, where citizens railed against their governments' cession of control over fiscal policies. The former judge's scepticism is unsurprising; Kirchhof wrote the GCC's *Maastricht decision*, and his opinions continue to reflect concern for the integrity of German sovereignty, constitutional identity and law. Accordingly, he argued that EU leaders' willingness to subordinate legal stability to economic and financial stability was misguided and dangerous. In fact, even the notion that there could be a neat trade-off between the two is a fallacy – legal stability is a necessary precondition of financial stability. It is the existence of reliable and enforceable legal norms that ensures that contractual obligations, including those surrounding the repayment of debt, will be honoured.

Kirchhof may have exaggerated the severity of the threat to the European *Rechtsstaat* posed by the euro rescue measures but he was right to warn that undermining the binding quality of law is a slippery slope. His central point was as simple as it was profound: a Union predicated on the rule of law cannot long survive its leaders' abandonment of legality in favour of expediency. The German Constitution's so-called 'eternity clause' was formulated precisely in recognition of the fact that no state of emergency can justify derogation from basic democratic principles. There is a real danger that, in addition to its economic fallout, the eurozone crisis has precipitated an inversion of the conventional story of integration through law. In other words, that it has opened up the possibility of a partial unravelling of European unity and stability prompted by a growing disregard for law and legality.

Mattias Kumm also affirmed the centrality of law to European integration. But, in contrast to Kirchhof's pessimism, he remained confident that 'more Europe' was the way forward. To that end, he urged the GCC to use its verdict on the ESM and Fiscal Compact to abandon what he viewed as the Court's unnecessarily narrow and defensive reading of the Basic Law and instead embrace that document's potential to facilitate the democratisation of European integration (Kumm 2012). Kumm's central contention was that, in its desire to protect democracy at the national level, the Court had not done justice to

Article 23 of the Basic Law, which requires German institutions to work towards the realisation of a democratic, united Europe. He called on the German Court to act as a *'gemeineuropäisches Verfassungsgericht'* (common European constitutional court), arguing that it had not only the capacity but also the *duty* to exert pressure on Europe's recalcitrant political leaders.

Kumm's most remarkable claim was implicit: that the GCC – an unelected body, whose remit is the interpretation and guardianship of Germany's Basic Law – should take a leading role in propelling the integration project forward, for the benefit of all Europeans. As the article's title proclaims, the GCC's verdict ought to have been 'a signal for Europe' (Kumm 2012). To some extent, Kumm's position may be understood in the context of German constitutional traditions, including the post-war judicialisation of the polity and empowerment of the constitutional court. From this perspective, Kumm's exhortation to the Court reflected what Robert van Ooyen described as the peculiarly German propensity to turn, in almost all situations, to the judicial branch as *'Ersatzkaiser-Ersatz'* (van Ooyen 2011: 59). Still, when applied to the EU, this reliance on courts also highlights persistent deficiencies in democratic politics at the European level (see, for example, Weiler 2011: 686–91). That it should fall to a constitutional court – or, for that matter, a central bank – to try to chart a course out of the most serious challenge that the EU has faced is especially an indictment of the European Parliament, which ideally would be the main forum for a public debate on Europe's future.

The Court's reaction to the euro rescue: yes, no and maybe

In the event, the GCC satisfied neither Kumm's wish for a strong statement on the German government's EU-democracy-promotion obligations, nor Kirchhof's desire for the euro rescue package to be struck down in the name of the *Rechtsstaat*. Instead the Court declined the plaintiffs' application for temporary injunctive relief on 12 September 2012, clearing the way for the entry into law of both the ESM Treaty and Fiscal Compact.[27] Following the Court's unusually quick 'summary review', it took another year and a half to deliberate on the principal proceedings, only handing down its final ruling on 18 March 2014.[28] Since the latter verdict essentially confirmed the preliminary ruling, I will discuss both together.

In contrast to the occasionally expansive rhetoric of its previous decisions on European integration, with the euro rescue verdicts the GCC restricted itself more explicitly to legal questions. When announcing the preliminary verdict, Court President Andreas Voßkuhle emphasised that the judges had not ascertained the suitability of the rescue package, which 'is and remains the task of politics' (Jahn 2012). Again, in the final ruling, the Court was at pains to point out the wide scope of the legislature's discretion when it comes to entering into European and international commitments, even when these commitments restrict domestic budgetary policy.[29] Nevertheless, the GCC also made clear that this discretion is still circumscribed by law and, while it gave its blessing to the rescue measures, it did not do so unreservedly.

The Court's focus in both the preliminary and principal proceedings was on the ESM Treaty (TESM). In admitting the plaintiffs' claims, the GCC acknowledged that the TESM had the potential to undermine the *Bundestag's* overall budgetary responsibility and, hence, violate the constitutionally guaranteed right to vote and precept of democracy. The Court had previously held that Article 38(1) of the Basic Law, which regulates the democratic election of the *Bundestag*, together with the principle of democracy, requires that decision-making power over public revenue and expenditure remains with the *Bundestag*. As such, the judges confirmed that the *Bundestag* had to 'individually approve every large-scale federal aid measure on the international or European Union level', and that it was prohibited from creating mechanisms that would delegate that power.[30] In other words, the legislature's discretion in exercising its budgetary competences did not extend to binding itself or its successors by assuming fiscal liabilities that were unlimited, automatic or irreversible.[31]

Nevertheless, despite sounding this note of caution, the Court concluded that neither the TESM nor the Fiscal Compact violated the *Budgestag's* overall budgetary responsibility, which was adequately safeguarded by EU and German law.[32] The Court's customary ' ... but' came in the form of several provisos, some fairly innocuous, some potentially more consequential. In its preliminary ruling, the GCC laid down two conditions for German participation in the ESM, both aimed at securing an appropriate level of parliamentary oversight of its activities. Firstly, the Court held that Germany could only ratify the TESM if the government ensured that Germany's contribution to the Stability Mechanism's capital stock (originally set at 190 billion euro) could not be increased without the agreement of the German representative to the ESM.[33] He or she, in turn, could not authorise an increase without the prior approval of the *Bundestag*, as is already provided by national law. Secondly, the Court stipulated that the TESM provisions on the inviolability of ESM documents and professional secrecy of staff must not infringe the German Parliament's right to be comprehensively informed about the activities of the Stability Mechanism.[34] The ESM member states responded on 27 September 2012 with a declaration that the relevant provisions of the TESM were to be interpreted in accordance with the Court's prescriptions. As its final ruling makes clear, this declaration was enough to assuage the GCC's concerns.[35]

Another issue raised by the complainants was the possibility of German voting rights in the ESM being suspended due to non-payment of committed funds, as provided for by Article 4(8) TESM. The Court acknowledged the potentially serious consequences of such a suspension – if the German representatives to the bodies of the ESM were unable to participate in their deliberations, then the link between *Bundestag* and ESM would be broken and the latter could potentially take decisions that affect Germany without the former's consent. However, the Court placed the onus squarely on the legislature to ensure that Germany would always be in a position to meet its financial obligations to the ESM, thus protecting its voting rights.[36]

Perhaps most intriguing was the way the GCC dealt with the complainants' assertion that the ESM could become a vehicle for unconstitutional state financing by the ECB. The Court reasoned that since state financing by the ECB is prohibited by Article 123 TFEU, the TESM could only be interpreted as *not* permitting the ESM's involvement in such borrowing operations.[37] In other words, the TESM cannot be interpreted as contravening a provision of EU Treaty law, because to do so would contravene EU Treaty law. This reasoning is circular and, at first glance, indicates an admission of lack of jurisdiction over the actions of EU institutions, as well as an unwillingness to interfere with a hard fought political bargain negotiated by the German government and endorsed by the German Parliament. However, on further consideration, this tautology may have been a forewarning of the Court's negative assessment of the legality of ECB interventions in euro area bond markets. Such an interpretation gained credence following the GCC's comments on the ECB's bond-buying programme in February 2014, discussed in the next section.

Reaction to the GCC's preliminary verdict – in many ways, the more important of the two, since it cleared the way for German ratification of the treaties – was swift. In Strasbourg, members of the European Parliament burst into spontaneous applause when informed of Karlsruhe's decision (Busse 2012). Chancellor Merkel certainly viewed the ruling as a vindication of her government's crisis management policies, telling the *Bundestag* that it sent a 'strong signal out to Europe and the world beyond' that 'Germany is decisively true to its responsibility in Europe as the largest economy and a reliable partner' (Kulish and Eddy 2012).

The rhetoric of Germany as 'reliable partner' harks back to the origins of the integration project and the desire to entrench firmly (West) Germany within Europe. As already noted, the obligation to work towards a united Europe even finds expression in the *Europarechtsfreundlichkeit* (pro-integration disposition) of the Basic Law, above all in Article 23. It is a historical irony, brought about by the euro crisis, that being a 'reliable partner' has come to mean taking the lead role in determining the fate of the currency union. It is a further irony that the German polity's twin commitments – to the *Rechtsstaat* and to European unity – are increasingly brought into conflict by attempts to rescue the euro that bend the rules of the EU treaties (Auer 2012: 61–62). It is precisely this thorny conflict that the GCC, as guardian of the Basic Law, must mediate, whilst observers are left to ponder whether the rules have already been bent too far. As much as Merkel may have wished otherwise, the Court's endorsement of the Fiscal Compact and ESM was far from the end of the story.

The GCC and the ECB – an addendum

Before it was even handed down, the Court's preliminary ruling on the ESM and Fiscal Compact was affected by external events. On 6 September 2012,

ECB Chief, Mario Draghi, announced a plan by the Bank to buy unlimited quantities of euro area government bonds under strict conditions (the so-called Outright Monetary Transactions (OMT) programme). This development was greeted in Germany almost immediately by another legal challenge, brought by Peter Gauweiler of the Christian Social Union (*Christlich-Soziale Union in Bayern*, CSU). Gauweiler filed an urgent motion requesting that the GCC delay its preliminary verdict in order to consider the ECB's move, which, he argued, 'created a totally new situation for assessing the constitutionality of the ESM Treaty' (*Die Zeit*, 2012).

The Court rejected Gauweiler's motion, opting to hand down its verdict on 12 September, as planned. However, it did reserve the right to consider the legality of the bond-buying programme in the course of the main proceedings. The Court held oral hearings on the ECB's activities on 11–12 June 2013, during which *Bundesbank* President, Jens Weidmann criticised the OMT programme as a violation of ECB independence and the prohibition on central bank financing of state deficits (Charter 2013). Then, in February 2014, the GCC opened a new chapter in its long-running dialogue with the ECJ by making a referral under the Article 267 TFEU procedure.[38] The OMT referral is one of the most interesting, and, potentially, consequential interactions between the courts because it intersects two conflicts that define EU constitutionalism: that between law and politics; and that between the national and supranational levels.

One of the clearest effects of the euro crisis has been to reconfigure the balance between law and politics in the EU. Politics (though not democratic contestation) is waxing, while law and courts are waning. Can the GCC buck the trend? If the court proceedings force the ECB to abandon or significantly modify OMT it would constitute something of a legal counter-revolution. However, the amount of time it will take for the ECJ to deliver its preliminary reference militates against such a view. Announcing the OMT programme was certainly a canny political move on the part of Mario Draghi, who sought to obviate the need for financial assistance to struggling euro area states by promising it in unlimited quantities. By the time the ECJ gives its opinion, the programme – legal or not – may well have served its purpose without ever being activated.

The OMT case also has the potential to trigger conflict along the national-supranational axis. By referring the case to Luxembourg, Karlsruhe has again raised the question of where power lies in a multilevel constitutional system. In the past, the GCC has expounded doctrines that flatly contradict ECJ jurisprudence on issues such as supremacy and competence-competence. As this chapter illustrates, the German Court has challenged the ECJ's authority without ever usurping it, and disputed the ECJ's legal interpretations without ever rejecting them (Kumm and Comella 2005: 475). The OMT case could realise this previously theoretical conflict. There is little space for constructive ambiguity in the GCC's strongly worded statement on the bond-buying programme. If the ECJ endorses OMT unreservedly, the GCC will have to choose between losing face and contradicting its own jurisprudence, and openly breaching the EU's uncodified constitution.

Thus, the GCC's preliminary referral should not be interpreted as a decision not to decide, or as an instance of buck-passing (Di Fabio 2014). The majority judgment is clear and sharp in its criticism of OMT. The bond-buying programme has no formal basis in EU law, and, in the Court's opinion, it appears to violate the EU treaties and the ECB's own charter. In particular, the GCC argued that OMT is inconsistent with Articles 119 and 127 TFEU, which grant the ECB a monetary policy mandate, but exclude it from pursuing its own economic policy, since the latter is a prerogative of member states. Moreover, the limitless nature of Draghi's promise, amongst other factors, suggests that OMT constitutes an unlawful circumvention of the prohibition on direct monetary financing of state budgets in Article 123 TFEU.[39] Having transgressed EU law in this way, the GCC suggests that OMT does meet the highly restrictive criteria laid down in *Honeywell* for a finding of *ultra vires*. That is, the programme constitutes a 'manifest violation' of powers that causes a 'structurally significant shift' in the allocation of competences between the national and supranational levels.[40]

If the ECB's transgression is so blatant, why involve the ECJ at all? By consulting the Court in Luxembourg, Karlsruhe has met one of the preconditions it set itself for returning a finding of *ultra vires*. Amidst the controversy surrounding the GCC's *Lisbon decision*, Frank Schorkopf (2009: 1239) observed that the case would be judged by the Court's ability 'to meet the standards it has set for itself'. Otherwise '[s]kepticism will be widespread that the Court will have achieved little but a wagging forefinger – a lot of sound and fury adding up to nothing'. That scepticism was only heightened when the GCC missed an apparently golden opportunity to put *Lisbon* into practice little over a year later in *Honeywell*. Instead, the Court used the latter case to qualify its jurisdiction over EU law, including by stipulating that the ECJ must be 'afforded the opportunity to interpret the Treaties, as well as to rule on the validity and interpretation of the acts in question' via an Article 267 TFEU referral *before* an *ultra vires* ruling is made.[41] Thus, pending the ECJ's next move, the GCC has, in fact, laid the groundwork for finding OMT illegal and preventing German participation in the programme.

While Luxembourg deliberates, the consequences of the GCC's stance will play out in the political realm. According to the majority of the Court, an *ultra vires* act 'creates an obligation [on] German authorities to refrain from implementing it and a duty to challenge it'.[42] These duties are not merely theoretical – they are owed to individual voters (whose constitutional rights would be imperilled by supranational usurpations of power) and they can be enforced before the Constitutional Court.[43] Even without further legal action, the articulation of these duties is a useful tool for those Germans opposed to the euro rescue measures to argue their illegitimacy. Beyond Germany, too, the decision may have repercussions, especially if markets come to doubt the solidity of Draghi's 'whatever it takes' pledge.

Thus, the German Court has ventured into deeply political territory. In separate opinions, the two dissenting judges argued that the complaints against OMT should have been rejected as inadmissible and beyond the realm of judicial competence.[44] Admittedly, the boundary between monetary and economic policy is blurred, and the Court was criticised for substituting its judgment for that of experts in the field (Schmieding 2014). Nevertheless, the ECJ cannot afford to dismiss the GCC's reasoning lightly. Despite frequently displaying a federalist bias, as seen recently, for example, in the *Pringle* case, the European Court must take national sensitivities into account. An open confrontation between national and supranational law would be damaging for both sides. The constitutional edifice constructed by the ECJ over the past 60 years derives its legitimacy from its unity and uniformity. Open rebellion by the GCC would strike at the very core of that edifice, already weakened by the de-legalisation that has accompanied the euro crisis.

Concluding remarks: the creation and recreation of EU constitutionalism through judicial contestation

The GCC's role in the integration project has been much more constructive than its critics suggest. Far from being a parochial actor, the Court is very much aware that its decisions have an effect beyond Germany.[45] It is justified in drawing attention to deficiencies in the EU's representative institutions and in the European public sphere. If the EU cannot transcend its constituent member states to create a supranational democratic government, it should instead recognise and support those states as the most important conduits of democratic legitimacy. The GCC's jurisprudence is consistent with pluralist assessments of EU constitutionalism and with certain elements of the Lisbon Treaty settlement, such as its allocation of a greater role to national parliaments and its strengthening of the principle of conferral.

While conventional legal theories seek systemic coherence from a constitutionally determined and universally accepted ultimate site of authority, the EU defies these expectations. Its constitutional framework has been shaped by a dynamic of '[r]esistance and response to legal integration' between national and European level actors (Davies 2012: 7). Constitutional coherence in the context of the EU does not require an absence of conflict, but rather effective conflict management. Unfortunately, this feature of the EU's uncodified constitutionalism has been undermined by the euro emergency, opening the way to more antagonistic relations between European and member state institutions, the German Constitutional Court amongst the latter.

Despite this constitutional reconfiguration, the GCC has not so far substantially impeded the euro rescue policies. Even its rebuke of OMT was not definitive because it came in the form of a referral to the ECJ. However, Karlsruhe's posture of conditional acquiescence could change. Remember, the GCC did have a get-out-of-jail-free card; it could have avoided the mega-political territory of ECB policymaking by finding the complaints against

OMT inadmissible. The judges of the majority were not forced to decide. The fact that they chose to do so indicates a willingness to challenge the subordination of judicial authority to political expediency that has characterised the post-2010 period. Whether the GCC follows through – and whether, and to what extent, it is assisted in this endeavour by the ECJ – remains to be seen.

Notes

1 *Internationale Handelsgesellschaft v Einfuhr-und Vorratsstelle für Getreide und Futtermittel (Solange I)* (1974) 2 CMLR 540.
2 *Brunner v The European Union Treaty* (1994) 1 CMLR 57 (*Maastricht decision*).
3 BVerfG, 2 BvE 2/08 vom 30.6.2009, Absatz-Nr. (1–421) available at www.bverfg. de/entscheidungen/es20090630_2bve000208en.html (*Lisbon decision*).
4 For example, in its *Lisbon decision*, the Court held that the accompanying legislation breached the Basic Law because it did not accord Parliament sufficient participatory rights. Such interventions reflect power dynamics amongst German government institutions, as well as between the GCC and EU institutions.
5 The GCC's stance on the EU institutions' lack of *Kompetenz-Kompetenz* reflects the member states' own preferences – the Lisbon Treaty strengthened the principle of conferral, whereby EU institutions may exercise only those competences conferred on them by member states in the treaties (see Article 5(2) TEU).
6 The similarities of form between British and EU constitutionalism – both uncodified and evolutionary – are ironic given that the latter is very much a product of continental Europe and has been the subject of much legal and political contention in Britain.
7 See, for example, *R v Secretary of State for Foreign and Commonwealth Affairs, ex parte Rees-Mogg* (1994) QB 552.
8 *Thoburn v Sunderland City Council* (2003) QB 151.
9 *Crotty v An Taoiseach* (1987) IR 713, (1987) ILRM 400. This case, which concerned Ireland's ratification of the Single European Act, also established the precedent whereby a referendum to amend the Irish Constitution is necessary before Ireland can ratify treaty changes that 'alter the essential scope or objectives of the Communities'.
10 Danish Supreme Court Decision of 6 April 1998, (1998) UfR 800.
11 In fact, the Danish Supreme Court articulated a principle very similar to the GCC's claim of an *ultra vires* review power over EU law: 'Consequently the Danish courts would be bound to rule that an EC measure was inapplicable in Denmark if the extraordinary situation should arise that it could be established that the measure, even if it had been upheld by the European Court of Justice, was based on an application of the Treaty which lay beyond the transfer of sovereignty brought about by the Act of Accession' (Oppenheimer 2003: 177–78).
12 Case 29/69, (1969) ECR 419.
13 Case 11/70, (1970) ECR 1125.
14 *Solange I* (1974) 2 CMLR 540.
15 *Application of Wünsche Handelsgesellschaft, Re ('Solange II')* (1987) 3 CMLR 225.
16 (1994) 1 CMLR 57 (*Maastricht decision*).
17 Robert van Ooyen (2011: 48) described the *Lisbon decision* as a re-affirmation of the 'holy Trinity' of 'state – sovereignty – (national) democracy' previously expounded in the *Maastricht decision*.
18 *Lisbon decision*, paragraph 249. See also the GCC's attempt, however imperfect, to catalogue these core competences:

> Particularly sensitive for the ability of a constitutional state to democratically shape itself are decisions on substantive and formal criminal law (1), on the

disposition of the monopoly on the use of force by the police within the state and by the military towards the exterior (2), fundamental fiscal decisions on public revenue and public expenditure, the latter being particularly motivated, *inter alia*, by social policy considerations (3), decisions on the shaping of living conditions in a social state (4) and decisions of particular cultural importance, for example on family law, the school and education system and on dealing with religious communities (5).

(Lisbon decision, paragraph 252)

19 If an imbalance between type and extent of the sovereign powers exercised and the degree of democratic legitimation arises ... it is for the Federal Republic of Germany because of its responsibility for integration, to endeavour to effect a change, and in the worst case, even to refuse further participation in the European Union.

(Lisbon decision, paragraph 264)

20 BVerfG, 2 BvR 2661/06 vom 6.7.2010, Absatz-Nr. (1–116), available at www.bverfg.de/entscheidungen/rs20100706_2bvr266106en.html (*Honeywell decision*).
21 *Honeywell decision*, paragraph 66.
22 The relevant treaties are the Treaty Establishing the European Stability Mechanism (TESM) and the Treaty on Stability, Coordination and Governance in the Economic and Monetary Union (TSCG).
23 *Thomas Pringle v The Government of Ireland, Ireland and the Attorney General* (2012) IESC 47.
24 In the *Lisbon decision*, paragraph 252. See further paragraph 256:

A transfer of the right of the *Bundestag* to adopt the budget and control its implementation by the government which would violate the principle of democracy and the right to elect the German *Bundestag* in its essential content would occur if the determination of the type and amount of the levies imposed on the citizen were supranationalised to a considerable extent. ... Not every European or international obligation that has an effect on the budget endangers the viability of the *Bundestag* as the legislature responsible for approving the budget. ... What is decisive, however, is that the overall responsibility, with sufficient political discretion regarding revenue and expenditure, can still rest with the German *Bundestag*.

25 The ESM was to have been launched on 1 July 2012. That deadline was missed because the agreement's entry into force required ratification by states representing 90% of its capital commitments. That, in turn, could not happen without the participation of Germany, which represented 27% of the total (*Spiegel Online*, 2012). Following approval by the GCC, the ESM was inaugurated on 8 October 2012. The Fiscal Compact came into force on 1 January 2013, as expected, having been ratified by at least twelve eurozone members by that date (Art. 14(2) TSCG).
26 See also Paul Kirchhof (2012a).
27 BVerfG, 2 BvR 1390/12 vom 12.9.2012, Absatz-Nr. (1–248), available at www.bverfg.de/entscheidungen/rs20120912_2bvr139012en.html (*euro rescue decision*). Following the Court's ruling, Federal President Joachim Gauck signed the relevant legal instruments into law the very next day.
28 BVerfG, 2 BvR 1390/12 vom 18.3.2014, Absatz-Nr. (1–245), available at www.bundesverfassungsgericht.de/entscheidungen/rs20140318_2bvr139012en.html (*euro rescue decision II*).
29 See, for example, *euro rescue decision II*, paragraph 168:

it is not from the outset anti-democratic for the budget-setting legislature to be bound by a particular budget and fiscal policy ... This can, in general, also take place by transferring essential budgetary decisions to bodies of a supra-national or international organisation, or by the assumption of corresponding obligations under international law ... It is primarily for the legislature to decide whether and to what extent this is sensible.

See also paragraph 173, where the Court affirms that it is not its role to 'usurp' the legislature's judgment in this respect.

30 *Euro rescue decision*, paragraphs 192–98.
31 *Euro rescue decision II*, paragraphs 161–65.
32 *Euro rescue decision*, paragraph 208; *euro rescue decision II*, paragraphs 223–24.
33 *Euro rescue decision*, paragraphs 220–22.
34 *Euro rescue decision*, paragraphs 223–29.
35 *Euro rescue decision II*, paragraphs 183, 188, 214.
36 *Euro rescue decision*, paragraphs 230–39; *euro rescue decision II*, paragraphs 158, 194–204.
37 *Euro rescue decision*, paragraphs 245–47.
38 BVerfG, 2 BvR 2728/13 vom 14.1.2014, Absatz-Nr. (1 – 105) available at www.bverfg.de/entscheidungen/rs20140114_2bvr272813en.html (*OMT referral*).
39 *OMT referral*, paragraphs 55–94.
40 *OMT referral*, paragraphs 36–43.
41 *Honeywell decision*, paragraph 60.
42 *OMT referral*, paragraph 44.
43 *OMT referral*, paragraphs 44–54
44 *OMT referral*, Dissenting Opinion of Justice Lübbe-Wolff, Dissenting Opinion of Justice Gerhardt.
45 The GCC often publishes official versions of its European integration-related verdicts in English.

References

Auer, S. (2012) *Whose Liberty is It Anyway? Europe at the Crossroads* (Calcutta: Seagull Books).

Baquero Cruz, J. (2008) 'The Legacy of the Maastricht-Urteil and the Pluralist Movement'. *European Law Journal*, Vol. 14, No. 4, pp. 389–422.

Beyer-Katzenberger, M. (2011) 'Judicial Activism and Judicial Restraint at the *Bundesverfassungsgericht*: Was the *Mangold* Judgement of the European Court of Justice an *Ultra Vires* Act?' *ERA-Forum*, Vol. 11, No. 4, pp. 517–23.

Bofinger, P., Habermas, J. and Nida-Rümelin, J. (2012) 'Einspruch gegen die Fassadendemokratie'. *Frankfurter Allgemeine Zeitung*, 3 August.

Bröhmer, J. (2009) '"Containment eines Leviathans" – Anmerkungen zur Entscheidung des Bundesverfassungsgericht zum Vertrag von Lissabon'. *Zeitschrift ZEuS*, Vol. 12, No. 4, pp. 543–57.

Busse, N. (2012) 'Postnationales Aufatmen'. *Frankfurter Allgemeine Zeitung*, 12 September.

Charter, D. (2013) 'Jens Weidmann Leads German Protest against Bond Scheme'. *The Times*, 12 June.

Cooper, I. (2010) 'Mapping the Overlapping Spheres: European Constitutionalism after the Treaty of Lisbon'. *ARENA Centre for European Studies Seminar Paper*, pp. 1–32.

Davies, B. (2012) *Resisting the European Court of Justice* (Cambridge: Cambridge University Press).

Dicey, A. V. (1959) *Introduction to the Study of the Law of the Constitution*, 10th edn (London: Macmillan).

Di Fabio, U. (2014) 'Die Weisheit der Richter'. *Frankfurter Allgemeine Zeitung*, 9 February.

Die Zeit (2012) 'Eilantrag soll Karlsruher ESM-Urteil verschieben'. 9 September.

Doukas, D. (2009) 'The Verdict of the German Federal Constitutional Court on the Lisbon Treaty: Not Guilty, but Don't Do It Again!'. *European Law Review*, Vol. 34, No. 6, pp. 866–88.

European Council (2011) *Conclusions*, Brussels, 20 April, document EUCO 10/1/11, Rev. 1.

Everson, M. (1998) 'Beyond the *Bundesverfassungsgericht*: On the Necessary Cunning of Constitutional Reasoning'. *European Law Journal*, Vol. 4, No. 4, pp. 389–410.

Ghaleigh, N. S. (2003) 'Looking into the Brightly Lit Room: Braving Carl Schmitt in "Europe"'. In Joerges, C. and Ghaleigh, N. S. (eds) *Darker Legacies of Law in Europe* (Oxford and Portland, OR: Hart Publishing).

Grimm, D. (1997) 'The European Court of Justice and National Courts: The German Constitutional Perspective after the *Maastricht Decision*'. *The Columbia Journal of European Law*, Vol. 3, No. 2, pp. 229–42.

——(2009) 'Defending Sovereign Statehood against Transforming the European Union into a State'. *European Constitutional Law Review*, Vol. 5, No. 3, pp. 353–73.

——(2010) 'Die grosse Karlsruher Verschiebung'. *Frankfurter Allgemeine Zeitung*, 9 September.

Halberstam, D. and Möllers, C. (2009) 'The German Constitutional Court Says *"Ja zu Deutschland!"*'. *German Law Journal*, Vol. 10, No. 8, pp. 1241–58.

Hartley, T. C. (2004) *European Union Law in a Global Context: Text, Cases, and Materials* (Cambridge: Cambridge University Press).

——(2010) *The Foundations of European Law* (Oxford: Oxford University Press).

Hoffmann, L. (2009) 'Don't Let the Sun Go Down on Me: The German Constitutional Court and Its Lisbon Judgement'. *Journal of Contemporary European Research*, Vol. 5, No. 3, pp. 480–88.

Jahn, J. (2012) 'Verfassungsrichter erlauben ESM und Fiskalpakt unter Auflagen'. *Frankfurter Allgemeine Zeitung*, 12 September.

Joerges, C. (1996) 'Taking the Law Seriously: On Political Science and the Role of Law in the Process of European Integration'. *European Law Journal*, Vol. 2, No. 2, pp. 105–35.

——(2012) 'Europe's Economic Constitution in Crisis'. *ZenTra Working Papers in Transnational Studies*, No. 06/2012, pp. 1–28.

Kirchhof, P. (2012a) *Deutschland im Schuldensog: Der Weg vom Bürgen zurück zum Bürger* (Munich: C. H. Beck).

——(2012b) 'Verfassungsnot!' *Frankfurter Allgemeine Zeitung*, 12 July.

Köcher, R. (2012) 'Das Bollwerk'. *Frankfurter Allgemeine Zeitung*, 21 August.

Kulish, N. and Eddy, M. (2012) 'In Victory for Merkel, German Court Ruling Favors European Bailout Fund'. *New York Times*, 12 September.

Kumm, M. (2012) 'Ein Signal für Europa'. *Frankfurter Allgemeine Zeitung*, 10 August.

Kumm, M. and Comella, V. F. (2005) 'The Primacy Clause of the Constitutional Treaty and the Future of Constitutional Conflict in the European Union'. *International Journal of Constitutional Law*, Vol. 3, No. 2–3, pp. 473–92.

MacCormick, N. (1995) 'The Maastricht-Urteil: Sovereignty Now'. *European Law Journal*, Vol. 1, No. 3, pp. 259–66.

Mahlmann, M. (2010) 'The Politics of Constitutional Identity and Its Legal Frame – the *Ultra Vires* Decision of the German Federal Constitutional Court'. *German Law Journal*, Vol. 11, No. 12, pp. 1407–20.

Marsh, D. (2011) *The Euro: The Battle for the New Global Currency* (New Haven, CT: Yale University Press).

Müller, J.-W. (2000) 'Carl Schmitt and the Constitution of Europe'. *Cardozo Law Review*, Vol. 21, No. 5–6, pp. 1777–95.

——(2011) *Contesting Democracy: Political Ideas in Twentieth Century Europe* (New Haven, CT: Yale University Press).

Oppenheimer, A. (2003) *The Relationship between European Community Law and National Law: The Cases* (Cambridge: Cambridge University Press).

Paterson, W. (2011) 'The Reluctant Hegemon? Germany Moves Centre Stage in the European Union'. *Journal of Common Market Studies*, Vol. 49, Annual Review, pp. 57–75.

Phelan, W. (2007) 'Can Ireland Legislate Contrary to European Community Law?' *Institute for International Integration Studies Discussion Paper*, No. 237, pp. 1–47.

——(2010) 'Political Self-Control and European Constitution: The Assumption of National Political Loyalty to European Obligations as the Solution to the *Lex Posterior* Problem of EC Law in the National Legal Orders'. *European Law Journal*, Vol. 16, No. 3, pp. 253–72.

Piris, J.-C. (2010) *The Lisbon Treaty: A Legal and Political Analysis* (Cambridge: Cambridge University Press).

Ragazzoni, D. (2011) 'Identity vs. Representation: What Makes "The People"? Rethinking Democratic Citizenship through (and beyond) Carl Schmitt and Hans Kelsen'. *Perspectives on Federalism*, Vol. 3, No. 2, pp. 1–30.

Sadurski, W. (2012) *Constitutionalism and the Enlargement of Europe* (Oxford: Oxford University Press).

Sarrazin, T. (2012) 'Geburtsfehler Maastricht'. *Frankfurter Allgemeine Zeitung*, 17 July.

Schmieding, H. (2014) 'Der Irrtum der Karlsruher Richter'. *Frankfurter Allgemeine Zeitung*, 31 March.

Schorkopf, F. (2009) 'The European Union as an Association of Sovereign States: Karlsruhe's Ruling on the Treaty of Lisbon'. *German Law Journal*, Vol. 10, No. 8, pp. 1219–40.

Selmayr, M. (2009) 'Endstation Lissabon? Zehn Thesen zum "Niemals"-Urteil des Bundesverfassungsgerichts vom 30. Juni 2009'. *ZEuS*, Vol. 12, No. 4, pp. 637–79.

Shore, C. (2006) '"Government without Statehood"? Anthropological Perspectives on Governance and Sovereignty in the European Union'. *European Law Journal*, Vol. 12, No. 6, pp. 709–24.

Spiegel Online (2012) 'Court May Take Longer to Rule on Euro Measures'. 10 July.

Van Ooyen, R. C. (2011) 'Mit "Mangold" zurück zu "Solange II"? Das Bundesverfassungsgericht nach "Lissabon"'. *Der Staat*, Vol. 50, No. 1, pp. 45–59.

Weiler, J. H. H. (1995) 'Does Europe Need a Constitution? Demos, Telos and the German Maastricht Decision'. *European Law Journal*, Vol. 1, No. 3, pp. 219–58.

——(2011) 'The Political and Legal Culture of European Integration: An Exploratory Essay'. *International Journal of Constitutional Law*, Vol. 9, No. 3–4, pp. 678–94.

Wessels, W. (2003) 'The German Debate on European Finality: Visions and Missions'. In Serfaty, S. (ed.) *The European Finality Debate and Its National Dimensions* (Washington DC: The Center for Strategic and International Studies).

4 EU constitutionalism's democracy gap

A law of intended and unintended consequences

Introduction: why the democratic deficit matters

Democracy is at the heart of Europe's self-understanding, a fact reflected in the EU's constitutional framework. The TEU, for example, contains numerous references to this core principle, including in the preamble, where democracy is described as part of the 'cultural, religious and humanist inheritance of Europe', and Article 2, which lists democracy as one of the Union's founding values.[1] Perhaps most striking is the quotation, taken from Thucydides, which opened the Draft Treaty Establishing a Constitution for Europe: 'Our Constitution ... is called a democracy because power is in the hands not of a minority but of the greatest number'.[2]

Yet, for all this professed commitment to the *ideal* of democracy, democratic principles have never played a large role in the organisation and functioning of the EU, itself. On the contrary, the Union is marked by a 'democratic deficit', which has become more burdensome as integrationist agendas have become more ambitious. The failed process of formal constitution making was aimed partly at addressing this shortcoming. In fact, the above quotation from Thucydides demonstrates the strong links between Europe's identity as natural cradle of democracy, and the constitutionalisation of that identity in the minds of the Constitutional Treaty's drafters. Nevertheless, the deficit remains and would have done so even if the CT had been successfully ratified, because it is deeply ingrained in the Union's political and legal culture (Weiler 2011). Moreover, since 2010 the democratic deficit has been magnified by the euro crisis in a way that threatens the sustainability of European integration.

Before turning to the consequences of the EU's democratic deficit, the term itself needs further explanation. Finding a concise definition is difficult, especially since there are so many sites of authority within this multi-level entity. The European Union is constituted by the member states plus the EU's own supranational layer of governance. These 'parallel and overlapping spheres' (Cooper 2010) are locked in a symbiotic relationship, their political and legal systems constantly shaping and being shaped by each other. Therefore, the member states, though liberal democracies in their own right, are not completely self-contained polities. The EU's system of governance, with all of its flaws, has implications for the practice of democracy at the national level too (Schmidt 2006). Conversely, the EU's institutional structure and governance arrangements, from their inception, were heavily influenced by the post-war West European predilection for checks and balances and a 'constrained' form of democracy, insulated from popular pressure (Müller 2012: 40–41).[3]

The founding fathers of European integration envisaged that the construction of an institutional edifice over and above its constituent member states would protect and nurture – rather than threaten – national democracies. All of the six founding members of the European Coal and Steel Community in 1952 and the European Economic Community in 1958 were either governed by fascist regimes prior to 1945, or were victims of fascist aggression during the war. The delegation of sovereign law-making power to supranational institutions was justified partly on the premise that it would secure liberal democratic arrangements and prevent relapses into authoritarianism (Müller 2012: 42–45). The fact that none of those institutions was directly representative of member state citizens, either severally or as a whole (the European Parliament was not directly elected until 1979), was not an oversight, but a deliberate choice. As was noted in Chapter 1 in the context of the judicialisation of post-war European politics, the institutional design of European integration was congruent with contemporary political theory, which called for a novel redefinition of liberalism and democracy in light of the continent's experience with totalitarianism (Müller 2012: 40–41). Nevertheless, the repercussions of those choices have echoed through the decades and their consequences have been, and continue to be, amplified by the expanding breadth and depth of the EU's powers.

Legitimacy with or without democracy: strategies for the EU polity

No system of governance – democratic or otherwise – is sustainable if it lacks legitimacy in the eyes of those who are subject to it (Holmes 1997: 43–58). This maxim is especially pertinent in relation to the European Union, whose absence of a separation between regime and entity means that any crisis of legitimacy threatens the system as a whole, because it cannot be quarantined to the government of the day and resolved by 'throwing them out' at the next election. Though the concepts are related, *democracy* and *legitimacy* are not identical. A political order may be regarded by its subjects as legitimate even if it is not democratic and, conversely, a democratic system of government may still fail for lack of legitimacy (this latter constellation doomed the Weimar Republic, for example). Nevertheless, the provision of opportunities for citizens to be involved in the processes of government either directly or through their elected representatives is an important means of legitimating a political order. In other words, *democratic legitimacy* is a subset of legitimacy and it is an important one for the EU as a Union of liberal democratic states.

Given its importance, then, whence does the Union derive its legitimacy? Max Weber (2004: 133–45) distinguished amongst three pure types of legitimate authority: traditional, charismatic and legal (or legal-rational) authority. Under the *traditional* mode of legitimation, exercised by monarchs, for example, leaders claimed the authority to rule based on long-standing tradition, often supplemented by some form of divine right. *Charismatic* authority, by contrast, was based on the personal attributes of the leader, and often applied to revolutionary figures. Finally, *legal-rational* authority denoted an impersonal form of legitimation, with legitimacy deriving from rules and laws rather than any particular individual charged with creating or discharging those laws. The legal-rational mode is, of course, the primary mode of legitimation in the modern state. Furthermore, as a community of law that lacks any form of strong personal leadership, the EU also relies on the legal-rational authority of its norms and institutions to legitimate its actions.

Weber thus provides a starting point for a discussion of the nature and effectiveness of EU legitimation strategies, as well as a useful reminder of the importance of law and legality to the European project. However, his pure types are insufficient to allow a comprehensive analysis of the EU's potential and actual sources of legitimacy. Therefore, they may be supplemented by several additional modes of legitimation, which were explicated by Leslie Holmes (1997: 43–44) in the context of the legitimation crises faced by the communist regimes of Central and Eastern Europe and the Soviet Union in the 1980s. Two legitimation strategies identified by Holmes are particularly relevant to a study of the contemporary EU. They are the goal-rational (or teleological) mode and the eudaemonic mode.

When applied to communist states, goal-rational legitimation involved a regime's attempts to base its legitimacy on its ability to steer the state and its people towards the end-goal of communism. Transferred to the EU, goal-rational legitimation is most obviously linked to federalist conceptions of the integration project, such as the United States of Europe famously envisaged by Joschka Fischer (2000), because of the teleological tendencies that such conceptions display. Moreover, and drawing on the European Commission's own rhetoric, efforts to present the EU as a post-national peace project also point to the same strategy. As Joseph Weiler (2011) argued, the goal-rational strands within the self-justificatory strategies of European integration can be traced back to the post-war origins of the project and, particularly, to the 'political messianism' inherent in its mission. Weiler used the term 'political messianism' to refer to the tripartite notion of the European project as a vision, a posited end goal, and as the mission to achieve that goal:

> In political messianism, the justification for action and its mobilizing force derive not from process, as in classical democracy, or from result and success, but from the ideal pursued, the destiny to be achieved, the promised land waiting at the end of the road.
>
> (Weiler 2011: 683)

This vision was already present in the Schuman Declaration, which called for the pooling of Franco-German coal and steel resources as a first step towards securing Europe's lasting peace, prosperity and happiness, and it has been the Union's most important and enduring source of legitimacy ever since (Weiler 2011: 683–86).[4] Even in the midst of a serious existential crisis, 'the mobilizing force' of 'the dream dreamt, the promise of a better future' (Weiler 2011: 683), continues to manifest itself in the EU's 'political culture of total optimism', which can only contemplate further progress towards political and economic union as the solution to Europe's problems (Majone 2011: 1).

It is this promise of a better future that links political messianism to the other mode of legitimation discussed by Holmes: the eudaemonic.[5] This form of legitimation is based on a regime's ability to 'deliver the goods'. It is, therefore, comparable to what is usually described in EU studies scholarship as *output legitimacy* (Scharpf 1999). Like goal-rational legitimation, the EU's focus on output legitimacy had its origins in choices made at the time of the establishment of the ECSC and EEC. As envisaged and executed by founding fathers such as Jean Monnet, European integration was to be an elitist endeavour, pursued for the general good of the people, but without consulting them through directly democratic procedures (Müller 2012: 40). In other words, this type of results-oriented legitimacy is based on the EU's purported ability to achieve more efficient and objectively 'better' outcomes than would be possible via other governance constellations (such as nation states acting alone or through less comprehensive forms of international cooperation). Indeed, the European project has always relied on a bold and ambitious rhetoric of results, from the big, overarching promises – peace, prosperity, stability, unity – to the 'European eudaimonia' (Chalmers 2009) that is reflected in a lot of secondary EU legislation. As noted in Chapter 1, one downside to the EU's excessive reliance on outputs is that it manifests itself in the infusion of ordinary pieces of legislation with extravagant self-justificatory claims that cannot be met, thereby leaving the EU unable to satisfy the standards it has set for itself (Chalmers 2009: 8). In the same way, the euro crisis – and the larger problem of stagnant growth and rising unemployment in Europe – is also a crisis of the EU's output legitimacy because it casts serious doubt upon the Union's ability to fulfil its promise of bettering European citizens' lives.

The European Union's heavy reliance on output legitimacy as an alternative to democratic, or input, legitimacy is problematic in other ways, too. Firstly, it gives EU policies a veneer of apolitical technocracy that belies the very real political choices involved in their drafting and implementation. Secondly, it assumes, without sufficient justification, that 'experts' in non-majoritarian institutions are better placed to deliver objectively 'good' outcomes than institutions that are subject to feedback from majoritarian processes (Bellamy 2010: 8–10). Thirdly, the lack of democratic inputs at the EU level runs counter to the EU's explicit proclamation of democracy as one of its founding values and as a standard to which prospective member states must adhere (Sadurski 2013: 11–14). Finally, it frustrates the expectations of Europeans, who – as the citizens of liberal democratic states – are conditioned to both assume and demand that the exercise of political powers that affect their lives is democratically qualified. It is not possible, then, to completely separate the EU's legitimacy from its democratic quality. As Weiler (2011: 682) put it, there is an air of *panem et circenses* (bread and circuses) to the notion that the EU's system of governance could effectively secure the well-being of the people with so little popular input. Bearing that in mind, I now turn to analyse the causes and characteristics of the EU's democratic deficit in more detail.

The impact of the democratic deficit at the national level

Despite the heavy bias towards non-elected institutions at the European level, it is arguably *within* the member states that the democratic deficit is most acutely felt. Vivien Schmidt (2009: 19–20) has pointed out that EU multi-level governance 'splits between supranational and national levels the four basic democratic legitimizing mechanisms that tend to operate simultaneously in any national democracy'. Building on Abraham Lincoln's famous definition of democracy, these are government *by, of, for*, and *with* the people. The first two mechanisms, which involve citizen participation in the political process and representation in its institutions, still operate mainly at the national and sub-national levels. On the other hand, EU-level legislative and administrative activities have focused on governance *for* the people, through efficient and effective rule making, and government *with* the people, via extensive engagement and consultation with interest groups.

The steady expansion of EU-level competences has meant that EU institutions govern *for* European citizens in more and more facets of their daily lives. The concomitant removal of policy areas from the national level has resulted in a substantive impoverishment of domestic politics, or as Schmidt (2006: 33, 163–71) described it, 'politics without policy'. Thus, representative democracy continues to function at the national level, but its quality is diminished. Citizens become frustrated at their perceived (and real) inability to influence policy choice, which may manifest itself in disengagement from the electoral process, or in electoral radicalisation. The latter trend is accentuated by the almost universal pro-EU consensus amongst mainstream political parties in all the member states, which pushes disgruntled voters towards the left and right fringes of politics (Hooghe and Marks 2009: 21).[6] The identification of mainstream parties, particularly governing parties, with pro-EU positions also helps to explain why referenda on European issues so often become occasions for protest votes that are only tangentially connected to the specific question being decided. Taken together, electoral apathy and electoral radicalisation may combine to erode the middle ground and destabilise the political system.

The rise in Greece of the extreme-right, neo-Nazi Golden Dawn Party provides a particularly troubling example of electoral radicalisation in an EU member state. Golden Dawn captured almost 7% of the vote in inconclusive May 2012 legislative elections, entering the Greek national parliament for the first time with 21 seats, which was slightly reduced to 18 seats following further elections in June 2012. The party continued to strengthen its position in Greek political and social life after those elections. Polling in late 2012 put its support at around 12% of the electorate, although its popularity was much higher amongst some sectors of society including, disturbingly, the police force (Mason 2012). As a social movement as well as a political party, Golden Dawn also became a much more visible presence on the streets, with its black-clad members – including serving parliamentarians – responsible for acts of violence and intimidation, largely targeted at migrants.[7]

Admittedly, this is an extreme case of electoral radicalisation, but it is also instructive. Golden Dawn's popularity was fuelled by Greece's dire economic downturn, which itself is compounded by the harsh austerity measures mandated by Greece's European and international creditors, particularly the 'troika' of the International Monetary Fund (IMF), European Commission and ECB. The hardship caused by austerity policies imposed from abroad has heightened Greek perceptions of a loss of control over their country and their destiny, creating a situation ripe for exploitation by extreme social and political movements. EU policies, up to and including the very decision to admit Greece into the currency union, are at least *partly* to blame for creating a situation in which the country is heavily indebted and perennially at a competitive disadvantage to more efficient and productive euro states.

It is not only Greece that is affected. The EU's policy failures have serious consequences for the stability of the Union as a whole. This is especially the case insofar as other heavily indebted states, such as Portugal and Cyprus, and even Italy and Spain (which are not under official bailout programmes), appear to follow the 'Greek path' of having to accept the dictates of the troika, leaving their citizens feeling disempowered and poorly represented by mainstream political parties. Even in 'Northern' creditor countries, populist parties are increasingly challenging the political establishment, which, because it maintains a pro-EU consensus, is unable to take account of public disaffection. Indeed, a study of West European member states by Robert Rohrschneider and Stephen Whitefield (2013) found that the euro crisis has had very little impact on the policy stances of centrist parties, whose positions on EU-related issues barely changed between 2008 and 2013. Since, on the other hand, public opinion on European integration *has* become more negative since the onset of the crisis, there is a growing representation gap that eurosceptic parties of various shades are well placed to fill.[8]

Returning to the Greek case, there are other episodes that illustrate the difficulty of reconciling European-level 'emergency' decision making with national-level democratic institutions and processes. Two examples will suffice to illustrate this point. The first concerns then-Prime Minister George Papandreou's announcement on 31 October 2011 that Greece's second proposed bailout plan would be put to the Greek people in a referendum

(Kitsantonis and Donadio 2011a). This may have been more a desperate attempt on Papandreou's part to improve his sliding political fortunes than a principled stand in favour of direct democracy, since it would have allowed him to shift responsibility for the unpopular austerity measures onto the electorate. Still, the decision to hold a referendum was primarily a domestic political matter. Thus, the angry and vocal reaction of Greece's European partners, perhaps understandable given the Greek government's vacillation, was also revealing of the extent to which the Greek state had ceded its sovereignty as a result of the crisis. Papandreou duly called off the referendum a few days later following a stern reproach from European leaders, including Angela Merkel and Nicolas Sarkozy, at the Group of 20 summit in France (Kitsantonis and Donadio 2011b). As well as further destabilising the Greek government (Papandreou stepped down as Prime Minister shortly afterwards), the affair reinforced the perception that democratic processes are not compatible with crisis management in the EU.

The second example of European leaders' disregard for the institutions and processes of Greek democracy concerns guarantees sought in the lead up to Greece's elections in May 2012. As already noted, in late October 2011 the Greek government and representatives of the troika had hammered out an agreement on the provision of further financial assistance from the latter in return for spending cuts and other austerity measures by the former. The cost of securing domestic parliamentary support for the package was Papandreou's resignation as Prime Minister. His interim replacement, the technocratic economist and former ECB Vice President Lucas Papademos, was sworn in on 11 November 2011 and charged with carrying out tax, social security and other reforms, a process underway but far from complete at the time of the elections.[9] Not wishing to jeopardise the bailout agreement, Greece's European partners demanded that all the major political parties sign a document committing them to implementing the reform programme regardless of the election results (Smith 2012).

As an attempt to drastically limit the range of options available to voters by locking in a deeply unpopular agreement negotiated by a deeply unpopular government, this initiative demonstrated contempt for the institution of democratic elections.[10] In the event, however, it was only an attempt, as not all party leaders undertook to continue implementation of the austerity measures. The two mainstream parties, Papandreou's socialist PASOK and the centre-right New Democracy both supported the bailout agreement, while several parties went to the elections on anti-austerity platforms, including Syriza, the far left coalition whose popularity has soared since the onset of the crisis (Smith 2012). Given the warnings emanating from Berlin, Paris and Brussels that no less than Greece's future in the eurozone was at stake, the May 2012 elections had something of the air of former Prime Minister Papandreou's aborted referendum after all.[11]

Carl Schmitt (2005: 5) famously defined the sovereign as 'he who decides on the exception'. Just where sovereignty now lies in Greece, which is in an economic state of emergency, is genuinely an open question. Are Greek citizens sovereign in their capacity as electors? Or has the range of options available to Greek lawmakers become so restricted that external authorities, such as the troika, are effectively determining Greece's political course? Most EU scholars would reject the application of Schmittian concepts and arguments to the politics of the post-national and *sui generis* EU, but they should not be so easily dismissed. Whether we like it or not, the euro crisis illustrates Schmitt's ongoing relevance well, particularly his concern with the limitations of law and the need for a sovereign able to take ultimate decisions in times of crisis. Moreover, the question of who is sovereign is not only relevant to Greece, but also to the EU as a whole. At the European level the 'Community method' – which is characterised by a high level of diffusion and constraint of political power – has been increasingly overshadowed by a hardnosed and German-dominated intergovernmentalism.

One of the great hopes associated with the creation of the EU and the supranational delegation of powers that it entailed was that it would lock in liberal democratic reforms (Müller 2012: 45). This hope was shared not only by the founding six, but also by post-authoritarian Greece, Spain and Portugal in the 1970s and 1980s, and the post-communist states of Central and Eastern Europe after 1989. Instead, in the case of Greece, the crisis and the EU's responses to it are compounding the country's pre-existing weaknesses. The faltering economy, fragile mainstream political parties, social unrest and the rise of extremist political elements are all combining to produce an unstable and, potentially, failing state (Featherstone 2011). Under such circumstances the EU's rhetorical commitment to democracy looks hollow indeed.

Even in less desperate circumstances than those of Greece, the phenomenon of 'politics without policy' can destabilise national political systems. It is problematic for moderate parties because political debates become less about substance and more about emotion and sentiment, which extreme parties are better placed to manipulate and channel. Member state governments themselves actually contribute to this problem by routinely engaging in 'blame-shifting and credit-taking' – blaming the EU for unpopular policies and claiming credit for popular ones (Schmidt 2009: 21–23). The fact that the activities of EU-level institutions are not well known or understood by the average European also makes them susceptible to misinformation and fear mongering. As was noted in Chapter 2, this certainly contributed to the defeat of the CT – a dense, long-winded and little-understood document with a provocative title into which eurosceptics of all stripes projected their fears and prejudices.

The French Socialist Party's stance on the CT illustrates well the difficulties moderate parties may face in dealing with European issues. The decision on whether or not to support the Constitution in the 2005 French referendum proved difficult and divisive for the party hierarchy, pitting their pro-integrationist instincts against the social and economic concerns of their members and voters. In the event, the party's official position was to support ratification of the text, although a number of high-profile Socialist figures broke ranks to oppose it (Brouard and Tiberj 2006: 263). The disunity at the top of the party was also reflected amongst rank and file party members and Socialist voters more generally. In fact, a majority of 'No' votes came from the left of the electorate and a majority of Socialist Party supporters voted 'No'.[12] The referendum, therefore, exposed a serious disconnect between the Socialist Party and its constituency. The party leadership failed to either correctly gauge the mood of its constituents or, alternatively, to convince them of the pro-CT case (Berezin 2006: 269).

On the level of domestic party politics, the Socialists' failure to develop and communicate a coherent position in relation to the CT was a missed opportunity. After all, the 'No' camp's victory was an embarrassment and credibility blow for centre-right President Jacques Chirac, who called a referendum where he did not have to and then campaigned unsuccessfully for the 'Yes' vote. The disarray caused by the referendum in the Socialist camp damaged the party's standing and meant that it was unable to capitalise on Chirac's bungled handling of the issue (Milner 2006: 260). In relation to the nexus between national level politics and EU level policymaking (or, in this case, treaty making), the episode confirmed the difficulty of winning citizens for Europe in the post-permissive consensus era. The CT was too easily portrayed by its opponents in France as a neo-liberal, Anglo-Saxon Trojan horse, which would undermine the social welfare state (Hainsworth 2006: 103–4, 108–9). Supporters of the proposed Constitution, on the other hand, failed to effectively counter such negative images with their own, positive narrative even though they were dealing with an overwhelmingly pro-EU electorate.[13] This gap between elites and publics is a recurring motif of EU politics. In the following section, I discuss how it plays out at the European level.

The impact of the democratic deficit at the European level

At the European level, the democratic deficit broadly refers to the unrepresentative nature of the EU's governing institutions, particularly the European Commission, and the lack of popular contestation over policies and political leadership. In other words, the problem lies with the ongoing weakness of European-level government *by* and *of* the people. Andreas Follesdal and Simon Hix (2006: 533–34) elucidated five main claims of what they described as the 'standard version' of the democratic deficit.

The first claim is that European integration has increased the power of the executive branch of government at the expense of national parliamentary control. This is one respect in which the EU is not so unique in comparison with other international organisations. Since national executives tend to have broad discretionary powers in matters of foreign affairs and diplomacy, they are able to dominate the activities of such organisations, largely free from domestic constraints. European-level policymaking is heavily populated by executive actors of various types. These include heads of government and national ministers in the European Council and Council of Ministers, government appointees in the European Commission and national bureaucrats in Coreper. When they are operating in the European institutions, these actors are all more insulated from parliamentary scrutiny than they would be when acting in comparable domestic settings and so democratic accountability is compromised (Follesdal and Hix 2006: 534–35).

The second claim is that the European Parliament is still too weak relative to national governments operating in the Council of Ministers (Follesdal and Hix, 2006, p. 535). To be sure, the EP has made great strides in increasing its powers since its inception as the Common Assembly of the ECSC and especially since the advent of direct elections in 1979. The co-decision procedure, which was introduced by the Maastricht Treaty, has been extended to new competences by every subsequent amending treaty and was renamed the 'Ordinary Legislative Procedure' (OLP) by the Lisbon Treaty (see Article 294 TFEU). Proponents of parliamentarisation regarded this last development as a particularly significant victory for the EP, with Berthold Rittberger (2012: 32), for example, claiming that the OLP's adoption reflected 'the institutionalization of the principle of representative democracy in the EU'. By 2009, therefore, the Parliament had become almost an equal co-legislator with the Council, at least on paper.

The EP has also made gains in terms of its powers of administrative and executive oversight. It has the power to censure and dismiss the Commission in its entirety, though not individual Commissioners (Article 17(8) TEU), and it votes to accept or reject the candidate for Commission President. In fact, under the Lisbon Treaty, the European Council must consider the results of EP elections when proposing a candidate for the post. This innovation was intended to increase interest and participation in the EP elections, as well as boosting their 'European' dimension, by giving voters key personalities on which to focus. It was also hoped that providing an electoral link, albeit indirect, between European citizens and the Commission would help to mitigate the democratic deficit. The measure's merits have been subject to much debate. Proponents argue that a partisan Commission President would, indeed, increase the Parliament's profile and improve EU democracy, while critics claim that it would undermine the Commission's impartiality and ability to work effectively with the Council, without necessarily delivering major benefits.[14] A further complication is the ambiguous wording of the treaty – the Council must *take into account* EP election results, but it is not obliged to nominate the Parliament's candidate.[15]

These complications were on full display when the provision was used for the first time as part of the process of selecting a successor to José Manuel Barroso, who will leave office in late 2014. In the lead up to the May 2014 European elections, each of the major party blocs nominated their candidate for Commission president. The main contenders – Jean-Claude Juncker for the centre-right European People's Party (EPP) and Martin Schulz for the centre-left Socialists and Democrats (S&D) – then engaged in a US-style campaign that included bus tours and televised debates. Nevertheless, the candidates' exposure to potential voters was still quite limited. An Ipsos poll conducted in 12 member states in April 2014 showed that over 60% of respondents had not heard of either Schulz or Juncker (Ipsos Mori Social Research Institute, May 2014). Even more damaging to the legitimacy of the 'leading candidates' idea was the European Council's reaction to the election results. While the EPP gained the highest number of seats in the new parliament, several heads of government – above all David Cameron – were resistant to the idea of nominating Juncker, insisting instead on the Council's right to choose its own candidate (Traynor 2014). This impasse remained unresolved at the time of writing, but a failure by the Parliament to get 'its' candidate nominated, or even the perception that the real decision was once again made behind the closed doors of the Council, would be a considerable blow to the legislature's prestige.

Thus, the EU is still far from having a parliamentary system of government as that term is traditionally understood. As Mattias Kumm (2008: 129) has noted, the EP, for all its progress, is still not the EU's central agenda setter; '[i]t is an editor, not the author, of European laws'. In terms of executive oversight, it remains the case that the Commission is not drawn from the EP, nor is it elected by it in any real sense, but rather the member states' preferences (for their individual Commissioners) are put forward for parliamentary confirmation. For that matter, there is not one clear site of executive authority in the Union; rather executive activities are carried out by a combination of the Commission, the Council, and numerous delegated agencies (Crum 2003: 376–79). Moreover, citizens' preferences (or at least those of the minority who do participate in EP elections) have only an indirect influence on EU policy outcomes. For all of these reasons, the EP is not an adequate supranational replacement for the influence lost by national parliaments.

The third plank of the democratic deficit is the ongoing lack of any genuinely 'European' elections. The procedural and substantive shortcomings in EP elections are manifold. The mode of proportional representation used, whereby contingents of parliamentarians are elected from individual member states in a way that only roughly corresponds to population size, forgoes the principle of electoral equality, or 'one person, one vote, one value' (Rose and Bernhagen 2010). This lack of electoral equality was identified by the GCC in its *Lisbon decision* as a major reason why the EP cannot be classified as a democratic representative body of a sovereign European people.[16] Furthermore, elections to the European Parliament are still well characterised as 'second-order national contests' given low participation rates and the prevalent use of such elections to register protest votes against national governing parties (Marsh 1998; Follesdal and Hix 2006: 536).

A related deficiency is the absence of pan-European parties to contest European elections. Although ideologically similar parties sit together in blocs once in parliament, they campaign separately. This means that EP elections, in effect, are the sum of a multitude of distinct national campaigns, each focusing on its own national issues rather than on potentially unifying threads. Again, the LT's innovation of linking EP election results to the office of Commission President was designed to promote greater unity and cohesion by giving each multi-national party bloc a single figurehead. It is too early to judge what effect, if any, this will have in transnationalising parties and election campaigns. As noted above, much will depend on whether the European Council follows through in nominating the Parliament's candidate. In the past, however, even where the same policy has been at issue in several member states, national mass media have tended to filter the discussion through domestic preferences so as to produce a series of insular, intra-state debates, rather than a truly transnational one.

The same trend is evident when it comes to EU treaty reform. For example, debates over the CT were 'domesticated' to a significant degree, even when they concerned European level developments (e.g. the drafting process) or events in other member states (e.g. the French referendum) (Statham and Trenz 2012: 55–78). Hence, the very same document was able to produce radically different discourses in different member states – what to the French was a harbinger of Anglo-Saxon style liberalisation, was perceived as a blue-print for the creation of an inefficient, bureaucratic superstate by the British (Baines and Gill 2006; Milner 2006). This problem of parallel, often mis- or under-informed national debates that do not speak to each other can be linked partly to the underdevelopment of the European public sphere, itself caused by language barriers, amongst other problems. Ironically, stimulation of a European public sphere capable of legitimating the European project was posited as one of the benefits of adopting a formal Constitution in the first place (Habermas 2001; Statham and Trenz 2012: 13–14).

EP elections, then, like national elections, tend not to be contested on European-level issues. To be sure, the euro crisis increased greatly the salience of EU policies in the lead up to the 2014 European elections, but to what end? Though the crisis has undoubtedly increased the relevance of European *policies*, it appears to be having the opposite effect on the European *Parliament*. In a reversal of the decades-long trend of its empowerment, the EP has been sidelined in all of the major initiatives undertaken over the last few years. Therefore, rather than encouraging European citizens' participation in the most significant supranational democratic outlet open to them, the crisis is actually adding another layer to the Union's democratic deficit (Fasone 2012).[17] It is, in effect, politicising EU policies without democratising EU policymaking. The success of eurosceptics and of far right and far left parties in the 2014 European elections (such groups will make up approximately 30% of the incoming parliament) indicates high levels of frustration amongst a certain segment of the population. On the other hand, overall turnout rose only slightly to 43.09% (from 43% in 2009), suggesting that apathy is still the prevailing attitude of most Europeans towards the Parliament, the crisis notwithstanding.

The fourth plank of the EU-level democratic deficit is the fact that the Union is simply too distant from European citizens for them to feel that their membership of it is meaningful. There are two distinct ways in which the concept of distance may be understood in this context – institutional and psychological. In institutional terms, it refers to the fact, discussed above, that the links between European citizens and the Council and Commission are indirect and mediated through several processes. In psychological terms, the concept of distance describes a lack of familiarity, whereby European citizens struggle to understand and identify with EU institutions because they are so unlike domestic institutions of governance. This last point relates especially to the European Commission, a hybrid executive and administrative organ that lacks national counterparts (Follesdal and Hix 2006: 536–37). The EU has tried to fill this identity lacuna in different ways, but the lack of strong ties of allegiance between citizens and Union institutions (and the EU *in toto*) remains a problem.

The fifth and final claim of the standard democratic deficit is that the EU's structures and processes produce 'policy drift' from voters' ideal preferences. Follesdal and Hix (2006: 537) explain that, '[p]artially as a result of the four previous factors, the EU adopts policies that are not supported by a majority of citizens in many or even most Member States'. Therefore, unlike the previous claims, this is a substantive criticism of EU-style democracy. It also tends to be a social democratic critique of what is regarded as a right-of-centre drift. The free market, neo-liberal emphasis of single market regulation (and deregulation) and the exclusive price stability mandate of the ECB are two commonly given instances of such a centre-right bias; though the wasteful and protectionist CAP may be cited as a counter-example. Fritz Scharpf (1999, 2009: 5–7), for example, has argued that the EU's institutional structure creates asymmetries that favour economic liberalisation; both by privileging 'policy-making by nonpolitical actors' (including courts) over European-level political action and by facilitating 'negative integration' (i.e. deregulation) whilst constraining positive integration. The result of these 'institutional asymmetries' is to undermine national social market economies and impede the creation of a European-level social market economy.

All five claims touch upon the EU-level counterpart to *intra*-state 'politics without policy': the equally problematic 'policy without politics' (Schmidt 2009: 20–24). Scharpf's claim that EU governance is structured in a way that favours policymaking by non-political actors is relevant here. In the early period of European integration, the asymmetry between the capacity for non-political and political action was not very pronounced. The 'foundational equilibrium' guaranteed national control over economic harmonisation and, besides, the original six member states had fairly similar welfare states, making it easier for national governments to aggregate their preferences in the Council. However, over time, enlargement and the growing diversity of national preferences made harmonisation of national rules through Community legislation more difficult, leading to political stagnation. As was described in Chapter 1, the ECJ stepped into this breach: if changing the treaties (via political action) proved to be an impossibly complex and drawn-out method of driving integration forward, then the treaties would need to be reinterpreted (via non-political judicial legislation). Through a combination of the doctrine of EU legal supremacy and the difficulty of formally amending the treaties, the Court's opinions were given far more weight than judicial pronouncements traditionally warrant, effectively becoming the higher law of the member states (Scharpf 2009: 7–13).

Thus, we come again to the downside of the judicialisation of the European project. A phenomenon that led to great progress in achieving 'ever closer union' amongst European peoples also entrenched non-majoritarian technocracy as the Union's *modus operandi*. Moreover, European-level 'policy without politics' is more accurately described as a *pretence* of depoliticised policymaking within EU institutions, not only the ECJ but also the European Commission and, increasingly, the ECB. In the pre-Maastricht Treaty period, law 'function[ed] as a mask for politics', allowing the achievement of policy results that could not have been obtained through political channels (Burley and Mattli 1993: 44). In a sense, law filled the role that neofunctionalists had postulated economics would play in promoting centralised regulation at the European level. The financial crisis, though, appears to be reversing that trend. In the face of the euro emergency, strict obedience to the rule of law is ceding ground to economic necessity as the driving force behind allegedly apolitical and exceptional measures.

A final point worth noting about European-level 'policy without politics' is that it is, to a large extent, a function of the lack of an EU government. The European Commission and much of EU studies scholarship treat 'European governance' as something positive and empowering for citizens, often by virtue of its supposedly post-national, *sui generis* nature. However, as Jan-Werner Müller (2012: 39) has pointed out, such rhetoric tends to obfuscate rather than illuminate the Union's *raison d'être*. In fact, it should be recognised and acknowledged that the diffuse institutions and processes covered by the term 'governance', as opposed to government, are not necessarily conducive to democracy. Ever-thickening layers of 'governance' tend to obscure lines of accountability, blurring the boundaries between EU and national competences in a way that leaves no one responsible and nowhere for citizens to turn to seek satisfaction on a particular issue (Shore 2006: 710, 720–21).

Why the European Union is more than a constrained technocratic body

The above notwithstanding, the proposition that the EU has a democratic deficit remains contested. One of the leading arguments for the Union's democratic *sufficiency* holds that its institutions and processes are appropriately constrained by law and an elaborate system of checks and balances, in keeping with the norms of liberal democracy. Andrew Moravcsik (2002, 2006) is a key proponent of this thesis. In an extension of his theory of liberal-intergovernmentalism, he has argued that the EU largely performs tasks of a technical and specialised nature that are suitable for delegation to non-majoritarian bodies. While acknowledging that the governance practices of the EU are not perfect, he has asserted further that when compared to real national democracies – rather than a non-existent ideal type – the Union is adequately, and even admirably, democratic (Moravcsik 2002: 621–22).[18]

Although this claim appears more relevant to the early European Community than the contemporary European Union, Moravcsik has maintained his views. In the early to mid-2000s, he argued that the CT was unnecessary because it aimed at the politicisation of a project that did not need to be politicised. Accordingly, he interpreted the CT's defeat not as a sign of serious tensions within the integration project, but rather as a reaffirmation of the strength, stability and vitality of the EU's uncodified 'constitutional settlement' (Moravcsik 2006: 221–26). Several years later, Moravcsik has drawn similar conclusions from the euro crisis. Thus, while acknowledging the scale of the problem (a fundamental lack of economic convergence within the eurozone) and the difficulty of implementing the solutions (Southern euro countries to become more 'German', and Germany and other Northerners to become more 'Southern'), he nevertheless concluded that, 'within the increasingly clear mandate of a stable constitutional settlement, Europe will continue to respond to the challenges of an increasingly interdependent world' (Moravcsik 2012: 68).

This claim lacks credibility in the current context. The EU's constitutional settlement is actually being *destabilised* by national and EU leaders' disregard for European legal norms and the rule of law in their rush to adopt a suite of *ad hoc* crisis relief measures (Joerges 2012: 1014–16). Moravcsik (2012: 60–61) praised the 'remarkable flexibility' with which European governments, the ECB and the troika acted to set up bailout funds and purchase the bonds of distressed euro countries, 'although doing so may have violated clauses of the Maastricht Treaty that ban bailouts and monetary financing of budget deficits'. Yet, it is difficult to see how the institutionalised violation of EU primary law promotes the stabilisation of EU constitutionalism. Moreover, in light of the multiple, interlinked crises facing the eurozone (Jones, 2012), it can no longer be plausibly argued that the EU only regulates issues of low public salience, that monetary policy is an entirely technocratic matter, or that its complete removal from the realm of national political contestation has not adversely affected democratic quality.

Nevertheless, Moravcsik (2012: 66) has continued to assert that complaints that the EU is undemocratic 'contain little truth', partly because '[t]he EU remains tightly controlled by elected national politicians'. This assessment ignores the predominance of *executive* politics throughout the crisis, which has marginalised legislatures and electorates. Furthermore, some national politicians are much more in control of the EU's collective destiny than others. Political leaders in countries such as Greece, Cyprus and Portugal have little influence over their own domestic policies, let alone 'the policies of other countries that affect [them]' (Moravcsik 2012: 66).

In giving the counter-argument, Follesdal and Hix (2006: 551–56) focused on the need for institutional reform to overcome the democratic deficit. They called, for example, for greater democratic contestation of European-level political leadership positions, such as the Commission President, and greater transparency in Council proceedings. Such reforms may be welcome attempts to better connect citizen preferences to EU policy outcomes. However, their success will be muted to the extent that the cause of the democratic deficit lies not in the failure to replicate national democratic institutions at the European level, but in the mismatch between expanding supranational competences and a limited – even shrinking – base of popular support (Majone 2012: 19). The first clear indication of the extent of this mismatch came with the difficult ratification of the Maastricht Treaty in the early 1990s. The Treaty was put to a popular vote in three member states – an attempted 'splash from the bottle of democratic legitimacy' that instead unleashed 'an apparent wave of popular opposition' (Franklin, Marsh and McLaren 1994: 456). The text won convincing support in the 1992 Irish referendum, but was rejected by Danish voters in June 1992 and only narrowly approved (with 51% of the vote) in a French referendum in September of that year.[19]

It was the passage of the Maastricht Treaty, then, that exposed a significant elite–public gap concerning perceptions of the EU's legitimacy and marked the end of the popular permissive consensus (Hooghe and Marks 2009: 21). Moravcsik (2012: 67) described Maastricht's ratification as the starting point of a 'two-decade-long trend toward the leveling off of European integration'. Perhaps, with hindsight, Maastricht did mark the EU at the height of its powers – confident to the point of hubris and about to embark upon a currency union that would prove detrimental to the goal of European unity in the medium term. However, the Treaty certainly did not indicate a levelling off of supranational European aspirations; aspirations that continue to outstrip the EU's democratic legitimacy.

If, then, the EU does have a democratic deficit and if that deficit cannot be resolved solely through institutional reform at the European level, what is to be done? The best solution may be to roll back EU competences and reaffirm the pre-eminence of the member states and, particularly, national parliaments, at least in some areas. By favouring constitutional pluralism over constitutional hierarchy, the Lisbon Treaty took a welcome step in that direction. Now the unfolding eurozone crisis is illustrating the value of such a pragmatic constitutional settlement just as the 'more Europe at any cost' mentality behind many of the crisis responses is undermining it (Gillingham 2012: 19–31).

Concluding remarks: the crisis of EU constitutionalism as a crisis for democracy in Europe

There is a paradox inherent within the EU's relationship to democracy: although it is a union of democratic states, and although the 1993 Copenhagen criteria enshrined the requirement that prospective member states have stable democratic systems, the EU's own institutions and processes fall short of democratic standards.[20] The EU's shortcomings in this respect are not simply the product of particular, contingent institutional arrangements, but rather are 'part of a deep-seated political culture' (Weiler 2011: 694). That is, they reflect choices made more than half a century ago to pursue European integration via non-majoritarian means, due partly to the absence of a European *demos* and partly to post-war concerns about the destructive potential of unconstrained democracy (Müller 2012). The deep entrenchment of non-majoritarian modes of governance in the EU means that there are no easy fixes for the democratic deficit; institutional reforms may alleviate some of the symptoms, but they cannot entirely cure the disease. This, in turn, has negative repercussions for the Union's legitimacy, which is also suffering from a perceived slide in the effectiveness of European-level outputs.

In his earlier work, Majone (1998: 5–7) argued that the democratic deficit was, in fact, 'democratically justified' insofar as it was in keeping with the preferences of a majority of Europeans, who favoured extensive economic integration but opposed the transformation of the EU into a federation. At the same time, he noted that the legitimacy of the EU as an 'inherently non-majoritarian' project rested on the strictest possible separation of economic integration from political integration, that is, on the depoliticisation of EU policymaking as the means to preserving national sovereignty and national parliamentary democracy. The notion that politics and economics could be kept separate was always problematic, but the advent of EMU made it completely unsustainable. As Majone (2012: 12) later acknowledged, '[s]uch a separation [between politics and economics] is much more difficult, not to say impossible, at the level of macroeconomic policymaking. This is because so much of what the modern welfare state does depends crucially on the way macroeconomic policies are designed and implemented'.

In a perverse way, then, the crisis of the eurozone – which now touches every aspect of economic and fiscal policymaking – has brought about the politicisation of European integration for which many euro-federalists had hoped. However, instead of contributing to the closure of the democratic deficit, politicisation is actually exacerbating it. The fifth and final chapter uses an analysis of the euro crisis to bring together the key themes of the book: the evolution of EU constitutionalism, the changing balance between law and politics in European integration, and the implications for national and European level democracy.

Notes

1 Further references to democracy include Art. 10(1) TEU, which states that '[t]he functioning of the Union shall be founded on representative democracy', Art. 11 on the principle of participatory democracy, and Art. 21(1), which requires that the EU's international relations be guided by its own founding principles, including democracy.

2 Armin von Bogdandy (2005: 300–301) aptly described this quotation, taken from Pericles's funeral oration, as a picture, rather than words, because it was presented

in the draft CT in ancient Greek, a language that only a tiny proportion of Europeans can read. As such, it functioned as a cipher, evoking ancient Greek culture and democracy as Europe's founding myth. However, the quotation was removed from the final version of the CT by the intergovernmental conference.

3 As noted in Chapter 1, one institutional manifestation of this predilection was the creation of powerful constitutional courts at both national and supranational levels.

4 For example, political messianic rhetoric featured heavily in the CT preamble, which was discussed in Chapter 2.

5 The term 'eudaemonic' means 'conducive to happiness'.

6 Notable exceptions to the mainstream pro-EU consensus include the British Conservative Party and Hungary's FIDESZ.

7 Following the murder of a left-wing musician by a Golden Dawn member in September 2013, there was a clampdown on the group and many of its senior figures were imprisoned awaiting trial (Smith 2013b).

8 The post-crisis decline in support for, and trust in, the EU and its institutions is borne out by Eurobarometer data. As summarised by Daniel Debomy (2013): 'Steadily consistent answers to several questions asked for Standard Eurobarometer opinion polls show that a decline in public opinion on the European Union observed since 2007 significantly worsened in 2011, bringing support to historically low levels which continue today.'

9 See Wolfgang Streeck (2012) for a critique of the crisis-induced promotion of technocratic administrators, at the expense of democracy, in countries such as Greece and Italy.

10 The situation in Cyprus in March 2013 demonstrated a similar disregard for parliamentary prerogatives. On March 19 the Cypriot parliament rejected a bailout negotiated between the government and the troika, which controversially involved a tax on all deposits over 20,000 euros. This hurdle was overcome by the negotiation, a few days later, of an amended package that no longer required parliamentary approval because losses to depositors would come about through bank restructuring rather than a levy or tax (Smith 2013a).

11 The results of the May elections were inconclusive and the subsequent failure to form a government led to a re-run in June 2012. Those elections produced a clearer outcome, with New Democracy securing just under 30% of the vote and 129 out of 300 seats (owing to a 50-seat bonus for the first-placed party). The anti-austerity Syriza also had a good showing, coming in second place with just under 27% of the vote and 71 seats (Psaropoulos 2012). Insofar as the election could be interpreted as a referendum on Greece's future in the eurozone (and that was certainly a popular reading in the media), a narrow plurality of Greeks chose austerity and the euro over default and a likely return to the drachma.

12 According to an IPSOS Exit Poll from 29 May 2005, 54.5% of 'No' voters declared themselves close to the parliamentary left or the extreme-left as opposed to 36.5% close to the right (of which 19.5% were close to the National Front) (Dehousse 2006: 153). In other words, the mainstream right largely supported President Chirac by voting 'Yes'.

13 As noted in Chapter 2, while there was some anti-EU rhetoric from the far left and far right, slogans such as '*Oui à l'Union; non à la Constitution*' give a better picture of the sentiments of more mainstream CT opponents (Milner 2006: 257–58).

14 For summaries of key arguments on both sides, see Pier Domenico Tortola (2013) and Heather Grabbe and Stefan Lehne (2013).

15 According to Article 17(7) TEU:

> Taking into account the elections to the European Parliament and after having held the appropriate consultations, the European Council, acting by a qualified majority, shall propose to the European Parliament a candidate for

President of the Commission. This candidate shall be elected by the European Parliament by a majority of its component members. If he or she does not obtain the required majority, the European Council, acting by a qualified majority, shall within one month propose a new candidate who shall be elected by the European Parliament following the same procedure.

16 *Lisbon decision*, paragraphs 279–81.
17 The euro crisis is both highlighting and exacerbating all facets of what Follesdal and Hix (2006) described as the 'standard version' of the democratic deficit. This is nowhere clearer than in relation to the weakening of parliaments; ironically only a few years after the entry into force of the LT marked a new zenith in the parliamentarisation of the EU. Cristina Fasone (2012: 1) put it succinctly:

> A new democratic deficit is likely to emerge (or, perhaps, it is already in place), since the fiscal sovereignty of national parliaments is put under severe constraints, whereas the EP, in the best hypothesis, is simply informed of the decisions taken by someone else at EU level, without its direct involvement.

18 Moravcsik (2002: 621) did presciently identify the structure and excessive independence of the ECB as a potential cause for concern. This has, in fact, been borne out by the eurozone crisis.
19 The Treaty was approved in Denmark in a second referendum in May 1993, the Danish government having obtained several concessions. See Mark Franklin, Michael Marsh and Lauren McLaren (1994) for analysis of the Maastricht Treaty referenda.
20 See Wojciech Sadurski (2012), particularly Chapter 3, for a discussion of the 'democracy paradox' in the context of the Central and Eastern European states' accession to the EU.

References

Baines, P. and Gill, M. (2006) 'The EU Constitution and the British Public: What the Polls Tell Us about the Campaign that Never Was'. *International Journal of Public Opinion Research*, Vol. 18, No. 4, pp. 463–73.

Bellamy, R. (2010) 'Democracy without Democracy? Can the EU's Democratic "Outputs" Be Separated from the Democratic "Inputs" Provided by Competitive Parties and Majority Rule?' *Journal of European Public Policy*, Vol. 17, No. 1, pp. 2–19.

Berezin, M. (2006) 'Appropriating the "No": The French National Front, the Vote on the Constitution, and the "New" April 21'. *Political Science & Politics*, Vol. 39, No. 2, pp. 269–72.

Brouard, S. and Tiberj, V. (2006) 'The French Referendum: The Not So Simple Act of Saying Nay'. *Political Science & Politics*, Vol. 39, No. 2, pp. 261–68.

Burley, A. and Mattli, W. (1993) 'Europe before the Court: A Political Theory of Legal Integration'. *International Organization*, Vol. 47, No. 1, pp. 41–76.

Chalmers, D. (2009) 'Gauging the Cumbersomeness of EU Law'. *LEQS Paper No. 2, May 2009*, pp. 1–37.

Cooper, I. (2010) 'Mapping the Overlapping Spheres: European Constitutionalism after the Treaty of Lisbon'. *ARENA Centre for European Studies Seminar Paper*, pp. 1–32.

Crum, B. (2003) 'Legislative-Executive Relations in the EU'. *Journal of Common Market Studies*, Vol. 41, No. 3, pp. 375–95.

Debomy, D. (2013) 'EU No, Euro Yes? European Public Opinions Facing the Crisis (2007–12)'. *Notre Europe Jacques Delors Institute*, Policy Paper 90, pp. 1–24.

Dehousse, R. (2006) 'The Unmaking of a Constitution: Lessons from the European Referenda'. *Constellations*, Vol. 13, No. 2, pp. 151–64.

Fasone, C. (2012) 'The Struggle of the European Parliament to Participate in the New Economic Governance'. *EUI Working Papers RSCAS 2012/45*, pp. 1–22.

Featherstone, K. (2011) 'The Greek Sovereign Debt Crisis and EMU: A Failing State in a Skewed Regime'. *Journal of Common Market Studies*, Vol. 49, No. 2, pp. 193–217.

Fischer, J. (2000) 'From Confederacy to Federation – Thoughts on the Finality of European Integration'. *Speech given at Humboldt University*, Berlin, 12 May.

Follesdal, A. and Hix, S. (2006) 'Why There Is a Democratic Deficit in the EU: A Response to Majone and Moravcsik'. *Journal of Common Market Studies*, Vol. 44, No. 3, pp. 533–62.

Franklin, M., Marsh, M. and McLaren, L. (1994) 'Uncorking the Bottle: Popular Opposition to European Unification in the Wake of Maastricht'. *Journal of Common Market Studies*, Vol. 32, No. 4, pp. 455–72.

Gillingham, J. (2012) 'The End of the European Dream'. In Zimmerman, H. and Dür, A. (eds) *Key Controversies in European Integration* (Basingstoke: Palgrave Macmillan).

Grabbe, H. and Lehne, S. (2013) 'Why a Partisan Commission President Would Be Bad for the EU'. *The Centre for European Reform*, October, pp. 1–8.

Habermas, J. (2001) 'Why Europe Needs a Constitution'. *New Left Review*, Vol. 11, Sep–Oct, pp. 5–26.

Hainsworth, P. (2006) 'France Says No: The 29 May 2005 Referendum on the European Constitution'. *Parliamentary Affairs*, Vol. 59, No. 1, pp. 98–117.

Holmes, L. (1997) *Post-Communism* (Cambridge: Polity Press).

Hooghe, L. and Marks, G. (2009) 'A Postfunctionalist Theory of European Integration: From Permissive Consensus to Constraining Dissensus'. *British Journal of Political Science*, Vol. 39, No. 1, pp. 1–23.

Ipsos Mori Social Research Institute (May 2014) *Ipsos European Pulse*, available at www.ipsos-na.com/download/pr.aspx?id=13648 (Accessed: 28 May 2014).

Joerges, C. (2012) 'Recht und Politik in der Krise Europas: Die Wirkungsgeschichte einer verunglückten Konfiguration'. *Merkur*, Vol. 66, No. 11, pp. 1013–24.

Jones, E. (2012) 'Europe's Threatened Solidarity'. *Current History*, Vol. 111, No. 743, pp. 88–93.

Kitsantonis, N. and Donadio, R. (2011a) 'Anxieties Stir As Greece Plans Referendum on Latest Europe Aid Deal'. *New York Times*, 31 October.

——(2011b) 'Greek Leader Calls Off Referendum on Bailout Plan'. *New York Times*, 3 November.

Kumm, M. (2008) 'Why Europeans Will Not Embrace Constitutional Patriotism'. *International Journal of Constitutional Law*, Vol. 6, No. 1, pp. 117–36.

Majone, G. (1998) 'Europe's "Democratic Deficit": The Question of Standards'. *European Law Journal*, Vol. 4, No. 1, pp. 5–28.

——(2011) 'Monetary Union and the Politicization of Europe'. *Keynote speech at the Euroacademia International Conference: 'The European Union and the Politicization of Europe'*, Vienna, 8–10 December.

——(2012) 'Rethinking European Integration after the Debt Crisis'. *UCL: The European Institute, Working Paper No. 3/2012*, June 2012.

Marsh, M. (1998) 'Testing the Second-Order Election Model after Four European Elections'. *British Journal of Political Science*, Vol. 28, No. 4, pp. 591–607.

Mason, P. (2012) 'Alarm at Greek Police "Collusion" with Far-Right Golden Dawn'. *BBC News*, 17 October.

Milner, H. (2006) '"YES to the Europe I Want; NO to this One." Some Reflections on France's Rejection of the EU Constitution'. *Political Science & Politics*, Vol. 39, No. 2, pp. 257–60.

Moravcsik, A. (2002) 'In Defence of the "Democratic Deficit": Reassessing Legitimacy in the European Union'. *Journal of Common Market Studies*, Vol. 40, No. 4, pp. 603–24.

——(2006) 'What Can We Learn from the Collapse of the European Constitutional Project?' *Politische Vierteljahresschrift*, Vol. 47, No. 2, pp. 219–41.

——(2012) 'Europe after the Crisis: How to Sustain a Common Currency'. *Foreign Affairs*, Vol. 91, No. 3, pp. 54–68.

Müller, J.-W. (2012) 'Beyond Militant Democracy?' *New Left Review*, Vol. 73, Jan–Feb, pp. 39–47.

Psaropoulos, J. (2012) 'Greece Results Bring Relief but No Remedy'. *Al Jazeera*, 18 June.

Rittberger, B. (2012) 'Institutionalizing Representative Democracy in the European Union: The Case of the European Parliament'. *Journal of Common Market Studies*, Vol. 50, No. S1, pp. 18–37.

Rohrschneider, R. and Whitefield, S. (2013) 'The Dog that Hardly Barked: The Stances of Political Parties about European Integration in Western Europe, 2008–13'. *Paper presented at the EUDO Dissemination Conference 'Elections in Europe in Times of Crisis'*, EUI, Florence, 28–29 November.

Rose, R. and Bernhagen, P. (2010) 'Inequalities in Representation in the European Parliament'. *Paper presented at the 5th ECPR Pan-European Conference on EU Politics*, Porto, Portugal, 23–26 June.

Sadurski, W. (2012) *Constitutionalism and the Enlargement of Europe* (Oxford: Oxford University Press).

——(2013) 'Democratic Legitimacy of the European Union: A Diagnosis and Some Modest Proposals'. *Sydney Law School Legal Studies Research Paper No. 13/29*, pp. 1–40.

Scharpf, F. (1999) *Governing Europe: Effective and Democratic?* (Oxford: Oxford University Press).

——(2009) 'The Double Asymmetry of European Integration. Or: Why the EU Cannot Be a Social Market Economy'. *Max-Planck-Institut für Gesellschaftsforschung, MPIfG Working Paper 09/12*, November.

Schmidt, V. A. (2006) *Democracy in Europe: The EU and National Polities* (Oxford: Oxford University Press).

——(2009) 'Re-Envisioning the European Union: Identity, Democracy, Economy'. *Journal of Common Market Studies*, Vol. 47, Annual Review, pp. 17–42.

Schmitt, C. (2005) *Political Theology: Four Chapters on the Concept of Sovereignty* (Chicago, IL: University of Chicago Press).

Shore, C. (2006) '"Government without Statehood"? Anthropological Perspectives on Governance and Sovereignty in the European Union'. *European Law Journal*, Vol. 12, No. 6, pp. 709–24.

Smith, H. (2012) 'Eurozone Crisis: Greek Left Leader Renounces Bailout Deal'. *The Guardian*, 8 May.

——(2013a) 'Cyprus Saved – but at What Cost?' *The Guardian*, 25 March.

——(2013b) 'Golden Dawn Leaders Brought to Court to Face Charges of Murder and Assault'. *The Guardian*, 1 October.

Statham, P. and Trenz, H.-J. (2012) *The Politicization of Europe: Contesting the Constitution in the Mass Media* (Oxford: Routledge).

Streeck, W. (2012) 'Markets and Peoples: Democratic Capitalism and European Integration'. *New Left Review*, Vol. 73, Jan–Feb, pp. 63–71.

Tortola, P. D. (2013) 'Why a Partisan Commission President Could Be Good for the EU'. *Centre for Studies on Federalism Policy Paper*, December, No. 2, pp. 1–13.

Traynor, I. (2014) 'EU Power Struggle as Cameron Tries To Stop Juncker Getting Top Job'. *The Guardian*, 28 May.

Von Bogdandy, A. (2005) 'The European Constitution and European Identity: Text and Subtext of the Treaty Establishing a Constitution for Europe'. *International Journal of Constitutional Law*, Vol. 3, No. 2–3, pp. 295–315.

Weber, M. (2004) 'The Three Pure Types of Legitimate Rule'. In Whimster, S. (ed.) *The Essential Weber: A Reader* (London: Routledge).

Weiler, J. H. H. (2011) 'The Political and Legal Culture of European Integration: An Exploratory Essay'. *International Journal of Constitutional Law*, Vol. 9, No. 3–4, pp. 678–94.

5   The euro crisis as a 'loud revolution'

The limits of law and the rise of new forms of technocracy

Introduction: Economic and Monetary Union and its crisis

EU constitutionalism has always been marked by the competing forces of centralisation and diffusion of political and legal power. It is the perpetual contestation within and between levels of governance – over authority, identity and meaning – that gives the integration project its constitutional character. However, the EU's model of progress through contestation is not without its limits. The Constitutional Treaty's defeat and, more recently, the euro crisis, have laid bare the contingent nature of European integration so that the contemplation of partial *disintegration* is no longer confined to committed eurosceptics (Webber 2013). Indeed, the task of conceptualising disintegration challenges the discipline of EU studies to maintain its relevance and explanatory power.

This book is an attempt to address that challenge, and this last chapter brings together its key themes. Above all, the euro crisis demonstrates the complex and changing relationship between law and politics in the EU, and the limits of law as an integrationist tool. EMU was a political undertaking but it was designed (and, to some extent, disguised) as a legal project. The currency union pushed integration-through-law to a new level, but its victory was Pyrrhic (Joerges 2012: 1014). The extent of the euro's failure was revealed little more than a decade after its introduction when, faced with a vicious cycle of compounding financial and economic crises, its legal framework could not cope. Since 2010, this has led to European leaders abandoning the strictures of the 'Community method' and instead adopting a series of stop-gap measures. Christian Joerges (2012: 1014–16) described the trend towards the replacement of 'legally structured actions' with *ad hoc* packages as the 'de-legalisation of the currency union' and it has serious implications for the future of European integration.

The euro crisis and integration theory: spillover or spillback?

In his declaration of 9 May 1950, Robert Schuman predicted that, 'Europe will not be made all at once, or according to a single plan. It will be built through concrete achievements which first create a *de facto* solidarity'. Schuman's statement foreshadowed the theory of neofunctionalism, which was the dominant theory of post-war European integration until the late-1960s, when its unidirectional logic was unable to explain stagnation in the integration process. Central to the neofunctionalist paradigm was the idea of 'spillover', whereby cooperation via Community institutions and processes in one area of economic activity would promote supranational integration in other, related areas. Moreover, it was postulated that economic integration would spillover into *political* integration, as progress in the economic realm generated demands for greater Community powers and as political interests and loyalties were gradually transferred from the national to the supranational level (Haas 1958, 1964; Schmitter 2004).

Certainly, there was something of the logic of spillover in the adoption of a common currency for the EU. EMU was introduced by the Maastricht Treaty as a key component of the political union that that document was meant to inaugurate. The Single European Market was due to be completed by the end of 1992 and, as the logic went, a true single market required a single currency, governed by a single monetary policy, administered by a single central bank. The euro crisis has not only exposed serious flaws in the neofunctionalist line of reasoning, it may even be presaging a kind of reverse-functionalism. In other words, rather than *integration* through spillover, the crisis is raising the possibility of *disintegration* through spillover; that is, the 'spillover', or spread, of crisis from one area of the EU to the next.

Already in the 1970s, Philippe Schmitter (1970: 840) theorised that spillover was not the only possible outcome of transnational or supranational cooperation in a given area. In fact, he noted that 'spill-back', whereby 'in response to tensions actors consequentially withdraw from their original objective, downgrading their commitment to mutual cooperation', was also possible. Elements of 'spill-back' are indeed evident in the euro crisis, which has tested the commitment of member states to common European interests and even the definition of those interests. Since 2010, doubts about the sustainability of the debt burdens of individual euro members have raised bigger questions about the efficacy of the EU's institutions and processes of economic governance. In addition, public disquiet over bailouts negotiated by executive governments and bureaucratic agencies, and austerity imposed through external pressure, point to a growing gap between European citizens and their governments over the pace and direction of integration. The crisis is political as well as economic, it engulfs creditor as well as debtor states, and it is leaving its mark on the EU's uncodified constitution. By contrast, previous crises tended to be more contained, and were tempered by progress in other areas of integration (Jones 2012: 89).

Giandomenico Majone (2011: 3) described EMU as a synecdoche of the European Union, a part that may be used to study the whole. It is, indeed, a microcosm of the integration project in its entirety – bold, ambitious, successful to a degree, but structurally flawed. The eurozone crisis is much more than a crisis of confidence in the stability of a currency; it is a crisis of confidence in the Union itself. A number of fundamental weaknesses in Europe's integration model have been exposed, including the EU's identity crisis and doubts about the sustainability of simultaneous deepening and widening.

The EU's 'identity crisis' refers to the enduring angst over what the Union is and what it should aspire to be. Though numerous visions have been put forward, European integration has no agreed upon *finalité politique*. The history of EMU neatly encapsulates why this uncertainty can be a handicap, especially when combined with bold political projects. It is generally agreed that the common currency was 'mainly political rather than economic in inspiration' (Marsh 2011: 46), yet it was created without the necessary political support structures. Moreover, when confronted with the possible collapse of the currency, European leaders hesitated, unwilling to move decisively towards a political union to match the troubled monetary union. Despite grave invocations of solidarity, national interests remain paramount and national taboos abound. The German government led by Chancellor Angela Merkel, for example, insisted that it would not countenance the mutualisation of debt via eurobonds (*The Economist*, 2012b). Thus, the EU is still 'a Europe of bits and pieces' (Curtin 1993), no closer to settling upon a coherent identity than it ever has been.

The eurozone crisis is also challenging the notion that deepening and widening go hand-in-hand in the process of European integration. Vast socio-economic discrepancies and significant political and cultural differences are an inescapable fact of the EU. While Europeans rightly prize their commitment to 'unity in diversity', enlargement inevitably places limits on the sorts of policies that can be pursued effectively at the supranational level. This is nowhere more evident than in relation to EMU, which was introduced without first securing the degree of economic convergence needed to make it work in the medium to long term, and which has not produced such convergence since its introduction (Louis 2010: 979–81; Marsh 2011).

As might be expected, the crisis has magnified pre-existing socio-economic discrepancies and made them more politically damaging. For example, Slovak parliamentarian and founder of the Freedom and Solidarity Party, Richard Sulik, questioned EU leaders' oft-stated claim that 'solidarity' obliged Greece's European partners to provide it with financial assistance. He cited Slovakia's much lower average income and welfare spending levels relative to Greece as reason for his opposition to expansion of the European Financial Stability Facility (EFSF) – opposition that, in October 2011, brought down the Slovak government and necessitated early elections (Auer 2013: 92–95).[1]

Another case in point concerned an ECB report on average levels of wealth across the eurozone. Contrary to popular assumptions and much to the consternation of Germans, the report revealed that Germany had the *lowest* median level of household wealth out of the 15 eurozone states for which there was data. In fact, at 51,000 euros per household, German median wealth was half that of Greece (102,000), less than a third that of Italy (174,000) and Spain

(183,000) and less than a fifth that of Cyprus (second only to Luxembourg at 267,000 euros per household) (Ruhkamp, 2013). Statistics, of course, must be interpreted with caution and in this case much lower levels of home ownership in Germany compared to the rest of the eurozone, combined with inflated property prices in some countries accounted for much of the difference.

Still, regardless of the explanatory factors, the report was highly provocative. The headline under which the *Frankfurter Allgemeine Zeitung* presented the data, '*Reiche Zyprer, arme Deutsche*' ('Rich Cypriots, Poor Germans') suggests that future calls for Germans to demonstrate 'solidarity' with their euro area partners will be viewed more warily. The timing of the report's release – it was delayed by the ECB until *after* the Cypriot bailout had been negotiated – was also controversial and lends weight to the theory that the Bank is being inappropriately politicised by its role in the crisis (Steltzner 2013a, 2013b).

The new economic governance: 'de-legalised' but not re-democratised

The relative speed with which a series of crisis response measures have been adopted by the member states and the variety of legal means used to anchor those measures challenge assumptions that EU constitutionalism has stabilised and reached maturity (cf. Moravcsik 2008: 181–82). The fact that EU leaders have largely sought to avoid EU law in their efforts to secure the eurozone's survival speaks to inadequacies in the Union's constitutional order and the mismatch between legal capabilities and political aspirations. My analysis will focus on the rescue packages, stability mechanisms and Fiscal Compact adopted between 2010 and 2012. These instruments relied upon 'the various legal toolboxes of public international law, European Union law and private law' (de Witte 2011: 5), and their adoption shows how the financial crisis is reconfiguring EU constitutionalism in a way that undermines its supranational character. What is emerging is a more flexible, less democratic, internationalised EU legal order in which member state executives are the key decision makers.

The immediate trigger for this constitutional transformation was the poor economic situation in Greece, which came to a head in early 2010 when the new government revealed that the country's budget deficit was far worse than had been previously reported. Once financial markets began to doubt the government's capacity to service its debt, Greece's access to capital markets dried up (Louis 2010: 971–72). A Greek default would have had dire consequences, not only for Greece, but also for the European banking system, market confidence in other heavily indebted eurozone economies, and the strength of the currency more generally. Thus, EU leaders began to discuss the possibility of putting together a Greek 'rescue package', though in a way that would avoid the potential legal roadblock of the TFEU's 'no-bailout clause' (Article 125). After much hesitation and uncertainty, euro area heads of state and government agreed the details of a financial assistance package in May 2010. The deal took the form of a series of bilateral loans between

Greece and other euro area states, meaning that it formally bypassed the framework of EU law.[2] However, the European Commission was tasked with supervising the lending operation, which somewhat muddied the issue of the EU's involvement with this bailout by another name (de Witte 2011: 5).

Though convenient, the bilateral loan model was only ever envisaged as a temporary solution, especially as the crisis engulfed Ireland and Portugal and threatened to spread further. Therefore, on 9 and 10 May 2010 at an extraordinary meeting of the Economic and Financial Affairs Council (Ecofin) two mechanisms were initiated in order to institutionalise more formally financial assistance arrangements. The first of these, the European Financial Stabilisation Mechanism (EFSM), was established by Council Regulation No. 407/2010 and based on Article 122(2) TFEU. That treaty provision allows the EU (as represented by the Council) to grant financial assistance to a member state that 'is in difficulties or is seriously threatened with severe difficulties caused by natural disasters or exceptional occurrences beyond its control'.

The second initiative involved the creation of an additional, and considerably larger, European Financial Stability Facility (EFSF) to coordinate loans and guarantees from euro area states. In contrast to the EFSM, the EFSF was established by a decision of the representatives of the euro area states only. Moreover, the representatives were wearing their intergovernmental hats and, as such, acting in their capacity as *states* rather than as members of the European Council.[3] Thus, the EFSF, like the first Greek bailout, did not formally involve the EU and was not given a legal basis in the treaties. It was established as a 'Special Purpose Vehicle', a private company based in Luxembourg (and so covered by Luxembourg law) and jointly controlled by euro area states. It was established for a period of three years, with a total lending capacity of 440 billion euros, compared to the EFSM's 60 billion euros. Following their establishment, the mechanisms were activated three times in 2010–11 – providing financial support in the form of loans and guarantees to Ireland, Portugal and Greece (again), respectively (Ruffert 2011: 1780–82).

Both of these financial assistance mechanisms were legally questionable. Two major objections could be raised against them; the first of which was the question of their compatibility with the 'no bailout' clause of Article 125(1) TFEU. That now-infamous provision reads as follows:

> The Union shall not be liable for or assume the commitments of central governments, regional, local or other public authorities ... A Member State shall not be liable for or assume the commitments of central governments, regional, local or other public authorities ... of another Member State.

Prima facie, it appears that Article 125 was breached, firstly by the Greek bailout of 2 May 2010 and later by the creation of the stability mechanisms (Ruffert 2011: 1785–87). Nevertheless, scholars and European leaders have advanced arguments for the consistency of the rescue measures with EU law.

These include the assertion that the phrase, 'shall not be liable for ... ' means that the Union and/or the member states shall not be *compelled* to assume the debts of another member state, but that the clause does not prohibit the *voluntary* assumption of such liability. However, this reasoning is contrary to the rationale behind Article 125, which was about using the discipline of financial markets to force member states to live within their means (Ruffert 2011: 1785–86). Another potential counter-argument is that the stability mechanisms facilitated the provision of loans and guarantees, rather than direct financial aid (de Witte 2011: 6), but, again, there is no plausible reason to interpret Article 125 so narrowly.

Potential justifications aside, the rescue packages were controversial because they violated the spirit, if not the letter, of Article 125. Similarly, they were not in keeping with public expectations of how the provision ought to be interpreted. The latter point was particularly true of Germany and other 'Northern' eurozone members, where the inclusion of Article 125 in the Maastricht Treaty was intended to placate critics who worried that the introduction of a common currency would lead to a 'transfer union', in which better performing states subsidised economically weaker members.

A prominent example of such opposition was the open letter signed in February 1998 by 155 German economists, which called for the euro's introduction to be postponed, and for Italy to be left out of the initial group of euro states (Hanke 1998). The signatories argued that the prospective EMU members had made insufficient progress towards economic convergence and that, under those circumstances, the Stability and Growth Pact would not be able to guarantee budgetary discipline. German politicians and officials, led by then-Chancellor Helmut Kohl, vehemently rejected the suggestion that Europe was not ready for a currency union (Karacs 1998), but many of the problems predicted by the critics have since proved accurate, adding to the chagrin of German citizens who feel they were deceived by their political leaders. Indeed, Ulrike Guerot (2012: 2) wrote of a 'narrative of betrayal' in German debates over the crisis, which has 'resulted in a sense of victimhood' amongst Germans despite the fact that, objectively, the country has benefitted greatly from the common currency, at least to date.

The second major query in relation to the legality of the measures adopted in May 2010 was whether or not Article 122(2) TFEU was really capable of supporting the EFSM (the EU law based pillar of the eurozone's financial firewall). At issue was what may constitute 'exceptional occurrences beyond [a member state's] control', which was the necessary condition for triggering financial aid. Since the governments of heavily indebted states had contributed to their own predicaments through economic mismanagement and poor decision-making, it could be argued that their circumstances were not beyond their control (de Witte 2011: 6; Ruffert 2011: 1787). However, more flexible interpretations of Article 122(2) were also advanced. Jean-Victor Louis (2010: 983–85), for example, argued that it ought to be interpreted as a '"counterweight" to the no-bailout clause', and, further, that the severe degeneration of conditions in Greece in 2010, the spread of the crisis to Ireland and the threat of further contagion, did mean that the situation was 'exceptional' and beyond the control of the Member States concerned.

At any rate, opinion was divided on the legality, not to mention legitimacy, of the temporary stability mechanisms. It was partly that uncertainty that prompted euro area states to create a permanent mechanism backed up by an amendment to the treaties. The German government was especially insistent on this point, as it was worried about the potential reaction of the German Constitutional Court. To this end, Merkel enlisted the support of the then French President, Nicolas Sarkozy, in return promising to soften the new, automatic sanctions regime for breaches of the Stability and Growth Pact – much to the annoyance of the Commission officials who had been drafting the stricter rules (Traynor 2010). The two leaders issued a joint declaration at Deauville on 18 October 2010, in which they called on European Council President Herman Van Rompuy 'to present ... concrete options allowing the establishment of a robust crisis resolution framework before ... March 2011' (de Witte 2011: 6–7). Thus, the Franco-German tandem was able to overcome the other member states' reluctance to reopen the treaties so soon after the long and torturous process of constitutional reform that had ended with the Lisbon Treaty.

The proposed amendment to Article 136 TFEU was tabled at the European Council meeting in December 2010. The new treaty paragraph specifically authorised the establishment of a stability mechanism by euro area states (rather than by the EU as a singular entity).[4] This paved the way for the new mechanism to be established and run along intergovernmental lines, as an institution of the euro area states in which non-euro area member states could participate on an *ad hoc* basis. The main decision-making body of the ESM is its Board of Governors, comprising the euro area Finance Ministers. EU institutions are represented at Board-level via the participation of the European Commissioner for Economic and Monetary Affairs and the President of the ECB as non-voting observers (Article 5 TESM).

The ESM is located in Luxembourg and is governed by public international law. Its legal framework leaves little scope for input from supranational institutions, such as the ECJ and European Parliament, through the channels traditionally provided by EU law. Indeed, it has been suggested that as the crisis cements a 'two-speed Europe', the ESM will become the nucleus of a set of euro-area-only institutions paralleling those of the EU-28 (Buras 2013).[5] The European Commission, however, was given an important role in facilitating the ESM's operation. In particular, it was tasked with assessing the public debt situation of a member state that requests financial assistance from the ESM, negotiating a 'financial assistance facility' for the state concerned and monitoring the state's compliance with the associated conditionality (Article 13 TESM).

The Article 136 TFEU amendment that authorised the ESM sits alongside the 'no bailout' clause – perhaps a little uncomfortably – but does not alter it.

Therefore, it still leaves several questions unanswered, not the least of which is what the new, overwhelmingly intergovernmental financial stability regime means for the future of the Community method of decision-making. I have already suggested that one consequence of the euro crisis is the *internationalisation* of European law. In other words, when confronted with a state of exception, the EU appears less like a *sui generis*, post-state entity and more like a traditional international organisation, which is dominated by executive actors. In this way, the crisis is reinforcing the first claim of the standard democratic deficit described by Follesdal and Hix (2006: 534–35) – the preponderance of executive power at the European level.

In fact, the EP did recommend some changes to the wording of the Article 136 amendment when it was consulted (along with the Commission and the ECB) on the Council's draft. The Parliament's suggestions were aimed at inscribing an explicit role for the EU institutions in the ESM's operation. In particular, the EP proposed that rules on conditionality be determined by an EU regulation, adopted under co-decision (de Witte 2011: 7). More fundamentally, the Parliament criticised the Council's decision to establish the ESM outside of the existing legal order, warning that it 'pose[d] a risk to the integrity of the Treaty-based system' (European Parliament, 23 March 2011, paragraph 7). However, the Council rejected the Parliament's advice and the Article 136 amendment was adopted with its original wording as European Council Decision 2011/199 on 25 March 2011. Following ratification by each of the member states, Decision 2011/199 entered into force on 1 May 2013.

It is somewhat ironic, given that the purpose of the amendment was to legitimise the ESM and inoculate it against legal challenges, that it only became operational several months *after* the permanent bailout fund itself.[6] Indeed, the ECJ considered the legality of this time lag in November 2012 on a preliminary reference from Ireland's Supreme Court. In a decision that endorsed the ESM Treaty's compatibility with EU law more generally, the Court held that the amendment to Article 136 TFEU only confirmed a power already held by member states and did not confer any new power. Accordingly, a member state's right to ratify the ESM Treaty was not subject to the amended TFEU provision's prior entry into force.[7]

On one level, the ECJ's verdict renders the new Article 136 superfluous – if member states were already competent to establish a stability mechanism then they need not have bothered changing the treaties. (Though, as noted, the enterprise was undertaken primarily with an eye to Karlsruhe, not the Court in Luxembourg.) More worrying, however, is the growing impression that the eurozone rescue measures are undermining the Union's legal coherence. The ECJ's approval of the ESM does nothing to assuage these concerns. In fact, the euro crisis is weakening the power and influence of the Court since it is *international* law, rather than European law, that 'is being used as a tool for the development of the European integration process' (de Witte 2011: 8). The implications of this trend are considered in the following section.

The other major treaty-based response to the crisis was the push to strengthen rules about public debt ratios, budgetary discipline and related matters via a Fiscal Compact. A tense overnight summit of the European Council on 9 December 2011 produced an almost unanimous commitment from the EU's heads of state or government to draw up just such an agreement, which would bind euro area states and non-euro area states alike. However, the refusal of the United Kingdom and Czech Republic to participate prevented the Fiscal Compact from being adopted under the auspices of EU law. Still, this did not mean that UK Prime Minister David Cameron had 'vetoed' the Fiscal Compact, as some British observers claimed (*The Economist*, 2011a).[8] Instead, the remaining 25 member states signed the document on 2 March 2012, and it came into force on 1 January 2013.

Thus, the Fiscal Compact, like the ESM, is an international treaty; formally outside the framework of EU law but intended by its drafters to be compatible with that framework, nonetheless.[9] Whether the fiscal regulation it envisages actually *is* compatible with the TFEU's rather narrow bases for economic governance (in Articles 121 and 126) is debatable. Above all, the fractious and painstaking process of the Compact's negotiation has highlighted the difficulty, in an EU of 28, of securing major treaty revisions (Amtenbrink 2012: 137–38).

From Beethoven to bailouts: the European Union in search of a 'constitutional moment'

It remains to be seen whether or not the rescue measures will succeed economically, but my key concern is how they will affect EU constitutionalism. Will the euro crisis revive the federalist project that was vanquished, or at least suppressed, by the Lisbon Treaty's constitutional settlement? Will the economic emergency succeed in fostering amongst Europeans a commonality of purpose, where the CT failed to do so with political symbolism? If the answer is yes, it would confirm Jean Monnet's sentiment, expressed by Robert Schuman, that European federation would be achieved via concrete steps rather than abstract statements of intent (Schuman 1950). Certainly, the creation of a currency union was one such step – though it was perhaps too great a leap from the core project of a common market. A legally binding commitment from member states to strengthen the EU's capacity for economic governance and coordination, including via budgetary oversight and large-scale financial transfers, could be another such step towards federalisation.

There is also a powerful symbolic element to attempts to rescue the common currency. Viewed through the lens of political symbolism, the question is whether the euro crisis could be the 'constitutional moment' that the EU has hitherto lacked.[10] Could it be the emergency that forges solidarity among European peoples and states, forcing the former to abandon apathy and parochialism and the latter their pretensions to national sovereignty in the face of the global markets? This is certainly the view taken by many

European officials at both the national and EU levels. Rather than questioning the efficacy of 'more Europe', they see the crisis as an opportunity to complete the process that the Maastricht Treaty and the introduction of the euro began – true political and economic union. Commission President José Manuel Barroso (2011), for example, implored Europeans to 'either unite or face irrelevance'. The *status quo*, he maintained, would not do; the EU must 'move on to something new and better'.[11]

Many scholars share this unwavering commitment to further integration as the only solution to Europe's problems. Ulrich Beck (2009) offered a particularly clear articulation of this doggedly pro-integration perspective at the outset of the crisis, proclaiming in *The Guardian* that his initial reaction to Europe's financial turmoil had been, 'my God, what an opportunity!'. An opportunity, that is, to establish the foundations of a 'new Europe', in which 'sharing sovereignty becomes a multiplier of power and democracy' (Beck 2011b). Indeed, Beck (2011a: 4, 10) went as far as to suggest that the 'predicable problems' of monetary union without political union were anticipated and even *intended* by the common currency's creators as a way of forcing national governments to move towards closer supranational integration, 'following the cosmopolitical imperative – cooperate or bust'. Similarly, Habermas (2011a) saw in the euro crisis the potential for European states and peoples to overcome national differences and pursue political integration backed by redistributive social welfare.

Nevertheless, reality belies such predictions and exhortations. It has proved almost impossible to have a full and inclusive debate on the lofty ideal of 'political union' while the euro crisis is in its emergency phase and European leaders are focused on pragmatic, day-to-day steps aimed at strengthening the currency and its governance. Thus, the undoubted sense of urgency that has gripped Europe's decision makers is not necessarily conducive to the grand plans of the 'euro-romanticists' (Guerot 2012: 5). Instead, the financial crisis has sparked the rise of a very peculiar type of cooperation, overwhelmingly intergovernmental rather than supranational, and dominated by a select few member states.[12] While Habermas (2011a, 2011b) bemoaned these trends, he insisted on viewing them as missed opportunities, the frustrating result of political narrow-mindedness, rather than questioning his underlying premises.

Still, the 'crisis as opportunity' narrative is not entirely without merit. In many respects, the crisis has supported Habermas's long-standing assertion that European integration is necessitated by the threats to national sovereignty and social democracy arising from globalisation (Habermas 1998: 106–7). Over the last several years, this has been shown especially by the role played by capricious market forces in determining the creditworthiness of nations, with all the economic and political implications that follow. Scholars such as Habermas and Beck are very much concerned with preserving and regenerating democracy in Europe. However, they are mistaken in promoting the EU as the only possible vehicle through which to achieve this goal.

Return to an isolationist 'national idyll' may well be impossible, but this is a far cry from embracing the still-undefined European space as the last best hope for European democracy's revival.

Proponents of ever-closer union often set up a false choice between 'more Europe and no Europe' (see, for example, Beck 2009; Barroso 2011). Amongst national leaders, Angela Merkel, in particular, has embraced such rhetoric. In May 2010, Merkel declared that the collapse of the common currency would mean the failure of the idea of European union, going on to argue – of course – that the crisis presented an opportunity to strengthen the integration project (*Spiegel Online*, 2010). As the eurozone's fiscal woes deepened, Merkel remained uncompromising, reiterating to her Christian Democratic Union (CDU) colleagues in November 2011 that, 'if the euro fails, then Europe fails' (*The Economist*, 2011b).

Such claims are misguided in their conceptualisation of the European project, which has evolved in a rather haphazard way and not according to any grand narrative. As Majone (2012: 3) noted, 'there is no political or economic reason why the failure of monetary union, in its present form, should entail the failure of "Europe"'. There is so much more to what the EU is, and what it does, than a currency union in which not all member states participate. On a practical, economic level, a single currency was not essential to ensure the smooth functioning of the common market when it was introduced and it is not essential on that basis today. Also, although it has been a potent and highly visible symbol of European unity, coins and banknotes are not the essence of 'EU-Europeaness' either. Certainly, the failure of the euro would be a very serious blow financially, logistically and to the Union's identity, credibility and self-belief, but it need not be fatal.

Somewhat ironically, it is the 'all-or-nothing' attitude displayed by many EU leaders towards the euro's fate that exacerbates the potential consequences of a currency union reconfiguration. At the 'nothing' end of the spectrum, talk of 'no euro, no EU' is dangerous precisely because of its potential to become a self-fulfilling prophecy. It dramatically narrows the space for discussion and irresponsibly closes off potential solutions. At the 'all' end of the spectrum, the view that the crisis is an opportunity to perfect economic and political union is just as unhelpful. The crisis does not present a stark choice between the end of European unity and its completion. It *does* present a good opportunity to honestly assess the integration project's flaws in a way that allows for the possibility that partial disintegration may be the best way forward. However, the genuine opportunity for the Union and its member states to benefit from a pragmatic approach to crisis management risks being missed as long as EU elites swing between the extremes of 'total optimism' and 'catastrophism' (Majone 2012: 1–3).

In my view, the euro crisis illustrates the dangers that 'more Europe' poses to European democracy much more readily than it points to europeanisation as the solution. Habermas (2011a), himself, acknowledged that 'more Europe' had come to mean more intergovernmental collaboration under Franco–German hegemony. The major legal and institutional measures adopted over the past several years, including the Fiscal Compact, the EFSF and its successor, the ESM, have largely bypassed both national and European parliaments. The Union has reverted to the type of elitist decision making that characterised the early, 'permissive consensus' decades of European integration. However, the permissive consensus is no more, and European leaders are dealing with matters of fundamental importance to their citizens. Thus, Europe's current politics of crisis resolution is putting democratic legitimacy under a level of pressure that will be difficult to sustain.

There are other factors militating against federalist interpretations of the euro crisis and its resolution. Just as the EU's formal constitutional project did, the euro has created and stoked conflicts that may not have otherwise existed. In the mid-2000s, the CT brought to the fore tensions between proponents of more and less integrated visions for Europe. The failure of the Constitution was a victory for those who favoured a looser union of states. Now the crisis of the eurozone is increasingly highlighting the vastly different economic and political philosophies, not to mention needs, of its member states. German thrift and Southern European profligacy; German concern for an independent central bank and French statism are coming into conflict where, without a common currency, they could have peacefully co-existed. Likewise, the emphasis on austerity measures may please Angela Merkel and the German electorate, but it will not resolve the underlying issues, including weak growth, rising unemployment and lack of competitiveness, which plague many eurozone economies.

From the outset of the crisis, economic pain combined with political disenfranchisement has fed anti-European sentiment across the Union, as populist parties sought to capitalise on citizens' frustrations. The rise of the extreme right Golden Dawn party in Greece, discussed in Chapter 4, is one of the most notable examples, but there are others. In Finland, the populist True Finns party was able to tap into widespread public dissatisfaction over European bailout policies in the April 2011 parliamentary elections, in which it polled third with 19% of the vote (Worth 2011). Finland's coalition government was concerned enough about the popular appeal of the True Finns – who, like Golden Dawn, combine anti-EU rhetoric with racist anti-immigrant sentiment – to take a tougher stance on the euro crisis, with Finland becoming the only country to demand collateral from bailout recipients in return for rescue funds (Milne 2012).[13] Longstanding populist figures, such as Marine Le Pen in France and Geert Wilders in the Netherlands, have also recalibrated their rhetoric, making the EU and eurozone policies much more prominent targets (Traynor 2013a, 2013b).

Populist political figures and tabloid media outlets have not only directed their vitriol at the EU and its institutions. More worryingly, the crisis has also brought ugly and divisive national stereotypes to the fore. For example, the German tabloid *Bild* (Germany's highest circulation newspaper) began a concerted campaign against 'lazy Greeks' in 2010, pushing the idea in article after article that Greeks and other feckless southerners were cheating hard-working Germans out of their money (Guerot 2012: 3). This produced a racially tinged tit-for-tat exchange, a lowlight of which was the use of Nazi imagery in the Greek press and calls from some Greek politicians for Germany to return gold allegedly stolen from the Greek central bank during the Nazi occupation (Crossland 2010). The danger is that efforts to create a more perfect fiscal union will only exacerbate these fundamental national differences.

From an institutional point of view, the marginalisation of the supranational European Parliament and the elevation of the European Council have been among the most striking consequences of the crisis (Tsoukalis 2011: 31–35). This suggests that the new economic governance architecture will not realise the failed CT's federalising potential. However, neither is it faithful to the Lisbon Treaty's constitutionally pluralist model of 'parallel and overlapping spheres' (Cooper 2010: 1–4), in which both member states and Union retain a hard core of legal autonomy. The Fiscal Compact's proposal to submit national budgets for external review, for example, is a direct threat to this requirement. It is also a significant usurpation of one of the most fundamental prerogatives of national parliaments. The Compact's centralised intergovernmentalism thus privileges the EU's largest and economically most powerful states at the expense of smaller and weaker states. Given Britain's non-participation, the treaty risks being resented by other European governments and electorates as a symbol of the Franco-German *directoire* that characterised the 2009–12 period (Fabbrini 2013: 1018–19).

Mattias Kumm (2006: 516) argued that when it came to the relationship between national and European law, to focus on the 'Schmittian question' – who has the final say? – was to miss the point. However, despite the remarkable inroads made by informal EU constitutionalism, *politics*, rather than law, ultimately governs the relationships among member states, and between them and the Union's supranational institutions. Therefore, the importance of the 'Schmittian question' cannot be underestimated, especially in times of crisis. There must always be an ultimate rule, even if it is only tested in emergencies. The euro crisis is, undoubtedly, an emergency and it is proving that, in the case of the EU, it is still national political institutions that have the final say (Abelshauser 2010: 1–2). The post-Lisbon Treaty constitutional settlement was able to accommodate this political reality within a legal framework of qualified EU supranationalism. In their efforts to save the common currency, European leaders ignore the lessons from the EU's almost decade-long project of constitutional reform at their own peril. The push towards a more centralised Europe may end up damaging the very project it seeks to further: European unity.

The end of integration via constitutionalisation: what role for courts in the euro crisis?

From the EEC's inauguration in 1958, the ECJ quickly established itself as a key pro-integrationist force and significant political actor, despite its ostensibly judicial mandate. More than five decades later, however, it seems that integration via court-led constitutionalisation has passed its high point. There are several reasons for this, chief amongst them the greater political salience of European issues in the age of constraining dissensus. The expansion of EU-level competences into politically sensitive areas helped to explode the fiction that Community (and, now, Union) law was merely the apolitical, technical instrument of a self-contained supranational legal system. Just as it was impossible to maintain a separation between economics and politics (Majone 2012: 12–14), so too it has proved with law and politics.

The euro crisis has further altered the dynamics of EU constitutionalism by creating a state of exception in the eurozone and the EU more broadly. Flexibility and decisiveness are critically important in a situation in which the solvency of individual states, and the stability of the currency union as a whole, hinges on the reactions of volatile markets. The urgency of the state of exception has exposed the limitations of the Union's legislative mechanisms, which work via a long and slow process of interest consultation and institutional bargaining amongst the Commission, Council and Parliament. The bypassing of those mechanisms, in turn, affects the ECJ's jurisdiction and its ability to play a role in the EU's future.

Thus, the euro crisis has expedited the ECJ's transformation from vanguard of European integration to laggard. *Pringle v Ireland* illustrates this point. The case arose out of a complaint brought by Thomas Pringle, an independent Irish parliamentarian, against the ESM Treaty.[14] Amongst other things, Pringle asserted that the Treaty's ratification should have been put to a referendum, as is required by Irish law whenever sovereign powers are transferred to an international organisation. The Irish government, however, had decided that a popular vote on the ESM Treaty was unnecessary, because it was authorised by an EU treaty provision (the amended Article 136 TFEU) that had been adopted under the simplified revision procedure in Article 48(6) TEU. As decisions taken under that procedure cannot increase the EU's competences, they should not trigger Ireland's referendum requirement. The Irish government argued that this logic extended to its ratification of the ESM Treaty.

Pringle's case eventually reached Ireland's Supreme Court, which found that the ESM Treaty did not involve an impermissible transfer of sovereignty. Nevertheless, it referred three questions to the ECJ for a preliminary ruling.[15] Firstly, was European Council Decision 2011/199, by which Article 136 TFEU was amended to allow for the creation of a euro area stability mechanism, valid? The Irish Supreme Court asked the ECJ to consider this question in light of the use of the simplified revision procedure and also having regard to whether the content of the amendment violated any existing provisions of EU law. Secondly, was a euro area state permitted to enter into an international agreement such as the ESM Treaty, having regard to the existing body of EU law? Thirdly and finally, if Decision 2011/199 were valid, was a member state's right to ratify the ESM Treaty subject to the prior entry into force of the amendment to Article 136 TFEU?[16]

The ECJ delivered its verdict on *Pringle v Ireland* on 27 November 2012. The Court's answers to the three questions were, respectively, yes, yes, and no. The decision was, therefore, a ringing endorsement of the ESM, though one given a full two months after the bailout fund entered into force. Less kindly, it could be described as an unnecessary (if still welcome) assurance given to a new EU vanguard rapidly disappearing from the ECJ's view. To be fair, by taking EMU out of the legal-constitutional realm, the euro rescue has left the Court in a difficult position. The *Pringle* decision suggests not that the ECJ has abdicated its privileged status, but that it has been deposed. Simply put, courts – slow, process-driven and dependent on legal norms – are not capable of deciding on the exception. As Jeremy Rabkin summarised:

> Remote, mysterious, essentially bureaucratic, the ECJ is a mirror of the EU, itself: it can process a vast range of technical questions but is not designed to face the supreme crises that may still confront Europeans in the course of human events.
>
> (Rabkin 2012: 94)

Rabkin's description of the ECJ is almost a negative mirror image of the picture drawn by Eric Stein (1981) more than thirty years ago. It is as though the physical and metaphorical aloofness that allowed the ECJ to implement a pro-integrationist agenda steadily and stealthily for so many years, has transformed into a disconnectedness, which handicaps the Court as it tries vainly to lead from behind.

The *Pringle* decision was also interesting for its implications for the ECJ's jurisdiction over the institutions and mechanisms created to counter the crisis. In relation to the second question referred by the Irish Supreme Court, it was submitted to the ECJ that it lacked jurisdiction to interpret provisions of the ESM Treaty, because it is an international treaty to which the EU is not a party. The ECJ circumvented the issue by stating that the real question to be answered was whether EU treaty law supported the creation of a stability mechanism by member states whose currency is the euro. As such, the Court was only required to interpret provisions of the TEU and TFEU and so was on solid jurisdictional ground.[17] The ECJ offered no comment on its jurisdiction, or lack thereof, in relation to the ESM and so the question remains open.

Though it may seem like a counterpoint to the ECJ's declining importance, the GCC's decision on the constitutionality of the ESM and Fiscal Compact is, in fact, further testimony to the inadequacy of judicial power in times of crisis. In comments made in the lead-up to Karlsruhe's preliminary verdict in September 2012, Court President Andreas Voßkuhle lamented the pace and frenzy of politics, claiming that it needed 'more moments of deceleration, [and] phases of reflection, in order to contemplate fundamental decisions' (Hildebrand and Jungholt 2012). Voßkuhle's sentiments were not shared by anxious EU officials and other observers. The description in *The Economist*

(2012a) of the GCC's judges as 'scandalously slow' was closer to the frustration felt by many at the Court's disproportionate influence over the eurozone rescue measures. At any rate, the Court's eventual delivery of another 'yes, but ... ' verdict continued the pattern of law's deference to politics and courts' deference to executive sovereign authority in matters of crisis resolution.

Even where national courts did exert their authority in a manner contrary to crisis imperatives, it was unclear how much influence their decisions would have over substantive policy outcomes. On 5 April 2013, the Portuguese Constitutional Court ruled that several of the austerity measures included in the government's 2013 budget were unconstitutional. The government had adopted the impugned measures in order to meet targets negotiated with the troika as part of Portugal's bailout, and their rejection by the Court caused considerable consternation in both Lisbon and Brussels (Minder 2013). Whilst the Portuguese government was quick to reassure its European partners of its commitment to meeting the agreed-upon austerity targets, the European Commission nevertheless felt compelled to comment on the situation, issuing a pointed reminder about the importance of Portugal fulfilling its obligations:

> The European Commission welcomes that, following the decision of the Portuguese Constitutional Court on the 2013 state budget, the Portuguese Government has confirmed its commitment to the adjustment programme, including its fiscal targets and timeline. Any departure from the pro-gramme's objectives, or their re-negotiation, would in fact neutralise the efforts already made and achieved by the Portuguese citizens, namely the growing investor confidence in Portugal, and prolong the difficulties from the adjustment ... The Commission reiterates that a strong consensus around the programme will contribute to its successful implementation. In this respect, it is essential that Portugal's key political institutions are united in their support.
>
> (European Commission, 7 April 2013)

Clearly, the Commission – as one of Portugal's creditors – had an interest in ensuring that the country complied with its austerity programme. However, its statement was remarkable for its willingness to interfere in a domestic matter and for its treatment of the Constitutional Court's verdict as a hindrance that could not be allowed to cause deviation from Portugal's troika-approved path. The Commission did not criticise the Court's verdict so much as it disregarded it, essentially reaffirming the primacy of emergency measures over law.

A new hero for a new mode of integration?

The diminishing importance of courts and the use of international treaties to establish crisis management tools are two examples of how the Community method has been bypassed during the course of the euro crisis. The politici-sation of the ECB is another manifestation of this trend. As the ability of courts to shape the integration project wanes, the ECB is emerging as a potential successor to the ECJ's pro-integrationist mantle. The same structural asymmetries that once privileged judicial law making (due to the difficulty of taking political action at the European level) (Scharpf 2009: 5–13), now favour a new group of economically focused eurozone institutions – though their promotion is also creating a new set of risks for European integration.

EMU was perhaps the most important symbol of the push for ever-closer union that was re-energised by the Maastricht Treaty. It represented both the denouement of Franco-German reconciliation and a bold, new step forward for a post-Cold War European project brimming with confidence and optimism. It was also symbolic of the presumed relationship between economic integration and political integration that has informed much of integration theory. In line with the neofunctionalist concept of spillover, many EU leaders and scholars thought that monetary union would be the first step towards economic and political union.[18] These hopes proved unfounded. Despite a significant narrowing of bond yields within the eurozone in the early years of monetary union, the creation of EMU did not lead to real economic convergence amongst national economies, or to greater supranational fiscal coordination amongst eurozone members. On the contrary, the 'sheer incongruousness of the euro's membership' proved to be a constant problem, which the crisis has only made much more visible (Marsh 2011: 47–48).

The decision to proceed with European-level monetary union without a commensurate level of fiscal and political union meant that the ECB was always operating in sub-optimal conditions. Though often viewed as technocratic regulatory institutions *par excellence,* national central banks are also important cogs in national political machines. Their monetary policy decisions do not operate in a vacuum, and cannot operate effectively without some degree of coordination with government macroeconomic policy decisions. They are also embedded in national debates, with interest rate decisions subject to media attention and public scrutiny. Hence, though formally independent, national central banks must operate with some level of responsiveness to public opinion (Bellamy 2010: 11).

The ECB, on the other hand, is 'politically and socially "disembedded"' (Majone 2012: 14). There is no EU finance minister and no EU government to administer fiscal policy for the eurozone. Instead, decisions on taxation and public spending are made by national governments on the basis of national priorities determined through national political contestation. Just as its lack of political entrenchment hampers its effectiveness, the absence of a European *demos* damages the ECB's legitimacy. This is especially so given the Bank's singular focus on price stability. Such an approach may be legitimate within a nation state such as Germany, where there is a broad consensus in favour of low inflationary policies, but it does not work at the European level where no such consensus exists.

This lack of embeddedness in a co-extensive political system is one of several interesting parallels between the ECB and the ECJ. Another similarity is that both have narrow bases of legitimacy, which rely on the assumption that they are adhering to rules that were negotiated and ratified by member state governments as the democratically elected representatives of European citizens. A third parallel is that both institutions are formally independent and apolitical, yet both have morphed into important political actors. This phenomenon may be illustrated in relation to the ECB by a few specific examples.

In May 2010, while member states were initiating the first Greek rescue package and the temporary stability mechanisms, the ECB was also moving to shore-up euro area economies. On 10 May, the Bank launched a programme to buy the debt instruments of struggling euro area states on secondary markets. According to then ECB President Jean-Claude Trichet, the so-called Securities Markets Programme was established in response to 'exceptional circumstances prevailing in the financial markets', including the dramatic widening of sovereign bond spreads and the almost total loss of liquidity in some government bond markets (Trichet 2010). By intervening in secondary markets, the ECB avoided the prohibition on direct monetary financing in Article 123 (1) TFEU and Article 18 of the Bank's Charter. However, the move was still highly controversial. Though the indirect purchase of euro area debt instruments is not strictly prohibited, such activities should not be used to circumvent the prohibition on direct financing (Ruffert 2011: 1787–88).

The Securities Markets Programme also raised questions about the strength of the Bank's much vaunted independence in the face of mounting external pressure to act. In this respect, the ECB's cause was not helped by inertia, uncertainty and division amongst European leaders, as the shortcomings of the EU's highly fragmented system of governance became abundantly clear. Trichet acknowledged as much at a speech in Vienna on 31 May 2010, when he urged euro area governments to live up to their responsibilities. After emphasising the importance of 'governments implement[ing] rigorously the measures needed to ensure fiscal sustainability', Trichet claimed that it was only 'in the context of these commitments' that the Bank had launched its initiative.[19] In the same speech, the President defended his institution against accusations that its actions were illegal. He claimed that the Bank's interventions were fully in line with its primary objective of price stability, since effective functioning of government bond markets was necessary for the proper transmission of ECB monetary policies to the real economy. Trichet argued further that the Securities Markets Programme aimed strictly at the correction of 'malfunctioning' markets and, as such, was not a substitute for proper budgetary discipline and could not and would not be used to circumvent the EU treaties (Trichet 2010).

Despite Trichet's protestations that the ECB was incapable of solving the eurozone's deeper problems, the Bank's activities have taken on an increasingly political character. At times, the ECB has appeared to be the only EU institution capable of showing decisive leadership. This is illustrated by the announcement on 6 September 2012 of a vastly expanded bond-buying programme by Trichet's successor, Mario Draghi. Under the new measure, called Outright Monetary

Transactions (OMT), the Bank would purchase the bonds of vulnerable eurozone members in unlimited quantities, albeit subject to strict conditions, including affected states' engagement of the ESM. In justifying the move, Draghi spoke in the same terms that Trichet had more than two years earlier, arguing that the bond purchases did fall within the ECB's mandate because they were necessary for the 'restoration of the proper functioning of monetary policy transmission' (Faigle and Uken 2012). Also like his predecessor, Draghi drew on the rhetoric of exceptional circumstances. In a speech before the German *Bundestag* in October 2012, he outlined the 'increasingly disturbed' state of the euro area financial system, which led the ECB to conclude that 'action was essential', despite the inevitable criticism that would follow (Draghi 2012).

Draghi, himself, has emerged as one of the key leaders of the European integration project and one of the few with the power and credibility to make claims about the eurozone's future. Hence the positive reaction of financial markets when, in July 2012, he declared that the euro was 'irreversible' and that, within its mandate, the ECB was ready to do 'whatever it takes' to preserve it (Moulds 2012). It was put to the ECB President in an interview with *Süddeutsche Zeitung* that the fact that he found it necessary to make such statements suggested an attempt to make up for the failures of EU governance (Hagelüken and Zydra 2012).[20] To be sure, Draghi denied this charge, but it is not without substance. The crisis has exposed inadequacies in the EU's designated political bodies – the Council and the Parliament – that are enabling, even pushing, the ECB to take a bigger role.

Thus, even putting aside the legality of the OMT programme, it is a remarkably bold move for a non-majoritarian and highly 'dis-embedded' institution to take. It cannot plausibly be argued that the ECB has simply selected the 'best' policy option in an objective manner; right or wrong, it is a profoundly political initiative. So far, the ECB has been relatively unscathed by the euro crisis. In fact, its reputation arguably has been enhanced, at least in the eyes of European elites, as evidenced by the fact that it was granted new competences in relation to banking union (Henning 2014). However, this reputational enhancement is based entirely on the ECB's outputs. The Bank has no input legitimacy to fall back on should it falter in delivering its mandate. Moreover, by becoming involved in banking supervision and regulation, the ECB has taken on considerable additional risks that are not mitigated by any degree of democratic accountability. A similar point may be made about OMT, which has worked so far because it has not been tested. It is an emergency parachute that, if actually pulled, may turn out to be an anvil that brings the ECB's credibility crashing to Earth.

The Bank's expanded role will also expose it to severe political pressure in the future, as its decisions on whether or not to offer support, and under what conditions to do so, could make or break a vulnerable euro state's financial viability, with the attendant consequences for the national economy and political and societal stability. The situation in Cyprus in March 2013 illustrated this danger. Having asked for financial aid from the troika, an agreement was struck between the Cypriot government and the Eurogroup, whereby Cyprus would receive a ten billion euro bailout, on the condition that it raised a further six billion euros itself, including through the unprecedented move of imposing a one-off levy on bank deposits over 20,000 euros. This deal fell through when it was voted down by the Cypriot parliament on 19 March 2013, following vociferous opposition within Cyprus and abroad, and amidst fears of a bank run. However, the ECB issued an ultimatum on Thursday 21 March, demanding that Cyprus secure an EU/IMF bailout before Monday 25 March, otherwise the Bank would withdraw its emergency liquidity assistance from the country's troubled banking sector, likely leading to its collapse (Wearden and Amos 2013).

There are, then, some echoes of the ECJ in the ECB's assumption of a more active role in shaping the integration project. However, the context in which the Bank operates today has changed dramatically from the Court's heyday. Unlike the 1960s, when the ECJ delivered some of its most famous and consequential constitutionalising verdicts, the europeanisation 'revolution' today is no longer quiet, and Frankfurt is certainly no 'fairyland Duchy of Luxembourg' (Stein 1981: 1). The big questions of European integration – How far should it go? What form should it take? – are very much contested within and across member states.[21] Entrusting so much responsibility for the financial management of the eurozone to the ECB may seem expedient, but it is not sustainable. Indeed, one wonders how long arguments predicated on the 'temporary' or 'exceptional' nature of the circumstances can hold their validity.

Concluding remarks: politicisation without democratisation

> European integration is a political process which is reversible once its output turns negative and/or the political support for it vanishes.
>
> (Zimmerman and Dür 2012: 2)

This may seem an obvious statement; certainly it is borne out by the EU's recent travails. Yet, as Hubert Zimmerman and Andreas Dür (2012: 3) noted, scholars have too often taken the integration project for granted, viewing the EU – for all its flaws – as an 'unambiguously positive force in European and global history'. Analyses based on such assumptions are incomplete, however, because by ignoring Philippe Schmitter's (2004: 47) observation that '[a]ny comprehensive theory of integration should potentially be a theory of disintegration', they preclude serious consideration of reforms that, though they involve less Europe, may improve the EU's stability and viability.

As the euro crisis entered its fourth year, several EU leaders confidently declared that Europe had turned the corner and was on the road to recovery.[22] Even if such claims prove accurate in relation to the acute phase of the crisis (i.e. the vicious cycle between heavily indebted sovereigns and weak banks), they certainly fail to grasp the broader constitutional reconfiguration that these events have triggered. Part of that reconfiguration affects the way in which law is deployed in pursuit of closer union. For several decades, law was a key instrument in the EU's construction, and those charged with interpreting and implementing EU law formed an integrationist vanguard. This has now changed to a significant degree. Since 2010, the eurozone – increasingly the EU's centre of gravity – has been de-legalised and EU law 'replaced by governmental and administrative operations outside the rule of law' (Joerges 2012: 1015–16). Unfortunately, as argued above, the main beneficiaries of this shifting balance of power have not been democratic political bodies, such as the European Parliament, but rather technocratic institutions, such as the ECB.

In fact, a principal irony of the EU's recent constitutional journey is the changing stance of its leaders towards the politicisation of European integration. The CT project was undertaken with the intention of engaging European citizens and encouraging their identification with the values and goals of *their* European Union. It was conceived of as an explicitly politicised antidote to the EU's effective, but dry, functional constitution. Yet, attempts to solicit public input into the CT at all stages from drafting to ratification were met largely with a mixture of apathy, ignorance and, ultimately, rejection. Therefore, part of the legacy of that crisis of EU constitutionalism – encapsulated in the form taken by the LT and the methods of its ratification – was a retreat from the CT's lofty ideal of democratisation via politicisation. Now, several years later, as a result of the second of the twin crises, the project of European integration has become well and truly politicised and European policies highly salient for national voters. However, this process has occurred largely against the will of EU leaders, who have sought technocratic solutions to what are inherently political problems. Thus, over the course of a decade the EU moved from an unsuccessful attempt at democratisation via politicisation, to an unintended politicisation without democratisation.

Joseph Weiler (1999: 4) described public dissent over the Maastricht Treaty as 'deliciously hostile', because it drew attention to a process that had too long gone unnoticed and unremarked by most Europeans. Popular debates sparked by Maastricht, particularly as they cut across national lines, were to be celebrated because they indicated the emergence, at long last, of a European public sphere. More than twenty years later, there is no shortage of public debate and hostility in relation to the handling of the euro crisis, but it is no longer delicious. On the contrary, the fragility of the financial and economic situation in the eurozone combined with inadequate EU-level democratic outlets and official policy responses that tend towards executive federalism, are fostering conditions under which the integration process may well become reversible.

Notes

1 In an opinion piece for the *Wall Street Journal*, co-written with Marian Tupy, Sulik argued:

After the fall of the Berlin Wall, Slovakia underwent painful but necessary economic reforms, with the burden of the transition to capitalism squarely on the shoulders of the Slovak people. Meanwhile, Greeks were enjoying artificial prosperity stimulated by government borrowing and spending. The average income in Slovakia was $17,889 in 2011; in Greece, it was $27,875. The average Slovak pension was $491 in 2010; in Greece, it was $1,775. Slovakia's national debt is 45% of GDP; Greek debt is approaching 160%. Yet Slovakia is now being asked to borrow in order to lend to Greece, thereby sacrificing its relatively high credit rating and low interest rates. Is this solidarity?

(Sulik and Tupy 2012)

2 Christine Lagarde, then French Finance Minister, was unusually candid about the dubious legality of the rescue, stating:

In the EU Treaty of Lisbon it stands: An EU state may not help another EU state that finds itself in financial difficulties. Yet the Greek-rescue plan leads exactly to that. Also the euro rescue package is not envisaged in the Lisbon Treaty. Nevertheless we have created a comprehensive rescue system – and have gone beyond the existing rules in order to achieve it.

(Kläsgen and Ulrich 2010)

3 Rather convolutedly, the decision was described in Council document 9614/10 of 10 May 2010 as a 'Decision of the Representatives of the Governments of the Euro Area Member States Meeting within the Council of the European Union'.
4 The amendment added the following text to Article 136 TFEU: 'The Member States whose currency is the euro may establish a stability mechanism to be acti-vated if indispensable to safeguard the stability of the euro area as a whole. The granting of any required financial assistance under the mechanism will be made subject to strict conditionality'.
5 Though, in a curious mixing of jurisdictions, there is provision for internal disputes to be adjudicated, in the last resort, by the ECJ (Article 37(3) TESM).
6 The ESM became effective on 27 September 2012, the date on which the General Secretariat of the Council received notification of German ratification. It was inaugurated by a meeting of the eurozone Finance Ministers in Luxembourg on 8 October 2012 (Kanter 2012).
7 See Case C-370/12 *Pringle v Ireland* [2012], paragraphs 183–85. This case is discussed further in the next section.
8 This episode also has repercussions for British–EU relations. It signals a deepening rift between the two parties that is being exacerbated by the pressure being placed on David Cameron by the eurosceptic wing of his own Conservative Party (*The Economist*, 2011a). The Prime Minister's speech on 23 January 2013, in which he called for a renegotiation of the EU treaties to be followed by an 'in or out' refer-endum on Britain's EU membership, is dramatic evidence of the escalation of this rift (Cameron 2013).
9 For example, Article 2(1) of the Fiscal Compact states that: 'This Treaty shall be applied and interpreted by the Contracting Parties in conformity with the Trea-ties ... and with European Union law ... '. Article 2(2) continues, '[t]he provisions of this Treaty shall apply insofar as they are compatible with the Treaties on which the Union is founded and with European Union law. They shall not encroach upon the competences of the Union to act in the area of the economic union.'
10 For a discussion of the importance of 'constitutional moments' in the American context, see Bruce Ackerman (1989). In the European context, Philippe Schmitter (2000: 45) noted that one problem with the EU's attempt at explicit constitutionalisation

was its timing – coming several decades after the Union's founding moment and in the absence of any national emergency akin to that which energised America's founding fathers in the 1780s.

11 German Social Democratic Party (SPD) leader, Sigmar Gabriel (2011), took a similar view that the crisis calls for political union. On the other hand, as noted, David Cameron saw a different sort of opportunity, flagging the possibility of using the crisis to push for a repatriation of powers from Brussels.

12 The supremacy of the Franco-German tandem became almost a caricature in the latter part of French President Nicolas Sarkozy's tenure, with he and German Chancellor Angela Merkel earning the collective moniker 'Merkozy'. The joint declaration made at Deauville in October 2010 regarding the need for an amendment to the treaties (described above) was just one example of the ability of the Franco–German partnership to virtually dictate the agenda to the other member states and EU institutions. Since 2012, however, France's role has receded, with Germany cementing its position as the EU's dominant power.

13 In an article in the *Financial Times*, a senior Finnish Social Democrat is quoted as saying of the True Finns: 'I wouldn't say we stole their clothing at all. But we did move a little in their direction, and I think that is in line with the mood of the Finnish people' (Milne 2012).

14 For a detailed account of Pringle's submissions on the incompatibility of the TESM with Union law, see Jonathan Tomkin (2013).

15 *Thomas Pringle v The Government of Ireland, Ireland and the Attorney General* [2012] IESC 47.

16 Case C-370/12 *Pringle v Ireland* [2012], paragraph 28.

17 Case C-370/12, paragraphs 78–81.

18 On the political ambitions that drove EMU, Marsh (2011: 46) quoted Ruud Lubbers, Dutch Prime Minister at the time of the Maastricht Treaty as saying: 'I thought that the euro would be so successful that it would lead to political union and that it would be attractive for other states to join. This was a mistake'.

19 Trichet stated further:

> Since our inception, we have always called upon governments to respect budgetary discipline. We had a lot of difficulty with several governments during the last ten years, both as regards their own national responsibilities and as regards their collegial responsibilities of peer surveillance in the Eurogroup. This period is over. We expect from governments strict respect for the principle of budgetary discipline and effective mutual surveillance.
>
> (Trichet 2010)

20 The interviewers suggested that Draghi was speaking like 'the Chancellor of Europe' by saying that the euro was irreversible. He responded as follows:

> I am communicating this message as the President of the ECB to all stakeholders, citizens, businesses and markets. Investors need a long-term vision because they undertake long-term commitments. For them, it is very important that our leaders and governments are determined to keep the euro irreversible. So, if I say this, *I am saying what our political leaders are fundamentally saying*.
>
> (Hagelüken and Zydra 2012, emphasis added)

21 Ulrike Guerot (2012: 7) observed in relation to Germany that political polarisation and legal uncertainty had created a situation whereby 'the government *de facto* leaves rescue actions to the ECB'.

22 In June 2013, Council President Herman Van Rompuy declared that the euro was no longer 'under existential threat', joining the likes of French President François Hollande and Spanish Prime Minister Mariano Rajoy who had previously asserted that the worst of the crisis had passed (Faiola and Cody 2013; Hope 2013).

References

Abelshauser, W. (2010) 'It's *Not* the Economy Stupid! Die politische Ökonomie der europäischen Integration in der Krise'. *Zeitschrift für Staats und Europawissenschaften*, No. 1, pp. 1–23.

Ackerman, B. (1989) 'Constitutional Politics/Constitutional Law'. *The Yale Law Journal*, Vol. 99, No. 3, pp. 453–547.

Amtenbrink, F. (2012) 'Legal Developments'. *Journal of Common Market Studies*, Vol. 50, Annual Review, pp. 132–64.

Auer, S. (2013) 'Richard Sulik: A Provincial or a European Slovak Politician?' *Humanities Research*, Vol. XIX, No. 1, pp. 81–100.

Barroso, J. M. (2011) 'The Speed of the European Union Can No Longer Be the Speed of the Most Reluctant Member'. *The Observer*, 13 November.

Beck, U. (2009) 'This Economic Crisis Cries Out to Be Transformed into the Founding of a New Europe'. *The Guardian*, 13 April.

——(2011a) 'Cooperate or Bust: The Existential Crisis of the European Union'. *Eurozine*, 29 September, pp. 1–11.

——(2011b) 'Europe's Crisis is an Opportunity for Democracy'. *The Guardian*, 28 November.

Bellamy, R. (2010) 'Democracy without Democracy? Can the EU's Democratic "Outputs" Be Separated from the Democratic "Inputs" Provided by Competitive Parties and Majority Rule?' *Journal of European Public Policy*, Vol. 17, No. 1, pp. 2–19.

Buras, P. (2013) 'The EU's Silent Revolution'. *ECFR Policy Brief*, Vol. 87, September, pp. 1–8.

Cameron, D. (2013) 'David Cameron's EU speech – Full Text'. *The Guardian*, 23 January.

Cooper, I. (2010) 'Mapping the Overlapping Spheres: European Constitutionalism after the Treaty of Lisbon'. *ARENA Centre for European Studies Seminar Paper*, pp. 1–32.

Crossland, D. (2010) 'Germans and Greeks Get Nasty over Debt'. *The National*, 28 February.

Curtin, D. (1993) 'The Constitutional Structure of the Union: A Europe of Bits and Pieces'. *Common Market Law Review*, Vol. 30, No. 1, pp. 17–69.

De Witte, B. (2011) 'The European Treaty Amendment for the Creation of a Financial Stability Mechanism'. *SIEPS European Policy Analysis*, No. 6, pp. 1–8.

Draghi, M. (2012) 'Opening Statement at Deutscher Bundestag'. *European Central Bank, Press and Information Division*, 24 October, available at www.ecb.int/press/key/date/2012/html/sp121024.en.html (Accessed: 25 March 2014).

European Commission (2013) *Statement by the European Commission on Portugal*, Brussels, MEMO/13/307, 7 April.

European Parliament (2011) *Resolution on the Draft European Council Decision Amending Article 136 of the Treaty on the Functioning of the European Union with Regard to a Stability Mechanism for Member States Whose Currency Is the Euro*, document P7_TA(2011)0103, 23 March.

Fabbrini, S. (2013) 'Intergovernmentalism and Its Limits: Assessing the European Union's Answer to the Euro Crisis'. *Comparative Political Studies*, Vol. 46, No. 9, pp. 1003–29.

Faigle, P. and Uken, M. (2012) 'Mario erklärt Makroökonomie'. *Die Zeit*, 24 October.

Faiola, A. and Cody, E. (2013) 'European Leaders Hail Breakthrough in Debt Crisis'. *The Washington Post*, 5 January.

Follesdal, A. and Hix, S. (2006) 'Why There Is a Democratic Deficit in the EU: A Response to Majone and Moravcsik'. *Journal of Common Market Studies*, Vol. 44, No. 3, pp. 533–62.

Gabriel, S. (2011) 'Was wir Europa wirklich schulden'. *Frankfurter Allgemeine Zeitung*, 13 December.

Guerot, U. (2012) 'The Euro Debate in Germany: Towards Political Union?' *European Council on Foreign Relations: Reinvention of Europe Project*, pp. 1–9.

Haas, E. (1958) *The Uniting of Europe: Political, Social and Economic Forces* (Stanford, CA: Stanford University Press).

——(1964) *Beyond the Nation-State: Functionalism and International Organization* (Stanford, CA: Stanford University Press).

Habermas, J. (1998) 'The European Nation-State: On the Past and Future of Sovereignty and Citizenship'. In Cronin, C. and De Greif, P. (eds) *The Inclusion of the Other: Studies in Political Theory* (Cambridge, MA: MIT Press).

——(2011a) 'Europe's Post-Democratic Era'. *The Guardian*, 10 November.

——(2011b) 'Merkels von Demoskopie geleiteter Opportunismus'. *Süddeutsche Zeitung*, 7 April.

Hagelüken, A. and Zydra, M. (2012) 'Interview with *Süddeutsche Zeitung*: Mario Draghi, President of the ECB', *Republished by European Central Bank, Press and Information Division*, 14 September, available at www.ecb.int/press/key/date/2012/html/sp120914.en.html (Accessed: 25 March 2014).

Hanke, T. (1998) '155 Professoren fordern die Verschiebung der Währungsunion'. *Die Zeit*, 12 February.

Henning, C. R. (2014) 'The ECB to the Rescue: The Brave New World of Central Banking in the Euro Area'. *Paper presented at the 21st International Conference of the Council for European Studies*, Washington DC, 14–16 March.

Hildebrand, J. and Jungholt, T. (2012) 'Alles zerrt am Verfassungsgericht'. *Die Welt*, 11 September.

Hope, C. (2013) 'The Euro Is Safe, Declares European Council Chief'. *The Telegraph*, 17 June.

Joerges, C. (2012) 'Recht und Politik in der Krise Europas: Die Wirkungsgeschichte einer verunglückten Konfiguration'. *Merkur*, Vol. 66, No. 11, pp. 1013–24.

Jones, E. (2012) 'Europe's Threatened Solidarity'. *Current History*, Vol. 111, No. 743, pp. 88–93.

Kanter, J. (2012) 'Europe Still at Odds over the Workings of Its Bailout Fund'. *New York Times*, 7 October.

Karacs, I. (1998) 'Kohl Fights to Restore Confidence after Call to Delay EMU'. *The Independent*, 10 February.

Kläsgen, M. and Ulrich, S. (2010) '"Wir werden bedingungslos sparen"'. *Süddeutsche Zeitung*, 23 December.

Kumm, M. (2006) 'Beyond Golf Clubs and the Judicialization of Politics: Why Europe has a Constitution Properly So Called'. *The American Journal of Constitutional Law*, Vol. 54, Fall, pp. 505–30.

Louis, J.-V. (2010) 'The No-Bailout Clause and Rescue Packages'. *Common Market Law Review*, Vol. 47, No. 4, pp. 971–86.

Majone, G. (2011) 'Monetary Union and the Politicization of Europe'. *Keynote speech at the Euroacademia International Conference: 'The European Union and the Politicization of Europe'*, Vienna, 8–10 December.

——(2012) 'Rethinking European Integration after the Debt Crisis'. *UCL: The European Institute, Working Paper No. 3/2012*, June.

Marsh, D. (2011) 'Faltering Ambitions and Unrequited Hopes: The Battle for the Euro Intensifies'. *Journal of Common Market Studies*, Vol. 49, Annual Review, pp. 45–55.

Milne, R. (2012) 'True Finns Keep Europe on National Agenda'. *Financial Times*, 24 September.

Minder, R. (2013) 'Portugal Warns Citizens of More Economic Pain'. *New York Times*, 8 April.

Moravcsik, A. (2008) 'The European Constitutional Settlement'. *World Economy*, Vol. 31, No. 1, pp. 158–84.

Moulds, J. (2012) 'Euro Is Irreversible, Declares European Central Bank President Mario Draghi'. *The Guardian*, 26 July.

Rabkin, J. (2012) 'The European Court of Justice: A Strange Institution'. In Zimmerman, H. and Dür, A. (eds) *Key Controversies in European Integration* (Basingstoke: Palgrave Macmillan).

Ruffert, M. (2011) 'The European Debt Crisis and European Union Law'. *Common Market Law Review*, Vol. 48, No. 6, pp. 1777–1806.

Ruhkamp, S. (2013) 'Deutsche sind die Ärmsten im Euroraum'. *Frankfurter Allgemeine Zeitung*, 9 April.

Scharpf, F. (2009) 'The Double Asymmetry of European Integration. Or: Why the EU Cannot Be a Social Market Economy'. *Max-Planck-Institut für Gesellschaftsforschung, MPIfG Working Paper 09/12*, November 2009.

Schmitter, P. C. (1970) 'A Revised Theory of Regional Integration'. *International Organization*, Vol. 24, No. 4, pp. 836–68.

——(2000) 'Federalism and the Euro-Polity'. *Journal of Democracy*, Vol. 11, No. 1, pp. 40–47.

——(2004) 'Neo-Neofunctionalism'. In Wiener, A. and Diez, T. (eds) *European Integration Theory* (Oxford: Oxford University Press).

Schuman, R. (1950) 'The Schuman Declaration'. Available at http://europa.eu/about-eu/basic-information/symbols/europe-day/schuman-declaration/ (Accessed: 25 March 2014).

Spiegel Online (2010) 'Merkel Warns of Europe's Collapse: "If Euro Fails, So Will the Idea of European Union"'. 13 May.

Stein, E. (1981) 'Lawyers, Judges and the Making of a Transnational Constitution'. *American Journal of International Law*, Vol. 75, No. 1, pp. 1–27.

Steltzner, H. (2013a) 'Arme Deutsche'. *Frankfurter Allgemeine Zeitung*, 9 April.

——(2013b) 'Reiche Zyprer, arme Deutsche'. *Frankfurter Allgemeine Zeitung*, 11 April.

Sulik, R. and Tupy, M. L. (2012) 'The Limits of European Solidarity'. *Wall Street Journal*, 15 February.

The Economist (2011a) 'Britain, Not Leaving but Falling out of the EU'. 9 December.

——(2011b) 'The German Problem'. 19 November.

——(2012a) 'The Flight from Spain'. 28 July.

——(2012b) 'The Future of the European Union: The Choice'. 26 May.

Tomkin, J. (2013) 'Contradiction, Circumvention and Conceptual Gymnastics: The Impact of the Adoption of the ESM Treaty on the State of European Democracy'. *German Law Journal*, Vol. 14, No. 1, pp. 169–90.

Traynor, I. (2010) 'France and Germany Hijack Strict New Eurozone Budget Regime'. *The Guardian*, 19 October.

——(2013a) 'Europe's Protest Parties on the March'. *The Guardian*, 1 March.

——(2013b) 'Le Pen and Wilders Forge Plan to "Wreck" EU from Within'. *The Guardian*, 13 November.

Trichet, J.-C. (2010) 'The ECB's Response to the Recent Tensions in Financial Markets'. *Speech given at the 38th Economic Conference of the Oesterreichische Nationalbank*, Vienna, 31 May.

Tsoukalis, L. (2011) 'The Shattering of Illusions – And What Next?' *Journal of Common Market Studies*, Vol. 49, Annual Review, pp. 19–44.

Wearden, G. and Amos, H. (2013) 'Cyprus Crisis: Politicians Race to Agree Details of "Plan B"'. *The Guardian*, 22 March.

Webber, D. (2013) 'How Likely Is It that the European Union Will *Dis*integrate? A Critical Analysis of Competing Theoretical Perspectives'. *European Journal of International Relations*, published online 4 January 2013. DOI: 10.1177/ 1354066112461286, pp. 1–25.

Weiler, J. H. H. (1999) *The Constitution of Europe: 'Do the New Clothes Have an Emperor?' And Other Essays on European Integration* (Cambridge: Cambridge University Press).

Worth, J. (2011) 'The True Finns Followed a Well-Known Recipe for Success'. *The Guardian*, 21 April.

Zimmerman, H. and Dür, A. (2012) 'Introduction: Key Controversies in European Integration'. In Zimmerman, H. and Dür, A. (eds) *Key Controversies in European Integration* (Basingstoke: Palgrave Macmillan).

Conclusion

Confronting the crisis of EU constitutionalism

The EU is a fundamentally contested project, a fact that is nowhere clearer than at the intersection of law and politics. In the second half of the twentieth century, judicially led constitutionalisation made remarkable inroads in establishing the EU as a cohesive and law bound polity, capable of extending its reach across new member states and policy areas. Nevertheless, integration through law peaked around the time of the Maastricht Treaty – although functionally successful, the EU's uncodified constitution was symbolically weak, lacking in democratic legitimacy and, therefore, unable to provide adequate support for an ambitious new phase of supranational integration.[1] Over the last decade, EU constitutionalism has been instead framed by the twin crises of the failure of the Constitutional Treaty and the near unravelling of the eurozone. Both the CT and EMU illustrate the tendency of EU policymakers to place undue faith in law as a means of furthering political objectives, and their crises form the backbone of this book's analysis of the integration project.

The CT was drafted with the interrelated aims of filling the symbolic lacuna of EU constitutionalism, facilitating the growth of an incipient European *demos*, and bringing the remote, mysterious and bureaucratic EU closer to its citizens. As Chapter 2 argued, its defeat in 2005 was a failure on all three counts, and served instead to highlight the large and growing elite–public gap over the desirable scope of further integration. Thus, the decision to abandon the form and rhetoric of a capital 'C' Constitution in favour of the tried and true method of intergovernmental treaty making was a significant setback to federalist conceptions of, and hopes for, the European Union (Christiansen 2008). Moreover, the shift from the CT to the LT also altered the EU's uncodified, functional constitution. Again, the shift was one from constitutional centralisation to constitutional diffusion, or from the idea of integration as hierarchy to integration as 'parallel and overlapping spheres' of national and European influence (Cooper 2010).

This shift not only struck a better balance between the EU's multiple sites of authority, it was also more in keeping with national understandings of the

EU legal system, as exemplified by the German example given in Chapter 3. The German Constitutional Court long has been a counterweight to the ECJ and to the federalist emphasis of its jurisprudence. It established a reputation for being a voice of caution, or even euroscepticism, within the German constitutional system with its decisions on the adequacy of supranational fundamental rights protections and the legality of the Maastricht Treaty. This is a role the Court has continued to play since the onset of the euro crisis, and which requires it to plot a course between safeguarding national democratic statehood and being open towards supranational integration, both imperatives that are enshrined in the Basic Law. The GCC's engagement with the euro crisis is made all the more fascinating by the fact that it takes place against the backdrop of Germany's contentious but, nevertheless, growing leadership role in the Union.

Across Europe, the crisis has fed perceptions that the EU is not able to effectively and efficiently address the economic, political and social challenges facing the member states; that, in fact, its overbearing and overly bureaucratic institutions and processes may be part of the problem. This is the political dimension of the economic crisis and, over the last few years, it has fuelled a significant rise in euroscepticism within the eurozone and beyond. At a European level, the effects of this trend were reflected in the results of the May 2014 EP elections. Eurosceptics and parties of the far left and right had their biggest successes in the UK, France, Denmark and Greece, where the elections were won by UKIP, the National Front, the Danish People's Party, and Syriza, respectively (Golden Dawn also won seats in Greece, coming in third place with just over 9% of the vote). Political forces hostile to European integration also made inroads in Austria, Italy, and Germany, amongst others, making up a total of around 30% of the new parliament.[2]

As Chapter 4 detailed, the growing prominence of populist and extremist parties can be explained partly by the impoverishment of national political spheres caused by the peculiar divide between European level 'policy without politics' and national level 'politics without policy' (Schmidt 2009). It also illustrates the fact, seized upon by opportunistic anti-Europeanists such as Marine Le Pen, that the symbolic value of the integration project has turned negative for many European citizens, for whom the EU is a meddlesome and mystifying overlord, rather than a guardian of common European values and custodian of a common European future.

Like the CT, the common currency project may be analysed in terms of the symbolic and functional dimensions of constitutionalism identified in Chapter 1. The euro was (and still is) both an emblem and an instrument of European integration. As with the formal Constitution's demise, the euro crisis also has consequences for both dimensions. Symbolically, the disintegration of the eurozone would be a major blow to the EU's self-perception as a project dedicated to the attainment and maintenance of peace, prosperity and unity for Europeans.[3] The functional implications of the faltering currency union are even more profound and even more dangerous to the idea of 'ever closer union'. They include institutional reconfiguration, the exacerbation of both national and European level democratic deficits and even the possibility of a member state exiting the EU.

Many of these problems have their origins in the design of the currency union – specifically in the decision to frame it in highly legalistic terms, despite the project's inherently political nature. The attempt to prescribe euro states' behaviour via the Maastricht Treaty and Stability and Growth Pact without the support of a commensurate political edifice overburdened the EU's legal order. Law's inadequacy to the task of securing a transnational monetary union was made clear little over a decade after the euro's 1999 launch when, faced with interlocking sovereign debt, banking, and macro-economic crises, EU leaders abandoned the strictures of rules such as the 'no bailout' clause in favour of a series of expediencies. This is what makes the eurozone crisis a Schmittian 'state of exception' (Schmitt 2005: 5–15). And this is what raises fundamental questions of power: who decides, and how legitimate is their authority to do so? EU leaders have repeatedly stated their determination to do 'whatever it takes' to save the currency union, but this vow comes with significant risks, including the risk of entrenching 'post-democratic, executive federalism' as the EU's primary mode of governance (Habermas 2012: 12, 50–53).

Critically, by compromising its commitment to the rule of EU law, the Union has compromised one of its most potent sources of legitimacy. Despite lacking democratic inputs, the EU could, in the past, at least 'lay claim to a formal commitment to the rule of law' (Shaw 1996: 251), framed by its con-stitutionalised founding treaties and implemented by the ECJ. However, even this claim to procedural legitimacy has been weakened by the suite of extra-treaty crisis response measures adopted since 2010. The EU's collective identity, which relies on the project's character as a community of law, is also under-mined by these developments. Remembering that the CT's failure exposed the frailty of symbolic markers of European identity, the weakening of the rules and norms that bind Europeans to each other and to the Union institutions is a serious blow. It will not be easy, either, to reverse this trend once the emergency phase of the crisis gives way to 'normality'.[4] Add the damage done to the EU's ability to deliver the goods by the economic downturn, and the long-term existential challenge posed by the crisis becomes clear.

My arguments should not be taken as a repudiation of the integral role of law in the European integration project. On the contrary, my intention is to highlight the need for a more realistic appraisal by European leaders and policymakers of what law is and what it can do. The rule of law is an important part of any liberal democratic constitutional order, but it is not a panacea and it cannot substitute for politics and political culture (Krygier 2011). The rules – regarding budget deficits, debt ratios, etc. – in the Maastricht Treaty and in the Stability and Growth Pact could not and did not prevent the euro crisis. Indeed, their legitimacy had been undermined by multiple unpunished violations, including by France and Germany, years before the crisis so openly revealed their flimsiness. There is little reason to think that the Fiscal Compact (a beefed-up Stability and Growth Pact) will be any more effective.

Where does this leave post-Lisbon EU constitutionalism? In some ways, the constitutional repercussions of the eurozone crisis appear to be furthering trends already evident in the LT, including the turn towards intergovernmentalism. However, the intergovernmentalism of the eurozone crisis response measures is very different from that envisaged by the LT – it is centralised at the European level, concentrating power in new non-majoritarian institutions, such as the ESM, and existing ones, such as the ECB. It is also very much executive and dominated by the preferences of a small group of powerful states, particularly Germany. Unfortunately, then, the crisis response measures have superseded, rather than advanced, many elements of the LT's constitutional settlement, including its parliament-friendly initiatives. Even the traditional method of amending the EU treaties via intergovernmental conferences (IGCs) had to be jettisoned in favour of international agreements to which not all EU member states are party and which, consequently, sit uncomfortably alongside the body of EU law.

The two crises of EU constitutionalism are also intertwined in terms of how they reflect the elite–public gap in perceptions of, and commitment to, European integration. Pre-existing discrepancies in this area, which were laid bare by the CT's defeat, have expanded over the last few years to the point where they constitute a significant constraint on policymakers' room to manoeuvre. Whereas elites still tend to assume that more Europe is the solution to current problems, national publics are increasingly sceptical. Popular feelings of disempowerment and disillusionment are not unjustified, either: one of the most significant developments of the crisis has been the growth of the EU's democratic deficit into a 'democratic default' (Majone 2012: 19–21). Technocratic institutions, such as the ECB, have taken on increasingly political roles, while political bodies have either been sidelined (in the case of parliaments, both national and European) or forced into technocratic straitjackets (in the case of eurozone countries hardest hit by the crisis). The latter trend was explicit in relation to Greece and Italy – two crisis-affected states that were directly governed for a time by unelected technocrats – and implicit in relation to countries such as Ireland, Spain, Portugal and Cyprus.

The strategies pursued by European leaders to resolve the crisis are all premised on securing the eurozone with its current membership.[5] This precludes serious consideration of the possibility that the single currency itself is part of the problem and prevents open contemplation of partial or total dissolution of the currency union in order to secure the long-term future of the EU. Unsurprisingly, then, all of the main pillars of EMU reform to date involve a greater centralisation of authority at the European level: banking union comprising a single supervisory mechanism (SSM) and single resolution mechanism (SRM), stricter economic and budgetary governance (focused on austerity), and a permanent bailout fund, backed by the ECB, to serve as the eurozone's financial firewall. How long it will take for these mechanisms to be fully operational, and how effectively they will work together are more difficult questions (Perrut 2013).

What next for European integration?

Bearing all of the above in mind, there are four, broad scenarios that we may contemplate for the EU's future. These are: a) completion of political and economic union on a democratically legitimate basis; b) entrenchment of a two-speed Europe, with eurozone membership the dividing line between a highly integrated core and loosely affiliated satellites; c) (partial) dissolution of the eurozone, combined with a broader reassessment of the balance of competences between the national and supranational levels; d) permanent crisis management – a version of the time-honoured EU tradition of 'muddling through'.

Scenario a) is in line with the 'crisis as opportunity' school of thought. However, its achievement seems no more likely now than in 2010 when the Greek crisis first broke, despite (or, perhaps, because of) the intervening years of political deadlock, interim measures and half steps. The endless procession of high-level summits, reports and resolutions has tended to alienate Europeans rather than galvanising them around a common cause, whilst illustrating the depth of governments' unwillingness to take radical action in one direction or another. Securing the long-term stability of the euro would require the institutionalisation of a transfer union – that is, large scale and semi-permanent transfers from creditor to debtor states of the sort that occur amongst differently performing regions within states. David Marsh (2013), in his book on the euro crisis, set out a blueprint for rescuing the euro via political union. Amongst other things, his ten point plan called for a centralised European finance ministry and treasury as part of a supranational government headed by a directly elected president and accountable to the EP, binding parameters for national budgets, debt mutualisation, a direct revenue raising capacity for EU institutions, full banking union, and transforming the ECB into a lender of last resort for eurozone governments.

From a theoretical point of view, such a course of action has much to commend it. Bringing EMU within a democratically legitimated framework (perhaps eventually encompassing a formal constitution) would not only stabilise the euro, but also go some way towards resolving other tensions within EU constitutionalism by bringing together its functional, symbolic and democratic threads. However, the fundamental – indeed, fatal – flaw in any plan for political union is its unpopularity across Europe. Marsh himself acknowledged that his plan is unrealisable. Both potential providers and recipients of funds are wary of any suggestion of institutionalising a transfer union within an overarching supranational political and economic framework. Citizens in creditor states resent the prospect of their hard-earned taxes being used to subsidise profligate euro members, while citizens in debtor states resent the harsh structural adjustments and restricted choices that are part of the package.

Therefore, the rhetoric of solidarity remains just that. It is difficult to envisage how it could be transformed into political will – on the part of both governments and electorates – to give up control over taxation and spending to the extent necessary to establish a true fiscal and political union. Individual measures that would be necessary in order to create such a union remain anathema to a large percentage of Europeans. For example, as of spring 2013, only 26% of Germans, 37% of Dutch and 39% of Austrians supported debt mutualisation in the form of Eurobonds (Standard Eurobarometer 79, Spring 2013). Satisfaction with both national and supranational governmental institutions is also at a low ebb, making it difficult for leaders to convince their electorates that political union is the right path.[6] In addition, as the experience of the CT illustrated, the sense of common European identity needed to underpin the whole enterprise remains weak. There are also legal obstacles to consider. As noted previously, the crisis management strategies undertaken so far have been challenged every step of the way in the German Constitutional Court. More radical, federalising initiatives would face the same fate and would likely require amendment of Germany's Basic Law, possibly ratified by a popular referendum. Legal challenges could also eventuate in other member states.

Some commentators see scenarios a) and b) as being linked. In other words, political and economic union will only be completed for a smaller, core group of member states, or at least it will begin there. Certainly, some of the proposals under debate, such as the creation of a separate budget for the eurozone, and further legal recognition of the Eurogroup and Euro Summit, have the potential to accelerate the formal establishment of a two-speed Europe, with euro membership as the dividing line. However, like the previous scenario, this too appears unrealisable. One of the key lessons of the CT's failure was that there is neither sufficient political will nor public support for political and economic union, even within a so-called 'core'. In fact, the EU is now beset by a number of crisscrossing fault lines – between euro ins and outs, between creditors and debtors, and amongst various visions for the eurozone's future involving more or less austerity, more or less direct ECB intervention, and so on. Under these circumstances, it hardly makes sense to speak of a 'core Europe' at all anymore.

I have already noted the rise of euroscepticism in a number of founding member states including the Netherlands, France, Italy and even Germany. In 2013, the Dutch government carried out a review of EU powers, similar to the British balance of competences exercise initiated by David Cameron. Influenced by deteriorating public perceptions of Dutch participation in the EU (and partly, perhaps, by the spectre of Geert Wilders), the government concluded that 'the time of an "ever closer union" in every possible policy area is behind us' and instead advocated a more modest EU based on the principle of 'Europe where necessary, national where possible'.[7]

Fractures have also appeared within the Franco-German tandem that has driven European integration since its inception. After having initially strengthened their joint dominance during the latter part of Nicolas Sarkozy's tenure, the crisis increasingly appears to be pushing the two countries in different directions. Germany, under Merkel, has become more willing to assert itself directly, lessening its need to act through partners, be they supranational institutions, such as the Commission, or other member states. At the same time, France's position relative to Germany has slipped over the past couple of years, as its political clout has been weakened by its stagnating economy. Ideologically, too, the gap between the two states has widened under Sarkozy's successor, Socialist President François Hollande, who has more openly questioned Germany's austerity focus. It is hard to believe, therefore, that even a small group of member states could find sufficient common ground to make political union viable.

Scenario c) may be unpalatable, but it must be given more serious consideration than it has so far received.[8] If European leaders do talk about the possibility of (partial) dissolution of the eurozone, it is only ever as a nightmare scenario to be avoided at all costs, and never as a policy option that could benefit individual euro states, as well as the integration project as a whole. Yet, the EU has a better chance of transitioning to a more democratically legitimate form of governance from within the legal mode that characterised the pre-crisis period than the technocratic mode that currently prevails. In other words, the integration project needs to be brought back within the constitutional framework that had previously legitimised it, at least in a formal, or procedural, sense. However, the protracted economic emergency in which the eurozone finds itself makes it unlikely that EMU could be 're-legalised'. Therefore, restructuring the currency union (e.g. through a reduction in membership, division into two or more parts, or even total dissolution), as part of a broader process of accepting that the EU must do less, may well be the most sustainable course of action, despite the very high short-term costs.

What does it mean to claim that EMU cannot be 're-legalised'? The crisis response, after all, has been accompanied by a whole new set of institutional and regulatory machinery. This machinery, however, is an appendage to the EU's established constitutional framework, rather than an embedded part of it. It is a tail that is increasingly wagging the dog. Anthony Giddens (2013: 6–7) described two structures of European Union governance, which illuminate the distinction between how things are supposed to be done (according to the treaties) and how they are actually done. He equated EU1 with the 'Monnet method', whereby policymaking is a joint enterprise involving the Commission, the Council, and to a lesser extent, the Parliament. The uncodified constitution described in Chapter 1 is the constitution of EU1. EU2, conversely, denotes a smaller coterie of decision makers who generally operate behind the scenes and who wield a great deal of power. These decision makers include some heads of state or government, primarily the German and French leaders, the ECB President, and often also the Council and Commission Presidents. EU2 has always coexisted alongside EU1, but it has really become the dominant governance structure since the onset of the euro crisis.

EU1 is handicapped both by a 'lack of democratic involvement' in its institutional processes and by an 'absence of effective leadership' (Giddens 2013: 211). During the euro crisis, EU2 – which corresponds closely to what Habermas (2012) critically described as 'executive federalism' – has supplied effective leadership, but not democratic involvement. In fact, the decision-making processes associated with EU2 are *less* transparent and accountable than those of EU1. A growing danger for the EU, as it attempts to move beyond the acute phase of the crisis, is that the exception will become the rule. All of the initiatives listed above, such as banking union, externally supervised austerity, and bailout funds have been driven by EU2, and it is difficult to see how their further institutionalisation could provide a basis for the future democratisation of European integration.

Insofar as past action is a good predictor of future action, scenario d) appears to be the most likely option for the immediate future, if not the most desirable. Marsh (2013), for one, has argued that the EU will continue to muddle through the crisis in an ineffective manner. He noted that the EU and its institutions have put a vast amount of resources into managing, but not resolving, the euro's problems. They may be able to sustain this holding pattern for a prolonged period of time, but at the expense of further – and perhaps irreparable – damage to the EU's democratic credentials and legitimacy. In addition to elevating technocracy, continuing on the same path of reactive and piecemeal reform would also likely strengthen German hegemony, which is not desirable either for Germany or for its European partners. In short, muddling through means further entrenching the decision-making processes that Giddens associated with EU2. It is not conducive to striking a stable long-term balance amongst the various European actors, interests and levels of governance.

The four options sketched above are *scenarios*, rather than solutions, for the simple reason that there are no easy answers to the problems that confront the EU. All of them are flawed in various ways. Scenario a) is hopelessly unachievable – there is neither elite political will nor mass public support for federal union. Scenario b) is also unrealistic given the growing fragmentation within so-called 'core Europe' so that there is just as much divergence within the eurozone as without. If, however, a fully institutionalised two-tier Europe were achieved, it would mean the end of the European dream of transcontinental unity as we know it. Scenario c) would have very high political and economic costs in the short term and possibly beyond. Scenario d) would further alienate citizens and entrench a situation of near total 'democratic default' in an EU dominated by technocrats.

Admittedly, this is a rather bleak assessment of where things stand. My primary aim, however, is to highlight the fact that the field of EU studies needs new theories and new understandings of European integration. I focus on the constitutional dimension of Europe's crises because it has been under-analysed and because a sustainable reorientation of the integration project needs to take seriously the task of rebalancing the relationship between law and politics in the EU. This rebalancing needs to include an acknowledgement that Europe must do less. The twin crises of twenty-first-century EU constitutionalism were both caused by overreaching, though in different ways. The CT was an unnecessary and hubristic attempt to codify EU constitutionalism, while EMU was never satisfactorily embedded within the EU's constitutional framework, but was instead undertaken in the vague, and vain, hope that it would promote political union of its own accord. Perhaps the challenge for the EU's leaders is to think smaller, but to do so boldly: to confront stark choices rather than continuing to muddle through in a blinkered fashion.

Notes

1 Even functionally, the (then) EC's constitution was not as well established and unquestioningly accepted as the ECJ would have it seem. Jo Shaw (1996: 237) noted that the Maastricht Treaty partly precipitated a new wave of critical legal studies that questioned 'the hitherto unassailable shibboleths about the "unity" of the EC legal order and about the "uniformity" of EC law, against the backdrop of the newly established Union'.

2 The election results were published on the European Parliament's website, available at www.results-elections2014.eu/en/election-results-2014.html (Accessed: 28 May 2014).

3 The very achievements lauded by the Norwegian Nobel Committee, which – somewhat ironically – awarded the 2012 peace prize to the EU in the midst of its most serious existential crisis (Cohen 2012).

4 In fact, it is seldom possible to demarcate clearly the boundary between a state of emergency and normality. Characteristics of the emergency phase are bound to become a part of the new *status quo* (White 2014). In the case of the EU, this may mean the permanent marginalisation of the Community method, particularly in matters of high importance and urgency.

5 And, indeed, on allowing for expansion – Latvia became the eighteenth member of the eurozone in January 2014.

6 Eurobarometer data from autumn 2013 found trust in EU institutions to be at an all-time low (39% of respondents tended to trust the Parliament, 35% the Commission and 34% the ECB). For each of the three institutions, distrust outweighed trust in some of the countries hardest hit by the euro crisis – Greece, Cyprus, Portugal, Spain and Italy – as well as in Germany and France. Overall, 58% of respondents tended not to trust the EU, compared to 31% who tended to trust it (the ratio was 62% compared to 28% in the eurozone). Regarding the way democracy works in the EU, 43% of respondents were satisfied, while 46% were not satisfied (the ratio was 40% satisfied to 51% not satisfied in the eurozone). The data also recorded falling satisfaction with national democracies; 46% of respondents were satisfied with the way democracy works in their country, while 52% were dissatisfied (Standard Eurobarometer 80, Autumn 2013).

7 An explanatory note on the Dutch 'subsidiarity review' stated:

> NL government is convinced that the time of an 'ever closer union' in every possible policy area is behind us – as the result of the 2005 referendum on the Constitutional Treaty made clear, the Dutch people were, and still are,

discontented with a Union that is continually expanding its scope, as if this were a goal in itself.

(*Ministerie van Buitenlandse Zaken*, 2013)

8 Some commentators have advocated orderly dissolution of the currency union in order to forestall a disorderly collapse, and to allow for the reinvestment of time, energy and financial resources into other areas of the integration project that have been neglected over the past few years. See, for example, the contribution of François Heisbourg (2013).

References

Christiansen, T. (2008) 'The EU Treaty Reform Process since 2000: The Highs and Lows of Constitutionalising the European Union'. *EIPA Scope 2008/1*, pp. 39–44.

Cohen, N. (2012) 'Greece Flirts with Tyranny and Europe Looks Away'. *The Observer*, 4 November.

Cooper, I. (2010) 'Mapping the Overlapping Spheres: European Constitutionalism after the Treaty of Lisbon'. *ARENA Centre for European Studies Seminar Paper*, pp. 1–32.

Giddens, A. (2013) *Turbulent and Mighty Continent: What Future for Europe?* (Cambridge: Polity).

Habermas, J. (2012) *The Crisis of the European Union: A Response* (Cambridge: Polity).

Heisbourg, F. (2013) *La Fin du Rêve Européen* (Paris: Stock).

Krygier, M. (2011) 'Four Puzzles about the Rule of Law: Why, What, Where, and Who Cares?' In Fleming, J. E. (ed.) *Getting to the Rule of Law* (New York: New York University Press).

Majone, G. (2012) 'Rethinking European Integration after the Debt Crisis'. *UCL: The European Institute, Working Paper No. 3/2012*, June.

Marsh, D. (2013) *Europe's Deadlock* (New Haven, CT: Yale University Press).

Ministerie van Buitenlandse Zaken (2013) *NL 'Subsidiarity Review' – Explanatory Note*, 21 June.

Perrut, D. (2013) 'Economic and Monetary Union Reform: Political Ambition or Division'. *Foundation Robert Schuman Policy Paper*, No. 297, 17 December, pp. 1–10.

Schmidt, V. A. (2009) 'Re-Envisioning the European Union: Identity, Democracy, Economy'. *Journal of Common Market Studies*, Vol. 47, Annual Review, pp. 17–42.

Schmitt, C. (2005) *Political Theology: Four Chapters on the Concept of Sovereignty* (Chicago, IL: University of Chicago Press).

Shaw, J. (1996) 'European Union Legal Studies in Crisis? Towards a New Dynamic'. *Oxford Journal of Legal Studies*, Vol. 16, No. 2, pp. 231–53.

Standard Eurobarometer 79 (2013) *Europeans, the European Union and the Crisis.* Survey Coordinated by the European Commission, Directorate General Communication, Spring.

Standard Eurobarometer 80 (2013) *Public Opinion in the European Union.* Survey Coordinated by the European Commission, Directorate General Communication, Autumn.

White, J. (2014) 'Authority after Emergency Rule'. *Paper presented at the 21st International Conference of the Council for European Studies*, Washington DC, 14–16 March.

Index